Praise for
Buddhism: One Teacher, Many Traditions

"Originating from a common source in the teachings of the historical Buddha, the southern Theravāda tradition, based on texts in Pāli, and the northern traditions of Tibet and East Asia, based largely on texts originally in Sanskrit, all developed their own unique systems of doctrine and practice. These are impressive in their philosophical insights into the nature of reality and in their understanding of the deep potentials of the human mind. In this book His Holiness the Dalai Lama and the American bhikṣuṇī Thubten Chodron jointly explore the commonalities and differences among these Buddhist traditions, doing so with exceptional precision. This book will reward those who study it carefully with a deep and wide understanding of the way these traditions have mapped their respective visions of the path to enlightenment."

—Bhikkhu Bodhi, translator of *In the Buddha's Words*

"His Holiness and Thubten Chodron have collaborated to create an invaluable modern-day resource that explores, illuminates, and clarifies the commonalities, synergies, and divergences within the major historical Dharma streams—especially regarding liberation, an analysis never before done in this way. It also shows how these profoundly ethical teachings can be skillfully applied in our present era to, in their words, serve humanity and benefit sentient beings both within the Buddhist community and beyond. It is a timely offering, at once compelling and wise."

—Jon Kabat-Zinn, author of *Full Catastrophe Living*

"*Buddhism: One Teacher, Many Traditions* is like a well-constructed bridge over a beautiful, deep river. People from all traditions will be able to find a clear view of both the Buddha's teachings and the vast, rich landscape those teachings have nourished. The spirit of respect and harmony expressed in this excellent book is inspiring."

—Sharon Salzberg, author of *Real Happiness*

"This is an invaluable survey of Buddhist civilizations—with their comprehensive histories, philosophical tenets, ethical disciplines, meditation trainings, and goals to be attained—all elucidated in one volume. A precious gift to all who love the Dharma."

—Tulku Thondup, coauthor of *Boundless Healing*

"Now that people around the world have unprecedented access to all traditions of Buddhism, a growing number of Buddhists find themselves drawn to theories and practices from different traditions. This makes this book especially valuable, for it presents clear and accurate comparisons between the Pāli-based and Sanskrit-based schools of Buddhism, showing the common ground and significant differences in their interpretations of key themes of the Buddhist path to liberation. I highly recommend this volume for everyone seeking a more global understanding of the many traditions of Buddhism, all inspired by the one Teacher, Buddha Shakyamuni."

—B. Alan Wallace, author of *The Attention Revolution*

BUDDHISM

BUDDHISM

One Teacher, Many Traditions

Bhikṣu Tenzin Gyatso
THE FOURTEENTH DALAI LAMA
and
Bhikṣuṇī Thubten Chodron

Foreword by Bhante Gunaratana

Wisdom

Wisdom Publications
199 Elm Street
Somerville, MA 02144 USA
wisdomexperience.org

Library of Congress Cataloging-in-Publication Data
Bstan-'dzin-rgya-mtsho, Dalai Lama XIV, 1935– author.
Buddhism : one teacher, many traditions / Bhikshu Tenzin Gyatso,
the Fourteenth Dalai Lama and Bhikshuni Thubten Chodron.
pages cm
Includes bibliographical references and index.
ISBN 1-61429-127-6 (cloth : alk. paper)
1. Buddhism—Doctrines. I. Thubten Chodron, 1950– II. Title.
BQ7935.B774B85 2014
294.3'4—dc23
2014007555

ISBN 978-1-61429-392-7 ebook ISBN 978-1-61429-151-0

23 22 21 20
5 4 3

Maps on pages xxvi–xxviii by XNR Productions, Inc.
Cover photograph by Vincent Marcil. Cover and interior design by Gopa&Ted2, Inc.
Set in Diacritical Garamond Pro 11/14.6.

Wisdom Publications' books are printed on acid-free paper and meet the guidelines for permanence and durability of the Production Guidelines for Book Longevity of the Council on Library Resources.

This book was produced with environmental mindfulness.
For more information, please visit wisdompubs.org/wisdom-environment.

Printed in the United States of America.

FSC www.fsc.org MIX Paper from responsible sources FSC® C011935

Please visit fscus.org.

Contents

Foreword

THE DALAI LAMA and I both embarked on our life's work early. He was identified as the leader of Tibetan Buddhism as a toddler, not long before I at age twelve became a monk in the Theravāda Buddhist tradition in my native Sri Lanka. Causes and conditions thus came together for each of us to begin our journeys to preserve and share the wisdom of the Buddha at around the same time.

I first met His Holiness the Dalai Lama in India in 1956 at the Buddhist holy site of Sanchi. He was visiting on one of his first trips outside his homeland, three years before he was forced to flee Tibet. We did not meet again until the 1993 Parliament of World Religions in Chicago. Even though I do not meet him very often, I continue to feel an inner connection with him because of his wisdom and fairness in sharing his Dhamma knowledge. So it is with deep appreciation and admiration of His Holiness's wisdom that I happily offer a few words at the front of this book that His Holiness and Venerable Thubten Chodron have written about our shared Buddhist tradition.

People today are generally more broadminded than those who lived before. Though the world is not without conflict, a unifying trend is emerging as we become more economically and culturally interconnected. Given this current trend, Buddhist unity is overdue. Although we Theravāda Buddhists have long met with other Buddhists, once the panel or conference is over, we go our separate ways, and nothing much happens.

Well-meaning books on the various traditions show our common points but, perhaps in order to be polite, say little about the differences among us. We need not consider it impolite to point out where we differ. Not only are there doctrinal differences among the various types of Buddhists, cultural practices also differ from country to country. Even within a single country, Buddhist practices may vary from region to region or group to group. Being able to honestly survey the traditions is a healthy sign of our strength and sincerity. There is nothing to hide in the Buddha's teaching. The present work is to be commended for its honest and systematic examination of the great overlap between the Pāli and Sanskrit Buddhist traditions while at the same time not shying away from discussing the many ways in which the teachings diverge.

Still, while it is healthy to discuss our differences openly, focusing on them to the exclusion of our shared heritage is also misguided. Both the Pāli and Sanskrit traditions have made tremendous efforts to bring more peace to the world through the sincere preservation of the teachings of the Buddha. It is rare, in either tradition, to find any call for violence to promote one tradition over the other. Thus religious politics is completely foreign to the Buddha's teaching, but sadly some Buddhists fail to practice what their religion teaches. Enthusiasm for the "real" Dhamma is sometimes so strong that the very basic instruction of the Buddha on how to teach the Dhamma without creating conflict is overlooked.

On this point, the *Simile of the Snake* (MN 22) is quite relevant. In this sutta, wrongly grasping the Dhamma is compared to catching a poisonous snake by its tail. A snake will bite and cause death or sickness if held incorrectly, but if the snake is caught correctly, the venom can be extracted for medicine and the snake released without harm. Like this, we must grasp the meaning of Dhamma correctly and not cling to it. Mishandling or clinging to the Dhamma can poison the mind just as a venomous snake can poison the body, and poisoning the mind is much more dangerous.

If we properly grasp the meaning of Dhamma, we can experience what is called the *miracle of education*. Because ignorance is so strong and deep, the Buddha at first wondered whether he would be able to help people understand Dhamma in order to free them from suffering. However, he began to teach, and using his wisdom, he turned vicious persons into saints, wicked persons into holy ones, and murderers into peacemakers. This potential for transformation is the miraculous power of education.

In order to experience the miracle of education for ourselves, we must look within. The truth within us that we can experience all the time is called the Dhamma. It is this Dhamma that invites us saying, "If you want to be free from trouble, look at me. Take care of me." The Dhamma within us talks to us constantly, even if we are not listening. Buddhas need not come to this world for the Dhamma to exist. The buddhas realize it and comprehend it, and having realized it, they teach it and make it known; but whether it is expounded or not, the Dhamma is there within us to be seen and heard, if we will only wipe the dust from our eyes and look at it.

We "come and see" the experience of peace the moment greed is abandoned. We "come and see" the experience of peace the moment hatred is abandoned. We must build up this habit to "come and see" what is really happening within us without pointing our finger at others. We do not preserve and promote the Buddhist tradition for its sake alone. Rather, we preserve the teachings of the Buddha handed down from generation to generation because they relieve suffering and promote happiness.

When we investigate Buddhism's major traditions, as the present book does, we can see that they have contributed to the world a rich tapestry of cultural, social, and spiritual knowledge. That knowledge offers deep insights into psychology, philosophy, and mental health. The broad recognition of this has fed today's global awakening to the importance of meditation. One needn't be Buddhist to enjoy the benefits that come from the practice of meditation.

Buddhism in all its forms draws the world's attention for its peaceful existence with other religions. Following this central message of the Buddha, every one of us should be a messenger of peace. This is our common bond. It is my wish that the present volume may help Buddhists everywhere release their clinging to views and engage in honest dialogue with mutual respect and that it may help all beings to experience the truth of the Dhamma that lies within. When our enthusiasm for the Dhamma is guided by love, compassion, joy, and equanimity, we honor the Buddha's central mission of peace.

Bhante Henepola Gunaratana
Founding Abbot, The Bhāvanā Society
High View, West Virginia

Prologue

Due to the great kindness of the Buddha, who taught the Dharma and established the Saṅgha, the teachings showing the path to liberation have been clearly set forth for sentient beings to follow. As the Buddha's doctrine spread throughout the Indian subcontinent and then into other countries, different Buddhist traditions emerged. In ancient times, and even into the modern era, transportation and communication among people from these various traditions were limited. While some may have heard about other traditions, there was no opportunity to check the accuracy of that information. Thus misconceptions arose and passed from one generation to the next.

Due to improvements in transportation and communication, in the twenty-first century, we followers of the Buddha have the opportunity to get to know each other directly. Thanks to new translations, we are now able to read the scriptures of each other's canons and the commentaries by our respective great masters. Since the translations available still represent only a fraction of the total scriptures, and the potential body of the sūtras and commentaries to read is quite extensive, we offer this humble volume as a bridge to begin learning about one another.

All of us Buddhists have the same Teacher, Lord Buddha. It would be to everyone's benefit if we had closer relationships with each other. I have had the great fortune to meet many leaders from the Christian, Muslim, Jewish, Hindu, Jain, and Sikh worlds, but I have had comparatively little opportunity to meet with the great teachers, meditators, and leaders of the different Buddhist traditions. Most Tibetan monastics and lay followers know little about other Buddhist traditions, and I believe the followers of other traditions know little about Buddhism as practiced in the Tibetan community. If our Teacher, the Buddha, came to our planet today, would he be happy with this? All of us, the Buddha's spiritual children, proclaim love for the same "parent," yet we have only minimal communication with our brothers and sisters.

In recent years this has fortunately begun to change. Many Buddhists from Asia and the West have come to Dharamsala, India, the center of the Tibetan community in exile; some Tibetan monks and nuns have also visited their countries. Communication with our Theravāda brothers and sisters had been particularly minimal, but some cracks in the centuries-old divisions are beginning to appear there as well. For example, two Burmese monks studying at a university in India came to visit me. They were interested in learning about Tibetan Buddhism so they could broaden their knowledge of the Buddhist world while continuing to practice in their own tradition. I admire their motivation, and I would like to encourage Buddhists from all traditions to gain a deeper understanding of the vastness of the Buddha's doctrine. This can only help us to appreciate even more the Buddha's exceptional qualities as a Teacher who has the wisdom, compassion, and skillful means to lead us all to awakening.

A central purpose of this book is to help us learn more about each other. All Buddhists take refuge in the Three Jewels; our teachings are based in the four truths of the āryas (the malaise of *duḥkha*, its origin, cessation, and path), the three higher trainings (ethical conduct, concentration, and wisdom), and the four immeasurables (love, compassion, joy, and equanimity). All of us seek liberation from *saṃsāra*, the cycle of rebirth fueled by ignorance and polluted karma. Learning about our similarities and differences will help us be more united.

Another purpose of this book is to eliminate centuries-old misconceptions about each other. Some Theravāda practitioners believe Tibetan monastics do not follow the *vinaya*—the monastic ethical code—and that as practitioners of tantra, they have sex and drink alcohol. Meanwhile Tibetan practitioners think the Theravāda tradition lacks teachings on love and compassion and characterize those followers as selfish. Chinese Buddhists often think Tibetans perform magic, while Tibetans believe Chinese Buddhists mainly do blank-minded meditation. All of these misconceptions are based on a lack of knowledge. We offer this book as a step toward alleviating these misconceptions.

Now in the twenty-first century East and West, South and North, are coming closer. We Buddhist brothers and sisters must also have closer contact and cultivate mutual understanding. This will benefit us as individuals, will help preserve and spread the Dharma, and will be an example of religious harmony for the world.

Bhikṣu Tenzin Gyatso, the Fourteenth Dalai Lama

June 13, 2014

Preface

A BOOK SHOWING the commonalities and unique points of various Buddhist traditions could have been approached from any number of perspectives. As Buddhists, we all bow to the Buddha, make offerings, and confess our ethical downfalls. We engage in meditation, chanting, study and recitation of sūtras, and listening to teachings. All of our communities have temples, monasteries, hermitages, and centers. Explaining the similarities and differences among these external activities would certainly aid our mutual understanding.

This book, however, focuses on the teachings—the shared tenets and the unique tenets of what we are calling the "Pāli tradition" and the "Sanskrit tradition." These are terms of convenience and should not be taken to imply that either tradition is homogenous. Both traditions trace their teachings and practices back to the Buddha himself. The Pāli tradition is descendant from the suttas and commentaries in Prakrit, in the old Sinhala language, and in Pāli. It relies on the Pāli canon and is currently found principally in Sri Lanka, Burma, Thailand, Cambodia, Laos, and parts of Vietnam and Bangladesh. The Sanskrit tradition descends from sūtras and commentaries in Prakrit, Sanskrit, and Central Asian languages and relies on the Chinese and Tibetan canons. It is currently practiced principally in Tibet, China, Taiwan, Korea, Japan, Mongolia, Nepal, the Himalayan region, Vietnam, and parts of Russia. Both traditions are found in Malaysia, Singapore, Indonesia, India, and in Western and African countries.

While stemming from the same Teacher, the Buddha, the Pāli tradition and the Sanskrit tradition each has its own distinctive features, unique contributions, and different points of emphasis. In addition, neither tradition is monolithic. The Buddhism of East Asia and Tibetan Buddhism, for example, are quite different in expression. But because they both stem from a similar body of Sanskrit texts and share many similar beliefs, they are included in the expression "the Sanskrit tradition."

Topics in this book are largely described from a prevalent viewpoint in each tradition. This may differ from how a subtradition or an individual teacher approaches a topic. In some instances, we had to select one presentation among many to put in this book. For example, in the chapter on selflessness (not self), among all the views in the Sanskrit tradition, we explained the Prāsaṅgika Madhyamaka view as presented by Tsongkhapa. In other cases, we explained a topic—for example, bodhicitta—according to the Tibetan presentation and then gave distinctive features from the Chinese presentation.

There is a tremendous body of literature in both traditions, and deciding what to include in this book was not easy. His Holiness the Dalai Lama and I would have liked to include or elaborate upon many more points, but the book would have become too lengthy. We apologize for not being able to discuss the wide variety of views, interpretations, and practices within each tradition and request your patience if certain topics you consider important are absent or condensed. Quotes from scripture we wanted to include have been omitted due to space concerns, as have titles and epithets.

Many of this book's readers will undoubtedly be learned in their own Buddhist tradition. When reading descriptions, or even textual translations, from traditions different than one's own, the thought may arise, "This is incorrect." At this time please recall that other traditions may use different words to express the same meaning as in one's own tradition. Recall also the benefit arising from knowledge of the diversity of the Buddha's teachings.

This volume was conceived by His Holiness to promote greater mutual understanding among Buddhists worldwide. I feel deeply fortunate that he has trusted me to carry out this most beneficial endeavor. His Holiness contributed most of the teachings from the Sanskrit tradition. I wrote them up from public teachings he gave as well as from a series of private interviews I had with him over the years. These were translated by Geshe Lhakdor, Geshe Dorji Damdul, and Geshe Thupten Jinpa. Geshe Dorji Damdul and Geshe Dadul Namgyal checked this part of the manuscript. Some of the sources for Chinese Buddhism were the writings of Chinese masters such as Zongmi, Yinshun, Hanshan Deqing, Shixian, Jizang, Taixu, and Ouyi Zhixu and interviews with Bhikṣu Houkuan, Bhikṣu Huifeng, Bhikṣu Dharmamitra, Bhikṣu Jian-hu, Dr. Lin Chen-kuo, and Dr. Wan Jing-chuang. Since I received bhikṣuṇī ordination in Taiwan, I have a heartfelt connection with that tradition. Reading the Pāli suttas, the writings of Buddhaghosa and Dhammapāla, and the teachings of contemporary authors such as Ledi Sayadaw, Ñāṇamoli Thera, Nyanaponika Thera, Soma Thera, Bhikkhu Bodhi, and Bhikkhu Anālayo opened my eyes to the beauty of the Pāli tradition. I studied Bhikkhu Bodhi's series of 123 talks on the Majjhima Nikāya, and he very generously clarified many points for me in personal correspondence. He also checked the parts of this book describing the Pāli tradition. His Holiness also asked me to visit Thailand and study and practice at a monastery there, which I did for two weeks.

Pāli and Sanskrit are linguistically similar but not identical. Because some terms, such as *meditative stabilization*, are unwieldy in English, the Pāli and Sanskrit terms—here *jhāna* and *dhyāna*—have sometimes been used instead. In some chapters the Pāli and Sanskrit presentations of a topic are given in separate sections; in other chapters they are presented in parallel. Whenever Pāli perspectives are given, the spelling of terms will be in Pāli; Sanskrit perspectives will contain Sanskrit spellings. When two terms are in parentheses, the first is Pāli, the second Sanskrit. When only one term is present, either it is the same in both languages, or it corresponds with the tradition whose perspective is discussed in that passage. Pāli and Sanskrit terms are usually given in parentheses only for the first usage of a word. When Pāli and Sanskrit terms are left untranslated, only initial usages are italicized.

The English "four noble truths" has been replaced by a more accurate translation—"four truths of the āryas (*ariyas*)," which is often abbreviated to "four truths."

There are several English terms that followers of the Pāli tradition may find different than what they are used to. On the first occurrence of such terms, I tried to reference the more familiar English term. There will be translation choices for Sanskrit words that are unfamiliar to some readers as well. This is unavoidable, and I request your tolerance.

All errors, inconsistencies, and any points that may be inappropriate are due to my ignorance alone, and I request your patience with these. They do not in any way reflect on His Holiness.

Appreciation

I pay homage to the Buddha as the Teacher, he who gave us these precious Dharma teachings that make our lives meaningful and lead us to true freedom from duḥkha. I also pay homage to the lineages of realized Buddhist masters in all traditions, due to whose kindness the Buddhadharma has flourished down to the present day.

In addition to the people mentioned above, I also deeply appreciate the help of Samdhong Rinpoche, Geshe Sonam Rinchen, Dr. Alexander Berzin, Traci Thrasher, the staff at His Holiness' office, the community at Sravasti Abbey, and Tim McNeill and David Kittelstrom at Wisdom Publications. All knowledge is a dependent arising, and the kindness and wise consul of these and many other *kalyāṇamitras* has made the present work immeasurably better.

Unless otherwise noted, henceforth the pronoun "I" refers to His Holiness.

Bhikṣuṇī Thubten Chodron
Sravasti Abbey, June 13, 2014

Abbreviations

Translations used in this volume, unless noted otherwise, are as cited here. Some terminology has been modified for consistency with the present work.

AN Aṅguttara Nikāya. Translated by Bhikkhu Bodhi in *The Numerical Discourses of the Buddha* (Boston: Wisdom Publications, 2012).

BCA *Bodhicaryāvatāra* by Śāntideva. Translated by Stephen Batchelor in *A Guide to Bodhisattva's Way of Life* (Dharamsala, India: Library of Tibetan Works and Archive, 2007).

Bv *Buddhavaṃsa.* Translated by I. B. Horner in *The Minor Anthologies of the Pāli Canon* (Lancaster: Pali Text Society, 2007).

C Chinese

CMA *Comprehensive Manual of Abhidhamma.* Translated by Bhikkhu Bodhi (Kandy: Buddhist Publication Society, 1993).

DN Dīgha Nikāya. Translated by Maurice Walshe in *The Long Discourses of the Buddha* (Boston: Wisdom Publications, 1995).

J Japanese

LRCM *The Great Treatise on the Stages of the Path* (*Lam rim chen mo*) by Tsongkhapa, 3 vols. Translated by Joshua Cutler et al. (Ithaca: Snow Lion Publications, 2000–2004).

MMK *Mūlamadhyamakakārikā* by Nāgārjuna

MN Majjhima Nikāya. Translated by Bhikkhu Ñāṇamoli and Bhikkhu Bodhi in *The Middle-Length Discourses of the Buddha* (Boston: Wisdom Publications, 1995).

RA *Ratnāvalī* by Nāgārjuna. Translated by John Dunne and Sara McClintock in *The Precious Garland: An Epistle to a King* (Boston: Wisdom Publications, 1997).

SN Saṃyutta Nikāya. Translated by Bhikkhu Bodhi in *The Connected Discourses of the Buddha* (Boston: Wisdom Publications, 2000).

TP *Treatise on the Pāramīs*, from the *Commentary to the Cariyāpiṭaka*. Translated by Bhikkhu Bodhi on www.accesstoinsight.org.

Ud *Udāna*

Vism *Visuddhimagga* of Buddhaghosa. Translated by Bhikkhu Ñāṇamoli in *The Path of Purification* (Kandy: Buddhist Publication Society, 1991).

Publisher's Acknowledgment

THE PUBLISHER gratefully acknowledges the generous contribution of the Hershey Family Foundation toward the publication of this book.

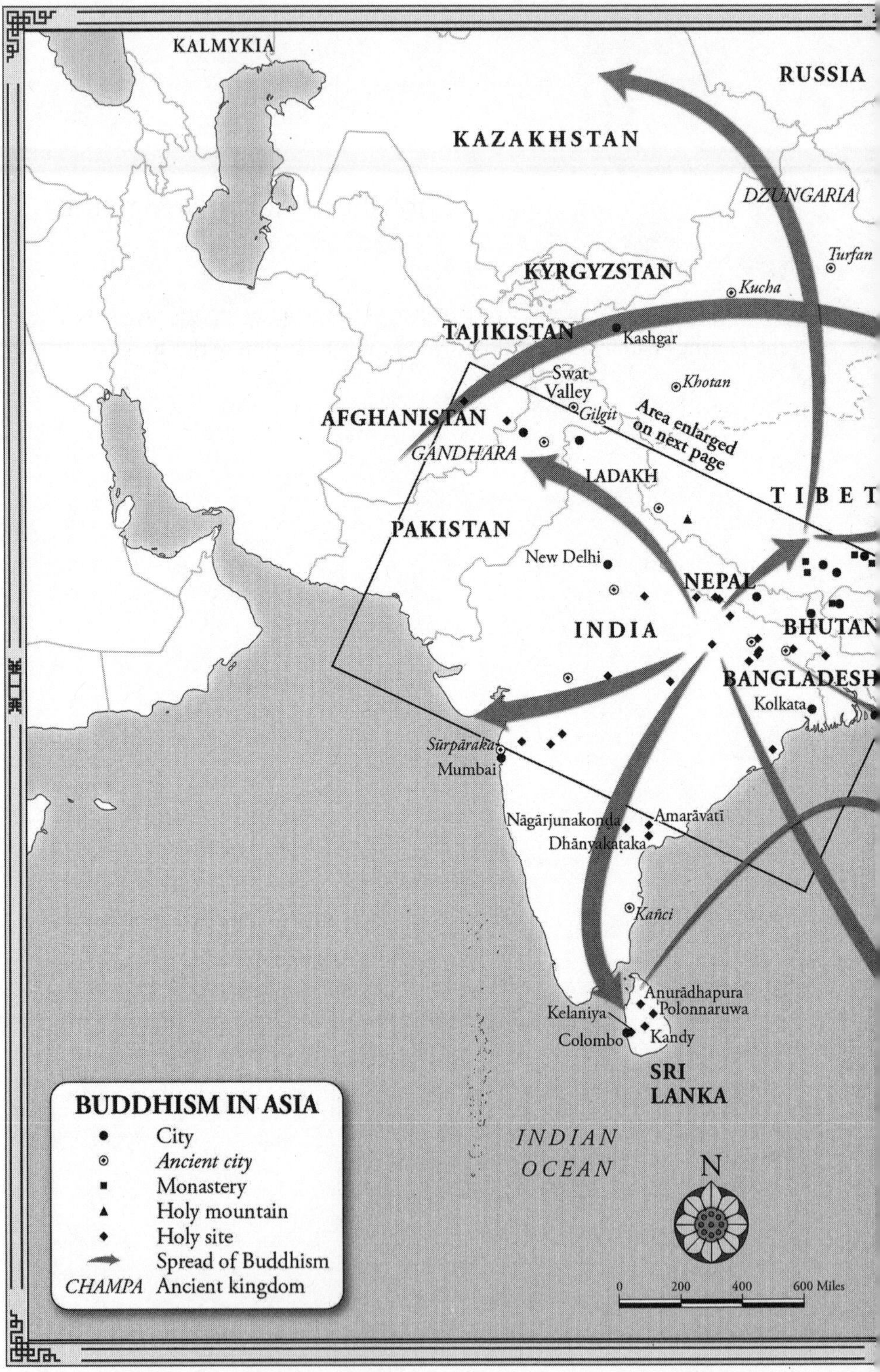
KALMYKIA
RUSSIA
KAZAKHSTAN
DZUNGARIA
Turfan
KYRGYZSTAN
Kucha
TAJIKISTAN
Kashgar
Swat
Valley
Khotan
Gilgit
Area enlarged
on next page
AFGHANISTAN
GANDHARA
LADAKH
TIBET
PAKISTAN
New Delhi
NEPAL
INDIA
BHUTAN
BANGLADESH
Kolkata
Sūrpāraka
Mumbai
Nāgārjunakonda
Amarāvatī
Dhānyakaṭaka
Kañci
Anurādhapura
Kelaniya
Polonnaruwa
Colombo
Kandy
SRI
LANKA
INDIAN
OCEAN
N
0
200
400
600 Miles
BUDDHISM IN ASIA
City
Ancient city
Monastery
Holy mountain
Holy site
Spread of Buddhism
CHAMPA Ancient kingdom

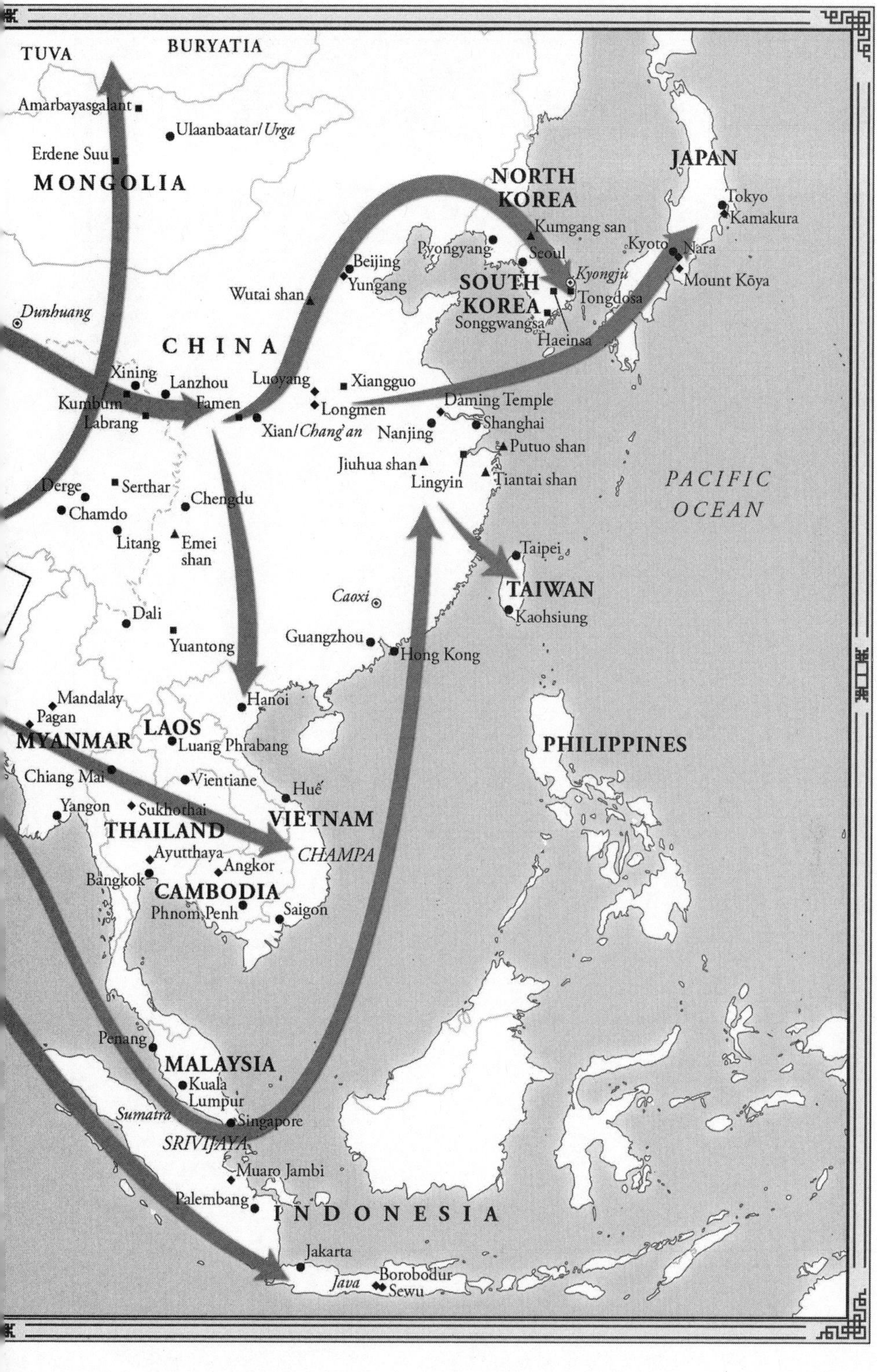

TUVA
BURYATIA
Amarbayasgalant
Ulaanbaatar/*Urga*
Erdene Suu
MONGOLIA
NORTH KOREA
JAPAN
Tokyo
Kamakura
Kumgang san
Pyongyang
Seoul
Kyoto
Nara
Beijing
Yungang
SOUTH KOREA
Kyongju
Mount Kōya
Wutai shan
Tongdosa
Dunhuang
Songgwangsa
Haeinsa
CHINA
Xining
Lanzhou
Luoyang
Xiangguo
Kumbum
Famen
Longmen
Daming Temple
Labrang
Xian/*Chang'an*
Nanjing
Shanghai
Putuo shan
Jiuhua shan
Lingyin
Tiantai shan
PACIFIC OCEAN
Derge
Serthar
Chengdu
Chamdo
Litang
Emei shan
Taipei
TAIWAN
Caoxi
Kaohsiung
Dali
Yuantong
Guangzhou
Hong Kong
Mandalay
Pagan
Hanoi
MYANMAR
LAOS
Luang Phrabang
PHILIPPINES
Chiang Mai
Vientiane
Huế
Yangon
Sukhothai
THAILAND
VIETNAM
CHAMPA
Ayutthaya
Angkor
Bangkok
CAMBODIA
Phnom Penh
Saigon
Penang
MALAYSIA
Kuala Lumpur
Sumatra
Singapore
SRIVIJAYA
Muaro Jambi
Palembang
INDONESIA
Jakarta
Java
Borobodur
Sewu

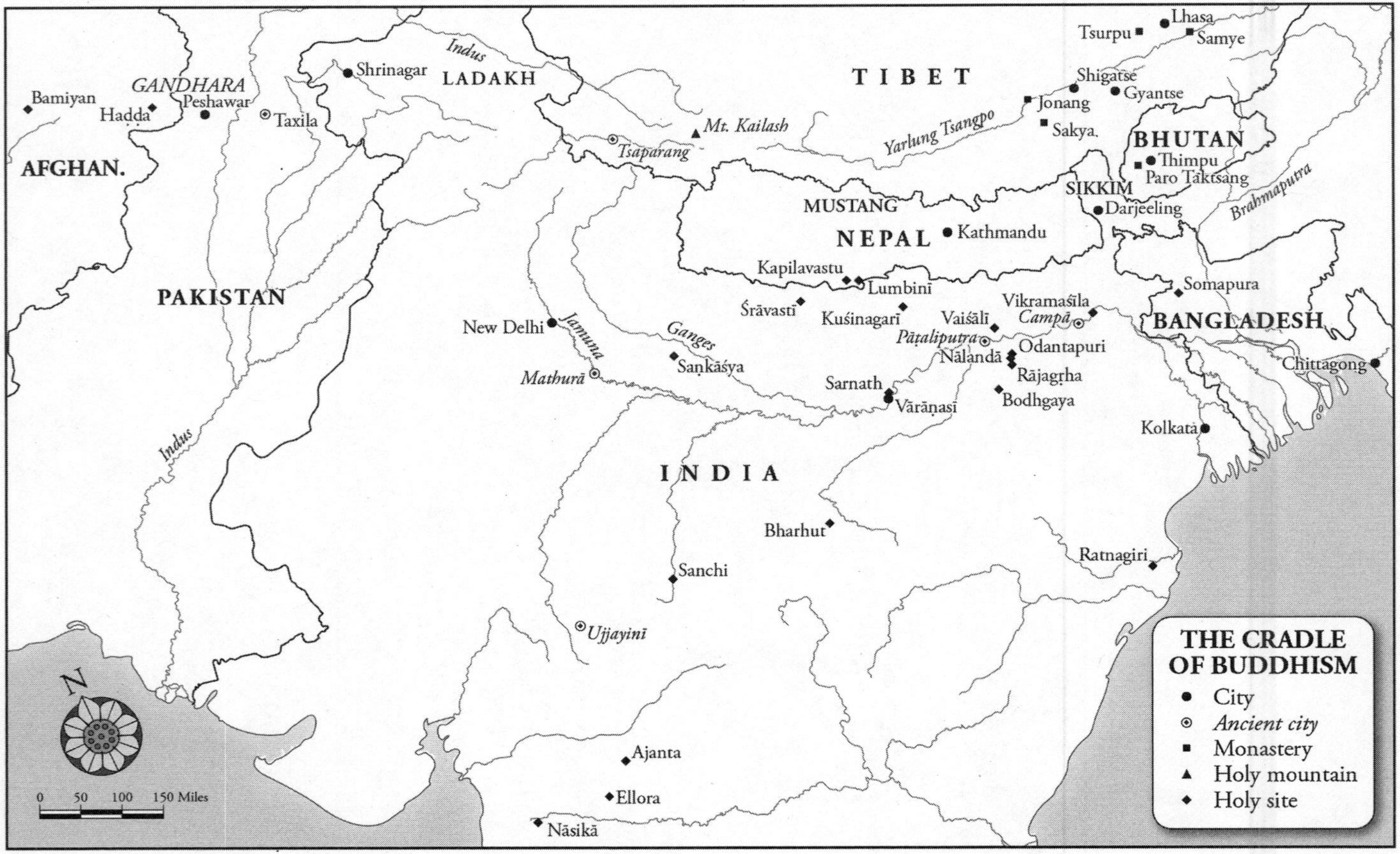
THE CRADLE OF BUDDHISM
City
Ancient city
Monastery
Holy mountain
Holy site
TIBET
NEPAL
INDIA
PAKISTAN
AFGHAN.
BHUTAN
SIKKIM
BANGLADESH
LADAKH
MUSTANG
GANDHARA
Bamiyan
Hadda
Peshawar
Taxila
Shrinagar
Indus
Tsaparang
Mt. Kailash
Yarlung Tsangpo
Tsurpu
Lhasa
Samye
Shigatse
Gyantse
Jonang
Sakya.
Thimpu
Paro Taktsang
Brahmaputra
Darjeeling
Kathmandu
Kapilavastu
Lumbinī
Śrāvastī
Kuśinagarī
Vaiśālī
Vikramaśīla
Campā
Pāṭaliputra
Nālandā
Odantapuri
Rājagṛha
Bodhgaya
Sarnath
Vārāṇasī
Somapura
Chittagong
Kolkata
New Delhi
Jamuna
Mathurā
Ganges
Saṇkāśya
Bharhut
Sanchi
Ujjayinī
Ratnagiri
Ajanta
Ellora
Nāsikā
N
0 50 100 150 Miles

1 | Origin and Spread of the Buddha's Doctrine

NOT ALL PEOPLE think alike. They have different needs, interests, and dispositions in almost every area of life, including religion. As a skillful teacher, the Buddha gave various teachings to correspond to the variety of sentient beings. We're going to look at the development of the two major Buddhist traditions containing these teachings, the Pāli and Sanskrit traditions.[1] But first, we begin with the life story of Śākyamuni Buddha.

The Buddha's Life

In the view common to both traditions, Siddhārtha Gautama, a prince from the Śākya clan, was born and grew up near what is now the India-Nepal border in the fifth or sixth century B.C.E. As a child, he had a kind heart and excelled in the arts and studies of his time. He lived a sheltered life in the palace during his early years, but as a young man he ventured out beyond the palace walls. In the town, he saw a sick person, an old person, and a corpse, prompting him to reflect on the suffering nature of life. Seeing a wandering mendicant, he considered the possibility of liberation from saṃsāra. And so, at age twenty-nine, he left the palace, shed his royal attire, and adopted the lifestyle of a wandering mendicant.

He studied with the great teachers of his time and mastered their meditation techniques but discovered they did not lead to liberation. For six years he pursued severe ascetic practices in the forest, but realizing that torturing the body doesn't tame the mind, he adopted the middle way of keeping the body healthy for the sake of spiritual practice without indulging in unnecessary comforts.

Sitting under the bodhi tree in what is present-day Bodhgaya, India, he vowed not to arise until he had attained full awakening. On the full moon of the fourth lunar month, he finished the process of cleansing his mind of all obscurations and developing all good qualities, and he became a fully awakened buddha (*sammāsambuddha, samyaksaṃbuddha*). Thirty-five years old at the time, he spent the next forty-five years teaching what he had discovered through his own experience to whoever came to hear.

The Buddha taught men and women from all social classes, races, and ages. Many of those chose to relinquish the householder's life and adopt the monastic life, and thus the saṅgha community was born. As his followers attained realizations and became skilled teachers, they shared with others what they had learned, spreading the teachings throughout ancient India. In subsequent centuries, the Buddhadharma spread south to Sri Lanka; west into present-day Afghanistan; northeast to China, Korea, and Japan; southeast to Southeast Asia and Indonesia; and north to Central Asia, Tibet, and Mongolia. In recent years, many Dharma centers have opened in Europe, the Americas, the former Soviet republics, Australia, and Africa.

I feel a deep connection to Gautama Buddha as well as profound gratitude for his teachings and for the example of his life. He had insights into the workings of the mind that were previously unknown. He taught that our outlook impacts our experience and that our experiences of suffering and happiness are not thrust upon us by others but are a product of the ignorance and afflictions in our minds. Liberation and full awakening are likewise states of mind, not the external environment.

Buddhist Canons and the Spread of the Dharma

Vehicle and *path* are synonymous. While they are sometimes used to refer to a progressive set of spiritual practices, technically speaking they refer to a wisdom consciousness conjoined with uncontrived renunciation.

The Buddha turned the Dharma wheel, setting forth practices of three vehicles: the Hearer Vehicle (Sāvakayāna, Śrāvakayāna), the Solitary Realizer Vehicle (Paccekabuddhayāna, Pratyekabuddhayāna), and the Bodhisattva Vehicle (Bodhisattayāna, Bodhisattvayāna). According to the Sanskrit tradition, the three vehicles are differentiated in terms of their motivation to attain a specific goal, their principal meditation object, and the amount of merit and time necessary to attain their goals. Teachings and practitioners of all three vehicles exist in both the Pāli and Sanskrit traditions. In general, those practicing the Hearer Vehicle principally follow the Pāli tradition, and those practicing the Bodhisattva Vehicle principally follow the Sanskrit tradition. Nowadays in our world, hardly anyone follows the Solitary Realizer Vehicle.

The Buddha's teaching spread widely in India in the centuries after the Buddha lived and was brought to Sri Lanka from India by King Aśoka's son and daughter in the third century B.C.E. The early suttas were transmitted orally by the *bhāṇakas*—monastics whose job it was to memorize the suttas—and according to Sri Lankan sources, they were written down about the first century B.C.E. to form what is now the Pāli canon. Over the centuries, beginning in India and later augmented by Sinhala monks in the old Sinhala language, a body of commentaries on the scriptures built up. In the fifth century the great translator and commentator Buddhaghosa compiled the ancient commentaries and translated them into Pāli. He also wrote his famous masterwork the *Visuddhimagga* and numerous commentaries. Another South Indian monk, Dhammapāla, lived a century later and also wrote many commentaries in Pāli. Pāli is now the scriptural language uniting all Theravāda Buddhists.

Beginning in the first century B.C.E., the Sanskrit tradition came into view and gradually spread in India. Philosophical systems in India—Vaibhāṣika, Sautrāntika, Yogācāra (a.k.a. Cittamātra or Vijñānavāda), and Madhyamaka—evolved as scholars developed divergent views on points not explained explicitly in the sūtras. Although many tenets of the Pāli tradition are shared with one or another of these four tenet systems, it cannot be equated with any of them.

Several monastic universities arose—Nālandā, Odantapuri, and Vikramaśīla—and there Buddhists from various traditions and philosophical schools studied and practiced together. Philosophical debate was a widespread ancient Indian custom; the losers were expected to convert to the winners' schools. Buddhist sages developed logical arguments and reasonings to prove the validity of Buddhist doctrine and to deflect the philosophical attacks of non-Buddhists. The renowned Buddhist debaters were also great practitioners. Of course not all Buddhist practitioners were interested in this approach. Many preferred to study the sūtras or to practice meditation in hermitages.

Nowadays, three canons exist: the Pāli, Chinese, and Tibetan; a Sanskrit canon was not compiled in India. Each canon is divided into three "baskets" (*piṭaka*)—or categories of teachings—which are correlated with the three higher trainings. The Vinaya basket deals chiefly with monastic discipline, the Sūtra basket emphasizes meditative concentration, and the Abhidharma basket is mainly concerned with wisdom.

The Chinese canon was first published in 983, and several other renditions were published later. The standard edition used now is the Taishō Shinshū Daizōkyō, published in Tokyo in 1934. It consists of four parts: sūtras, vinaya, śāstras (treatises), and miscellaneous texts originally written in Chinese. The Chinese canon is very inclusive, sharing many texts with both the Pāli and Tibetan canons. In particular, the Āgamas in the Chinese canon correspond to the first four Nikāyas in the Pāli canon.

The Tibetan canon was redacted and codified by Buton Rinpoche in the fourteenth century. The first rendition of the Tibetan canon was published in 1411 in Beijing. Later editions were published in Tibet in Nartang in 1731–42 and later in Dergé and Choné. The Tibetan canon is composed of the Kangyur—the Buddha's word in 108 volumes—and the Tengyur—the great Indian commentaries in 225 volumes. Most of these volumes were translated into Tibetan directly from Indian languages, chiefly Sanskrit, although a few were translated from Chinese and Central Asian languages.

Pāli Tradition

Buddhism spread to Sri Lanka, China, and Southeast Asia many centuries before coming to Tibet. As our elder brothers and sisters, I pay respect to you.

Modern-day Theravāda was derived from the Sthaviravāda, one of the eighteen schools in ancient India. The name Theravāda does not seem to have indicated a school in India prior to Buddhism having gone to Sri Lanka. The Sinhala historical chronicle *Dīpavaṃsa* used the name Theravāda in the fourth century to describe the Buddhists on the island. There were three Theravāda subgroups, each with a monastery bearing its name: Abhayagiri (Dharmaruci), Mahāvihāra, and Jetavana. Abhayagiri Theravādins had close connections with India and brought in many Sanskrit elements. The Jetavanins did this as well, but to a lesser extent, while the Mahāvihārins maintained the orthodox Theravāda teachings. In the twelfth century the king abolished the Abhayagiri and Jetavana traditions and amalgamated those monks with the Mahāvihāra, which has since remained prominent.

Buddhism suffered greatly after the Sri Lankan capital fell to the Coḷa forces in 1017. The bhikkhu and bhikkhunī orders were destroyed, although the bhikkhu order was restored when the Sri Lankan king invited monks

DHAMEKH STUPA, SITE OF THE BUDDHA'S FIRST TEACHING, SARNATH, INDIA

from Burma to come and give the ordination. The Buddhadhamma thrived once again in Sri Lanka, and Sri Lanka came to be seen as the center of the Theravāda world. When the state of Theravāda teachings or its ordination lineages in one country were adversely affected, leaders would request monks from another Theravāda country to come and give ordination. This has continued up to the present day.

In late eighteenth-century Thailand, King Rāma I began to remove elements of Brahmanism and tantric practice, although traces live on today with many Thai Buddhist temples hosting a statue of four-faced Brahmā in their courtyard. King Rāma IV (r. 1851–68), a monk for nearly thirty years before ascending the throne, witnessed the relaxed state of monastic discipline and Buddhist education and instituted a wide range of saṅgha reforms. Importing an ordination lineage from Burma, he began the Dhammayuttikā Nikāya, unified the other sects into the Mahā Nikāya, instructed both sects to keep the monastic precepts more strictly, and placed both under a single ecclesiastical authority. Revamping monastic education, he wrote a series of textbooks expressing a more rational approach to Dhamma and eliminated elements of non-Buddhist folk culture attached to Thai

Buddhism. As Thailand became more centralized, the government assumed the authority to appoint preceptors to give ordination. The Saṅgha Act of 1902 brought all monastics under royal control by centralizing administrative authority for the entire saṅgha in the Supreme Saṅgha Council (*Mahathera Samakhom*) headed by the *saṅgharāja*. King Rāma V's half-brother, Prince Wachirayan, wrote new textbooks that were the basis for national saṅgha exams. These exams improved the monks' knowledge as well as distinguished the monks who would advance in ecclesiastical rank.

Colonialism hurt Buddhism in Sri Lanka, but the interest of a few Westerners in Buddhism, especially Theosophists Helena Blavatsky and Henry Olcott, spurred lay Buddhists such as Anagārika Dhammapāla to present Buddhism in more rational terms and to connect with Buddhists internationally. Buddhism provided a rallying point for Sri Lankans in dealing with colonialism and establishing an independent nation.

Colonialism did not harm Buddhism in Burma as much, and it actually stimulated the king to request monks to teach vipassanā meditation in the court. Soon laypeople from all social classes were learning to meditate. The monks Ledi Sayadaw (1846–1923) and Mingon Sayadaw (1868–1955) set up lay meditation centers, and Mahasi Sayadaw (1904–82) passed his teachings to lay teachers. This meditation style is now popular in Burma.

The means to select a saṅgharāja differ. In Thailand, they are generally appointed by the king. In other countries monastic seniority or a semi-democratic process are used. The authority of saṅgharājas varies: some are figureheads; others such as the late Mahā Ghosananda of Cambodia have great influence by virtue of their practice, beneficial works, and advancement of social change. Thailand's saṅgharāja, a position existing since the eighteenth century, is part of a national hierarchy handling issues of importance to the saṅgha. He has legal authority over monastics, works with the secular government, and is assisted by the Supreme Saṅgha Council. In Cambodia the saṅgharāja position disappeared during the Khmer period, but in 1981 the government reestablished it.

In many cases, national governments instituted changes that had the side effect of lessening the saṅgha's traditional roles as teachers and doctors and supplanting them with secular systems of modern education and medicine. As a result, Theravāda monastics, as well as their brethren in countries following the Sanskrit tradition, have had to rethink their role in society in the face of modernization.

Buddhism in China

Buddhism entered China in the first century C.E., first via the Silk Road from Central Asian lands where Buddhism flourished and later by sea from India and Sri Lanka. By the second century, a Chinese Buddhist monastery existed, and translation of Buddhist texts into Chinese was under way. Early translations employed inconsistent terminology, leading to some misunderstanding of Buddhist thought, but by the fifth century, translation terms became more settled. The early fifth century also marked the translation of more vinaya texts. For many centuries, emperors sponsored translation teams, so a wealth of Buddhist sūtras, treatises, and commentaries from India and Central Asia were translated into Chinese.

Chinese Buddhism contains a diversity of schools. Some views and practices are common to all schools, while others are unique to individual schools. Some schools are differentiated based on their philosophical tenets, others on their manner of practice, others by their principal texts. Historically, ten major schools developed in China.

1. *Chan* (J. *Zen*) was brought to China by the Indian meditation master Bodhidharma in the early sixth century. He was the twenty-eighth Indian patriarch and the first Chinese patriarch of this school. Currently, two sub-branches of Chan exist: Linji (J. *Rinzai*) and Caodong (J. *Sōtō*). Linji primarily uses *hua-tous* (koans)—puzzling statements that challenge practitioners to go beyond the limits of the conceptual mind—and speaks of sudden awakening. Caodong focuses more on "just sitting" and takes a more gradual approach.

   Early Chan masters relied on the *Laṅkāvatāra Sūtra* and on Prajñāpāramitā sūtras such as the *Vajracchedikā Sūtra*, and some later adopted *tathāgatagarbha*, or "buddha essence," ideas. The *Śūraṅgama Sūtra* is popular in Chinese Chan. Nowadays most Korean Chan practitioners and some Chinese ones learn Madhyamaka—Middle Way philosophy. Dōgen Zenji and Myōan Eisai were instrumental in bringing Zen to Japan in the thirteenth century.
2. The *Pure Land* (C. *Jingtu*, J. *Jōdo*) school is based on the three Pure Land sūtras—the smaller and larger *Sukhāvatīvyūha* sūtras and the *Amitāyurdhyāna Sūtra*. It emphasizes chanting the name of Amitābha Buddha and making fervent prayers to be reborn in his

pure land, which provides all circumstances necessary to practice the Dharma and attain full awakening. The pure land can also be viewed as the pure nature of our own minds. Chinese masters such as Zhiyi, Hanshan Deqing, and Ouyi Zhixu wrote commentaries on the Pure Land practice, discussing how to attain serenity and realize the nature of reality while meditating on Amitābha. After the ninth century, Pure Land practice was integrated into many other Chinese schools, and today many Chinese monasteries practice both Chan and Pure Land. Hōnen took the Pure Land teachings to Japan in the late twelfth century.

3. *Tiantai* (J. *Tendai*) was founded by Huisi (515–76). His disciple Zhiyi (538–97) established a gradual progression of practice from the easier to the most profound, with the ultimate teachings found in the *Saddharmapuṇḍarīka Sūtra*, the *Mahāparinirvāṇa Sūtra*, and Nāgārjuna's *Mahāprajñāpāramitā-upadeśa*. This school balances study and practice.
4. *Huayan* (J. *Kegon*) is based on the *Avataṃsaka Sūtra*, translated into Chinese around 420. Dushun (557–640) and Zongmi (781–841) were great Huayan masters. Huayan emphasizes the interdependence of all people and phenomena and the interpenetration of their worlds. The individual affects the world, and the world affects the individual. Huayan philosophy also emphasizes the bodhisattvas' activities in the world to benefit all beings.
5. The *Sanlun* (J. *Sanron*) or Madhyamaka school was founded by the great Indian translator Kumārajīva (334–413) and principally relies on the *Mūlamadhyamakakārikā* and *Dvādaśanikāya Śāstra* by Nāgārjuna and the *Śataka Śāstra* of Āryadeva. Sometimes Nāgārjuna's *Mahāprajñāpāramitā-upadeśa* is added as the fourth principal Sanlun text. Sanlun relies on the Prajñāpāramitā sūtras and follows the *Akṣayamatinirdeśa Sūtra* in asserting that these sūtras reveal the definitive meaning of the Buddha's teachings.
6. *Yogācāra* (C. *Faxiang*, J. *Hossō*) is based on the *Saṃdhinirmocana Sūtra* and on the *Yogācāryabhūmi Śāstra*, *Vijñaptimātrasiddhi Śāstra*, and other treatises by Maitreya, Asaṅga, and Vasubandhu. Xuanzang (602–64) translated these important texts and established this school after his return from India.

7. *Vajrayāna* (C. *Zhenyan*, J. *Shingon*) is based on the *Mahāvairocana Sūtra*, *Vajraśekhara Sūtra*, *Adhyardhaśatikā Prajñāpāramitā Sūtra*, and *Susiddhikara Sūtra*, which explain yoga tantra practices. Never widespread in China, this school was brought to Japan by Kukai (774–835) and is still extant there.
8. The *Vinaya* (C. *Lu*, J. *Ritshū*) school was founded by Daoxuan (596–667) and principally relies on the Dharmaguptaka vinaya, translated into Chinese in 412. Four other vinayas were also translated into Chinese.
9. The *Satyasiddhi* (C. *Chengshi*, J. *Jōjitsu*) school is based on the *Satyasiddhi Śāstra*, an Abhidharma-style text that discusses emptiness among other topics. Some say it emphasizes the Śrāvaka Vehicle, others say it bridges the Śrāvaka Vehicle and Bodhisattva Vehicle. This school is not extant now.
10. *The Abhidharma* (C. *Kośa*, J. *Kusha*) school was based on the *Abhidharmakośa* by Vasubandhu and was introduced into China by Xuanzang. While this school was popular in the "golden age of Buddhism" during the Tang dynasty (618–907), it is small now.

Some of the ten schools still exist as separate schools. The tenets and practices of those that do not have been incorporated into existing schools. Although the Vinaya school does not exist as a separate entity now, the practice of vinaya has been integrated into the remaining schools, and the saṅgha is flourishing in Taiwan, Korea, and Vietnam. While no longer distinct schools, the Abhidharma, Yogācāra, and Madhyamaka philosophies are studied and meditated upon in the indigenous Chinese schools as well as in Korea, Japan, and Vietnam.

Changes in society in the early twentieth century spurred Buddhist reform and renewal in China. The fall of the Qing dynasty in 1917 stopped imperial patronage and support of the saṅgha, and the government, military, and educational institutions wanted to confiscate monasteries' property for secular use. Buddhists wondered what role Buddhadharma could play in their encounter with modernity, science, and foreign cultures.

This social change provoked a variety of reactions. Taixu (1890–1947), perhaps the most well-known Chinese monk of that time, renewed the study of Madhyamaka and Yogācāra and began new educational institutes for the saṅgha using modern educational methods. He also incorporated the best from secular knowledge and urged Buddhists to be more socially engaged. Traveling in Europe and Asia, he contacted Buddhists of other traditions and established branches of the World Buddhist Studies Institute. He encouraged Chinese to go to Tibet, Japan, and Sri Lanka to study, and he established seminaries in China that taught Tibetan, Japanese, and Pāli scriptures. Taixu also formulated "Humanistic Buddhism," in which practitioners strive to purify the world by enacting bodhisattvas' deeds right now as well as to purify their minds through meditation.

Several young Chinese monks studied Buddhism in Tibet in the 1920s and 30s. Fazun (1902–80), a disciple of Taixu, was a monk at Drepung Monastery, where he studied and later translated into Chinese several great Indian treatises and some of Tsongkhapa's works. The monk Nenghai (1886–1967) studied at Drepung Monastery and, upon returning to China, established several monasteries following Tsongkhapa's teachings. Bisong (a.k.a. Xing Suzhi 1916–) also studied at Drepung Monastery and in 1945 became the first Chinese *geshe lharampa*.

The scholar Lucheng made a list of works in the Tibetan and Chinese canons to translate into the other's language in order to expand Buddhist material available to Chinese and Tibetan practitioners and scholars. In the first half of the twentieth century, Chinese lay followers had increased interest in Tibetan Buddhism, especially in tantra, and invited several Tibetan teachers to teach in China. They and their Chinese disciples translated mostly tantric materials.

Taixu's disciple Yinshun (1906–2005) was an erudite scholar who studied the sūtras and commentaries of the Pāli, Chinese, and Tibetan canons. A prolific writer, he was especially attracted to Tsongkhapa's explanations. Due to Yinshun's emphasis on Madhyamaka and the Prajñāpāramitā sūtras, many Chinese Buddhists have renewed interest in this view. He developed the schema of the major philosophical systems in Chinese Buddhism today: (1) False and unreal mind only (C. *Weishi*) is the Yogācāra view. (2) Truly permanent mind only (C. *Zenru*) is the tathāgatagarbha doctrine, which is popular in China and has a strong impact on practice traditions. (3) Empty nature, mere name (C. *Buruo*) is the Madhyamaka view based on the Prajñāpāramitā sūtras. Yinshun also encouraged Humanistic Buddhism.

Buddhism in Tibet

Tibetan Buddhism is rooted in Indian monastic universities such as Nālandā. Beginning in the early centuries of the Common Era and lasting until the early thirteenth century, Nālandā and other monastic universities consisted of many erudite scholars and practitioners emphasizing different sūtras and espousing a variety of Buddhist philosophical tenets.

Buddhism first came to Tibet in the seventh century through two wives of the Tibetan monarch Songtsen Gampo (605 or 617–49), one a Nepali princess the other a Chinese princess, who brought Buddhist statues to Tibet. Buddhist texts in Sanskrit and Chinese soon followed. From the late eighth century onward, Tibetans preferred the texts coming directly from India, and these formed the bulk of Buddhist literature translated into Tibetan.

Buddhism flourished in Tibet during the reign of King Trisong Detsen (r. 756–ca. 800), who invited the monk, Madhaymaka philosopher, and logician Śāntarakṣita from Nālandā and the Indian tantric yogi Padmasambhava to come to Tibet. Śāntarakṣita ordained Tibetan monks, establishing the saṅgha in Tibet, while Padmasambhava gave tantric initiations and teachings.

Śāntarakṣita also encouraged the Tibetan king to have Buddhist texts translated into Tibetan. In the early ninth century, many translations were done, and a commission of Tibetan and Indian scholars standardized many technical terms and compiled a Sanskrit-Tibetan glossary. However, Buddhism was persecuted during the reign of King Langdarma (838–42), and monastic institutions were closed. Since Dharma texts were no longer available, people's practice became fragmented, and they no longer knew how to practice all the various teachings as a unified whole.

At this crucial juncture Atiśa (982–1054), a scholar-practitioner from the Nālandā tradition, was invited to Tibet. He taught extensively, and to rectify misconceptions, he wrote the *Bodhipathapradīpa*, explaining that both sutra and tantra teachings could be practiced by an individual in a systematic, noncontradictory manner. As a result, people came to understand that the monastic discipline of the Vinaya, the bodhisattva ideal of the Sūtrayāna, and the transformative practices of the Vajrayāna could be practiced in a mutually complementary way. Monasteries were again built, and the Dharma flourished in Tibet.

The Buddhism in Tibet prior to Atiśa became known as the Nyingma or "old translation" school. The new lineages of teachings entering Tibet beginning in the eleventh century became the "new translation" (*sarma*) schools, and these slowly crystallized to form the Kadam, Kagyu, and Sakya traditions. The Kadam lineage eventually became known as the Gelug tradition. All four Tibetan Buddhist traditions that exist today—Nyingma, Kagyu, Sakya, and Gelug—emphasize the Bodhisattva Vehicle, follow both the sūtras and tantras, and have the Madhyamaka philosophical view. Following the example of Śāntarakṣita, many Tibetan monastics engage in rigorous study and debate in addition to meditation.

Some misnomers from the past—the terms "Lamaism," "living buddha," and "god king"—unfortunately persist. Westerners who came in contact with Tibetan Buddhism in the nineteenth century called it Lamaism, a term originally coined by the Chinese, perhaps because they saw so many monks in Tibet and mistakenly believed all of them were lamas (teachers). Or perhaps they saw the respect disciples had for their teachers and erroneously thought they worshiped their teachers. In either case, Tibetan Buddhism should not be called Lamaism.

Lamas and tulkus (identified incarnations of spiritual masters) are respected in Tibetan society. However, in some cases these titles are simply social status, and calling certain people tulku, rinpoche, or lama has led to corruption. It saddens me that people put so much value on titles. Buddhism is not about social status. It is much more important to check a person's qualifications and qualities before taking that person as one's spiritual mentor. Teachers must practice diligently and be worthy of respect, whether or not they have titles.

Some people mistakenly believed that since tulkus are recognized as incarnations of previous great Buddhist masters, they must be buddhas and thus called them "living buddha" (C. *huofo*). However, not all tulkus are bodhisattvas, let alone buddhas.

"God king" may have originated with the Western press and was attributed to the position of the Dalai Lama. Since Tibetans see the Dalai Lama as the embodiment of Avalokiteśvara, the bodhisattva of compassion, these journalists assumed he was a "god," and since he was the political leader of Tibet, he was considered a king. However, since I currently hold the position of Dalai Lama, I repeatedly remind people that I am a simple Buddhist monk, nothing more. The Dalai Lama is not a god, and since the Central Tibetan Administration located in Dharamsala, India, is now headed by a prime minister, he is not a king.

Some people mistakenly think the position of the Dalai Lama is like a Buddhist pope. The four principal Tibetan Buddhist traditions and their many sub-branches operate more or less independently. The abbots, rinpoches, and other respected teachers meet together from time to time to discuss issues of mutual interest under the auspices of Central Tibetan Administration's Department of Religion and Culture. The Dalai Lama does not control their decisions. Similarly the Dalai Lama is not the head of any of the four traditions. The Gelug is headed by the Ganden Tripa, a rotating position, and the other traditions have their own methods of selecting leaders.

Our Commonalities and Diversity

Sometimes people mistakenly believe that Tibetan Buddhism, especially Vajrayāna, is separate from the rest of Buddhism. When I visited Thailand many years ago, some people initially thought that Tibetans had a different religion. However, when we sat together and discussed the vinaya, sūtras, abhidharma, and such topics as the thirty-seven aids to awakening, the four concentrations, four immaterial absorptions, four truths of the āryas, and noble eightfold path, we saw that Theravāda and Tibetan Buddhism have many common practices and teachings.

With Chinese, Korean, and many Vietnamese Buddhists, Tibetans share the monastic tradition, bodhisattva ethical restraints, Sanskrit scriptures, and the practices of Amitābha, Avalokiteśvara, Mañjuśrī, Samantabhadra, and Medicine Buddha. When Tibetan and Japanese Buddhists meet, we discuss the bodhisattva ethical restraints and sūtras such as the *Saddharmapuṇḍarīka Sūtra*. With the Japanese Shingon sect we share the tantric practices of the Vajradhātu maṇḍala and Vairocanābhisaṃbodhi.

While there are differences in the texts that comprise each canon, there is considerable overlap of the material discussed in them. In subsequent chapters we will explore some of these in greater depth, but here are a few examples.

The Buddha spoke at length about the disadvantages of anger and the antidotes to it in the Pāli suttas (e.g., SN 11:4–5). The teachings for overcoming anger in Śāntideva's *Bodhicaryāvatāra* echo these. One sutta

Reclining Buddha, Thailand

(SN 4:13) recounts the story of the Buddha experiencing severe pain due to his foot having been cut by a stone splinter. Nevertheless, he was not distressed, and when prodded by Māra, he responded, "I lie down full of compassion for all beings." This is the compassion generated when doing the taking-and-giving meditation (Tib. *tonglen*) taught in the Sanskrit tradition, where a practitioner imagines taking the sufferings of others upon himself and giving others his own happiness.

Furthermore, the altruistic intention of bodhicitta so prominent in the Sanskrit tradition is an extension of the four *brahmavihāras*, or four immeasurables, taught in the Pāli canon. The Pāli and Sanskrit traditions share many of the same perfections (*pāramī, pāramitā*). The qualities of a buddha, such as the ten powers, four fearlessnesses, and eighteen unshared qualities of an awakened one are described in scriptures from both traditions. Both traditions speak of impermanence, the unsatisfactory nature, selflessness, and emptiness. The Sanskrit tradition sees itself as containing the teachings of the Pāli tradition and elaborating on certain key points—for example, by explaining true cessation according to the Prajñāpāramitā sūtras and the true path according to the Tathāgatagarbha sūtras and some of the tantras.

The terms Thai Buddhism, Sri Lankan Buddhism, Chinese Buddhism, Tibetan Buddhism, Korean Buddhism, and so on are social conventions. In each case, Buddhism in a country is not monolithic and contains many Buddhist practice traditions and tenet systems. Within these, there are subgroups consisting of monasteries or teachers with various affiliations. Some subtraditions emphasize study, others meditation. Some stress practicing serenity (*samatha, śamatha*), others insight (*vipassanā, vipaśyanā*), and others both together.

While one country may have many traditions in it, one tradition may also be practiced in many countries. Theravāda is practiced in Sri Lanka, Thailand, Burma, Laos, Cambodia, and is also found in Vietnam. Within Theravāda countries, some follow early Buddhism—the suttas themselves—without relying on the commentaries very much, while others follow the explanations in the commentarial tradition. Even the robes in one country or in one tradition may vary.

Similarly, Chan is practiced in China, Taiwan, Korea, Japan, and Vietnam. While Chan practitioners in all these countries rely on the same sūtras, the teachings and meditation style vary among them.

In Western countries, Buddhism from many different traditions and countries is present. Some groups consist primarily of Asian immigrants, and their temples are both religious and community centers where people can speak their native language, eat familiar food, and teach their children the culture of their homeland. Other groups in the West are composed mostly of Western converts. A few are mixed.

As followers of the Buddha, let's keep these variations in mind and not think that everything we hear or learn about another tradition applies to everyone in that tradition. Similarly not everything we hear about how Buddhism is practiced in a particular country applies to all traditions or temples in that country.

Indeed we are a huge and diverse Buddhist family following the same wise and compassionate Teacher, Śākyamuni Buddha. I believe our diversity is one of our strengths. It has allowed Buddhism to spread throughout the world and to benefit billions of people on this planet.

2 | Refuge in the Three Jewels

All Buddhist traditions agree that taking refuge in the Three Jewels is the demarcation of becoming a Buddhist. While people may take refuge in the Three Jewels for a variety of reasons, stable refuge comes from knowing and understanding the teachings through reasoning and experience, thus confirming for ourselves that the Buddha's teachings are true.

The chief way the Buddha leads us is by teaching the path to liberation and awakening. The *Samādhirāja Sūtra* says:

> Buddhas do not wash away negativities with water,
> clear away beings' duḥkha with their hands,
> or transfer their own knowledge to others;
> they liberate by teaching the truth of reality.

We must follow this path and practice it ourselves; no one else can do it for us. The Buddha himself encouraged us to understand his teachings, not to follow them blindly. This is especially so in the twenty-first century, when literacy and education are widespread and people are not content with blind belief. People have access to literature from many religions, and if the younger generation finds the explanations of older Buddhists superficial, inadequate, or superstitious, they will not be convinced. Thus to benefit future generations, we must learn and practice the Dharma well and then teach it to others, showing the benefit that Buddha's doctrine brings through the example of how we live.

To be able to take refuge in a proper way, we need to identify and have a clear understanding of the Three Jewels. To do that, understanding the four truths of the āryas is important. Based on taking refuge, we continue to learn, contemplate, and meditate on the Buddha's teachings, thus deepening our refuge. That deeper refuge inspires us to learn and practice more, and so we progress, with taking refuge and understanding the teachings mutually aiding each other.

Existence of the Three Jewels

In the Pāli and Sanskrit sūtras, the Buddha said that whoever sees the interdependent nature of phenomena sees the Dharma, and whoever sees the Dharma sees the Tathāgata. Nāgārjuna explained that the key to verifying the existence of the Three Jewels is understanding the interdependent nature of phenomena.

Upon examination we find that persons and phenomena are dependent. There are three aspects of dependence: (1) Conditioned things depend on their causes and conditions—a sprout arises from a seed, and our experiences depend on our previous actions or karma. (2) All phenomena—both the impermanent and the permanent—depend on their constituent parts.[2] Our body is made of parts such as arms, legs, and internal organs, and these are made of other parts. Our mind is composed of a sequence of tiny moments of mind that form its continuum. (3) On the subtlest level, all phenomena depend on the mind that conceives and designates them. On the basis of two arms, two legs, a torso, a head, and so on, a mind conceives and designates "body." In dependence on the collection of a body and mind, we impute "person."

Ignorance, the root of saṃsāra, grasps all persons and phenomena as having a "self"—an independent, inherent essence unrelated to anything else such as causes and conditions, parts, and the mind that conceives and designates them. Because all persons and phenomena exist dependent on other factors, they are empty of independent or inherent existence. Thus ignorance is an erroneous mind since it lacks a valid basis. Wisdom, on the other hand, is a reliable mind since it apprehends reality; it realizes that all persons and phenomena are empty of inherent existence because they exist dependent on other factors. Wisdom's apprehension of reality can overpower ignorance, and with repeated meditation, wisdom can completely eradicate ignorance from our mindstream, making liberation possible.

In this way, knowledge of dependent arising helps us to understand the four truths that form the basic framework of the Buddha's teachings. Ignorance misapprehending reality gives rise to afflictions, which create karma and lead to duḥkha. This is the truth of duḥkha and the truth of its origin, the first two truths of the āryas. Knowledge of dependent arising also enables us to understand emptiness and selflessness: persons and other phenomena are empty of independent existence because they are dependent. Emptiness and dependent arising are established by reasoning and can be directly experienced. The wisdom understanding emptiness is the fourth truth, true path, which counteracts the ignorance, wrong views, and afflictions that are founded on the misapprehension of reality. In this way, we can actualize a state in which all ignorance and afflictions have been removed. This is nirvāṇa, true cessation, the third truth.

Thus the four truths of the āryas exist. The last two of the four truths—true cessations and true paths—are the Dharma Jewel. Persons who have actualized at least some of these paths and cessations in their continuum are the Saṅgha Jewel. When they progress to the point where all afflictions and obscurations have been eliminated and all paths and qualities brought to perfection, they become the Buddha Jewel. Thus, beginning with the fact that all phenomena are empty of independent existence yet arise dependent on other factors, we can prove the existence of the Three Jewels. For this reason, the Buddha said that those who see interdependence see the Dharma, and those who see the Dharma see the Tathāgata.

Understanding this increases our faith in the Three Jewels because we understand the possibility of mental development that leads to actualizing the Three Jewels. In this way, understanding the four truths gives us confidence that not only can we trust the Three Jewels as spiritual guides leading us to full awakening, but we can also become the Three Jewels ourselves.

The historical order of the existence of the Three Jewels and their order of generation for individual practitioners differ. Historically, the Buddha appeared first. He then gave Dharma teachings. On the basis of practicing these, people gained realizations. Disciples possessing realizations are āryas, the Saṅgha.

An individual practitioner first actualizes the Dharma Jewel by cultivating true path and actualizing true cessation. Thus, he becomes the Saṅgha Jewel. By further enhancing the Dharma Jewel in his mind until he is fully awakened, he becomes the Buddha Jewel.

The Tathāgata's Qualities

Learning about the qualities of the Three Jewels and especially of the Buddha increases our confidence in their ability to guide us from the dangers of saṃsāra. Both the Pāli and the Sanskrit traditions extensively praise the Tathāgata's qualities by expressing his four types of fearlessness, ten powers, and eighteen unshared qualities.

Candrakīrti quotes (*Madhyamakāvatāra* 6.210cd) a passage, also found in the Pāli canon (MN 12:22–26), describing the *four kinds of self-confidence* or *fearlessness* of the Tathāgata that enable him to "roar his lion's roar in the assemblies." The Buddha sees no ground on which any recluse, brahman, god, or anyone else could accuse him of (1) claiming to be fully awakened although he is not fully awakened to certain things, (2) claiming to have destroyed pollutants (*āsava, āśrava*) that he has not destroyed, (3) calling things obstructions that are not obstructions, and (4) teaching a Dharma that does not lead someone who practices it to complete destruction of duḥkha. These four enable the Tathāgata to teach the Dhamma with perfect self-confidence free from all self-doubt because he is fully awakened regarding all aspects, has destroyed all pollutants, correctly identifies obstructions on the path, and gives teachings that lead those who practice them to nirvāṇa.

The *ten powers* are a set of exceptional knowledges exclusive to the Tathāgata. They enable him to do a Buddha's unique activities, establish his doctrine in the world, skillfully teach sentient beings, and lead them to awakening. Spoken of in both the Pāli (MN 12) and Sanskrit sūtras (*Daśabhūmika Sūtra*), these ten are exalted wisdoms that have abandoned all obscurations and know the infinite objects of knowledge. Unless otherwise noted, the explanations below are shared by both traditions.

1) With direct, unmistaken perception the Tathāgata knows *the tenable and the untenable*, the relations between actions and their results as well as the implications of actions done by āryas and ordinary beings.

2) Only the Tathāgata fully and accurately knows *the intricacies of past, present, and future karma and their results*, including subtle causes leading to a particular experience in the beginningless lives of each sentient being.

3) The Tathāgata knows *the various destinations of ordinary beings*—the saṃsāric realms—and the paths leading to rebirth there. He also knows the destination of the āryas of the three vehicles—nirvāṇa—and the paths leading to that.

4) He fully understands *the world and the various elements* (*dhātu*) that compose it—the eighteen constituents (*dhātu*), six elements, external and

DAIBUTSU, KAMAKURA, JAPAN

internal sources (*āyatana*), twelve links (*nidāna*) of dependent arising, twenty-two faculties (*indriya*),[3] and so on—with wisdom seeing them as impermanent, conditioned, and dependent processes.

5) He knows *the different inclinations of beings* (*adhimutti, adhimokṣa*)—their spiritual aims and the vehicles they are attracted to. This enables him to teach them the Dharma according to their individual faculties, abilities, and aspirations.

6) He knows *the strength of each being's faculties* (*indriya*) of faith (*saddhā, śraddhā*), effort (*viriya, vīrya*), mindfulness (*sati, smṛti*), concentration (*samādhi*), and wisdom (*paññā, prajñā*) and teaches each being accordingly.

7) Because the Buddha has mastered the jhānas, the eight meditative liberations (*vimokkha, vimokṣa*),[4] and the nine meditative absorptions (*samāpatti*), he knows the defilements, cleansing, and emergence (Pāli: *sankilesa, vodāna, vuṭṭhāna*) regarding them. *Defilements* are impediments hindering a meditator from entering a meditative absorption or, having entered, make it deteriorate. *Cleansing* is the method for removing the impediment. *Emergence* is the way to come out of a state of meditative

absorption after having entered it. He is able to guide others to attain these meditative states without their becoming attached to the bliss of concentration and urge them to continue practicing the path to nirvāṇa.

8) The Tathāgata *recollects in detail his manifold past lives with their aspects and particulars.* This and the next power are the last two of the five superknowledges (*abhiññā, abhijñā*). Thus he knows his previous relationships with each sentient being and what types of relationship would be most beneficial to have with them now and in the future.

9) With the divine eye, he sees beings dying and being born according to their karma. Knowing this, he does whatever is most beneficial to guide each being on the path to awakening.

10) Realizing with direct knowledge, the Tathāgata here and now *enters upon and abides in the unpolluted liberation of mind* (*cetovimutti, cittavimukti*) *and liberation by wisdom* (*paññāvimutti, prajñāvimukti*)[5] *and knows that all defilements have been eradicated.* He also knows the level of realization and attainment of each being of the three vehicles. The last three powers are the three higher knowledges (*tevijjā, trividyā*) that the Buddha gained while meditating during the night prior to his awakening.

Both the Pāli tradition (in later commentaries) and the Sanskrit tradition (in the Prajñāpāramitā sūtras) describe *eighteen qualities of a buddha not shared by other arhats* (*aṭṭhārasāveṇikabuddhadhammā, aṣṭādaśāveṇikabuddhadharma*):

Six unshared behaviors

1. Due to mindfulness and conscientiousness, a buddha has no mistaken physical actions, whether he is walking, standing, sitting, or lying down. He acts in accordance with what he says, and his speech satisfies what each sentient being who is listening needs to understand in that moment.
2. Always speaking appropriately, truthfully, and kindly, he is free from mistaken speech and idle chatter. A buddha does not dispute with the world, nor does he complain about what others have done.
3. He is free from any kind of lack of mindfulness interfering with the jhānas and exalted wisdom, or with viewing all sentient beings and teaching them appropriately.
4. His mind always abides in meditative equipoise on emptiness, and simultaneously he teaches sentient beings the Dharma.
5. He does not perceive any discordant appearances of a self and of inherent

existence and thus recognizes all phenomena as sharing the one taste of emptiness. He also does not treat sentient beings with bias.

6. He abides in perfect equanimity, knowing the individual characteristics of each phenomenon.

Six unshared realizations

1. Due to his all-encompassing love and compassion, a buddha never experiences any decline of his aspiration and intention to benefit all sentient beings and to increase their virtuous qualities.
2. He never loses joyous effort to lead others to awakening. A buddha experiences no physical, verbal, or mental fatigue and continuously cares for the welfare of sentient beings without getting tired, lazy, or despondent.
3. A buddha's mindfulness effortlessly remains constant and uninterrupted. He is mindful also of the situations each sentient being encounters in the past, present, and future and the methods to subdue and help them.
4. He continuously remains in samādhi, free from all obscurations and focused on the ultimate reality.
5. His wisdom is inexhaustible and never declines. He perfectly knows the 84,000 Dharma teachings and the doctrines of the three vehicles, as well as how and when to express them to sentient beings.
6. It is impossible for him to lose the state of full awakening free from all obscurations. He knows the mind to be naturally luminous, and he lacks any dualistic appearance or grasping at duality.

Three unshared awakening activities

1. Imbued with exalted wisdom, a buddha's physical actions are always done for the benefit of others. He emanates many bodies that appear wherever sentient beings have the karma to be led on the path to awakening. Whatever a buddha does has a positive effect on sentient beings, subduing their minds.
2. Knowing the dispositions and interests of each sentient being, he teaches the Dharma in a manner appropriate for that person. His speech flows smoothly, is accurate and lovely to listen to. It does not deceive or lead others astray but is clear, knowledgeable, and kind.
3. Filled with undeclining love and compassion, his mind encompasses all beings with the intention to do only what is of the highest benefit. He is effortlessly and continuously cognizant of all phenomena.

Three unshared exalted wisdoms
A buddha's exalted wisdom knows everything in the three times—past, present, and future—without any obscuration or error. His knowledge of the future does not mean that things are predetermined. Rather, a buddha knows that if a sentient being does a particular action, this particular result will follow, and if another course of action is taken, a different result will come. He knows all buddhafields and realms of sentient beings as well as all the beings and their activities there.

Reading such passages from the sūtras gives us an idea of a buddha's exceptional qualities. Contemplating them brings joy and expands our mental horizons. These passages also give us an idea of the qualities we will attain if we practice the Dharma as the Buddha instructed.

While the descriptions of the four fearlessnesses and ten powers in the Pāli and Sanskrit traditions do not differ considerably, the Sanskrit tradition emphasizes how these abilities benefit sentient beings.

Three Jewels: Pāli Tradition

All Buddhists take refuge in the Three Jewels and not in a particular Buddhist tradition, lineage, or individual teacher. Our refuge is in general the Three Jewels. The Pāli tradition's and the Sanskrit tradition's descriptions of the Three Jewels contain many common points as well as points unique to each tradition. First we'll examine the Pāli tradition.

The *Buddha Jewel* is the historical Buddha who lived approximately 2,600 years ago and turned the Dhamma wheel for the benefit of sentient beings. To refer to himself the Buddha frequently used the term *Tathāgata*, the "one thus gone," because he has gone to nibbāna, the unconditioned state, by perfecting serenity and insight, the paths and the fruits. *Tathāgata* also means the "one thus come": the Buddha has come to nibbāna in the same way all the previous buddhas have, by perfecting the thirty-seven aids to awakening, completing the ten perfections; giving away his body and possessions in charity to others, and acting for the welfare of the world.

A Tathāgata has fully awakened to the nature of this world, its origin, its cessation, and the way to its cessation. He has fully understood and can directly perceive all things that can be seen, heard, sensed, known, cognized, and thought about, knowing them just as they are. Everything a Tathāgata says is true and correct. His words and actions accord with each other; he is free from hypocrisy. He has conquered the foes of the afflictions and is not conquered by them. Thereby, he possesses great power to benefit the world.

The Tathāgata has realized two great principles: dependent arising and nibbāna. Dependent arising applies to the entirety of the conditioned world of saṃsāra of true dukkha and true origins. All worldly things arise dependent on their specific conditions (*idappaccayatā, idampratyayatā*) and are impermanent. Nibbāna is the unconditioned—true cessation—which is realized by true paths. Together dependent arising and nibbāna include all existents, so understanding them is understanding all existents.

The Buddha is praised as the one who actualized the Dhamma and taught it to others. A famous passage in the Pāli canon describes the relationship of the Dhamma and the Buddha. When speaking to the monk Vakkali, who was gravely ill and regretted not having been able to see the Buddha sooner, the Buddha replied (SN 22:87):

> Enough, Vakkali! Why do you want to see this foul body? One who sees the Dhamma sees me; one who sees me sees the Dhamma.

Seeing and knowing the Buddha is not done physically but through mental development. Being close to the Buddha means actualizing the same true paths and true cessations he has. The extent to which our minds have been transformed into the Dhamma is the extent to which we see the Buddha. Regarding this quotation, in his commentary the *Sāratthappakāsinī*, Buddhaghosa explains:

> Here the Blessed One shows [himself as] the Dhamma body (*dhammakāya*), as stated in the passage "The Tathāgata, great king, is the Dhamma body." For the ninefold supramundane Dhamma [the four ariya paths, their fruits, and nibbāna] is called the Tathāgata's body.

The *Dhamma Jewel* consists of true cessation and true path. *True cessation* is the ultimate aim of spiritual practice. It is the unconditioned, nibbāna, the deathless state. Nibbāna is not produced by causes and conditions; it is not impermanent and does not change in each moment. Four synonyms of nibbāna describe it from different angles: (1) It is *destruction*—of ignorance, attachment, anger, and especially of craving. (2) It is *dispassion*, the absence of attachment, desire, greed, and lust. (3) It is the *deathless*, free from saṃsāric birth, aging, sickness, and death. (4) It is *excellence*—supreme, never-ending, and inexhaustible.

True path refers to the supramundane noble eightfold path (*ariya aṭṭhaṅgika magga, āryāṣṭāṅgamārga*) that leads to nibbāna. To develop this, we first cultivate the ordinary eightfold path by practicing ethical conduct, the four establishments of mindfulness, and mundane right concentration. As our concentration increases and our understanding of the body, feelings, mind, and phenomena being impermanent, unsatisfactory, and not self deepens, we will reach a point where the breakthrough by wisdom (*paññāya abhisamaya*) arises and realizes nibbāna. While the mind dwells in concentration, wisdom penetrates the ultimate truth. Certain defilements are extinguished, and when one emerges from that concentration, one is an ariya and a stream-enterer. This concentration is praised beyond all other samādhis because it leads to lasting beneficial results, while worldly samādhis lead to rebirths in the material (form) and immaterial (formless) realms.

The *Saṅgha Jewel* is the community of ariyas—those who have realized nibbāna, thus becoming "noble"—which consists of eight types of persons subsumed in four pairs—those approaching and those abiding in the states of stream-enterer (*sotāpanna, srotāpanna*), once-returner (*sakadagami, sakṛtāgāmi*), nonreturner (*anāgāmi*), and arahant (arhat). During the approach phase of each pair, a practitioner is in the process of developing the *path* that will culminate in its corresponding *fruit*, or result. Each path is marked by a breakthrough in which one sees nibbāna ever more clearly and thus subdues or eradicates a certain portion of defilements. The four pairs of persons are called *sāvakas* (*śrāvaka*), literally "disciples" or "hearers," and due to their spiritual realizations they are worthy of offerings. Those who make offerings to the ariya sāvakas accumulate great merit that brings them upper rebirths and circumstances conducive to practicing Dhamma.

Realization of the four truths is the essence of the ariya path. Until people are spiritually mature, the Buddha teaches them other Dhamma topics. Full penetration of the four truths comes about through practicing the thirty-seven aids to awakening and cultivating serenity and insight. The moment one becomes a stream-enterer, one experiences a breakthrough called the *arising of the eye of the Dhamma*, because for the first time one directly sees the Dhamma, the truth of the Buddha's teaching, nibbāna. One now changes lineage from being an ordinary person to being an ariya.

Through directly realizing nibbāna, stream-enterers completely abandon three fetters (*samyojana, saṃyojana*): (1) They no longer have the *view of a personal identity* (*sakkāyadiṭṭhi, satkāyadṛṣṭi*) that grasps a real self existing in relation to the five aggregates. Such a self could be a self that is identical to one of the aggregates, possesses the aggregates, is possessed by the aggregates, is inside the aggregates (like a jewel in a box), or contains the aggregates (like a box containing five jewels). (2) *Doubt* (*vicikicchā, vicikitsā*) in the Buddha, Dhamma, and Saṅgha being reliable sources of refuge vanishes due to having direct experience of the Dhamma taught by the Buddha. (3) They eliminate the view of rules and practices (*sīlabbataparāmāsa, śīlavrataparāmarśa*). Stream-enterers maintain precepts and perform various ceremonies but do not cling to rules or to the idea that correct performance of ceremonies has special power in and of itself to bring liberation.

Stream-enterers may be monastics or lay practitioners. The former keep their monastic precepts very well, and the latter keep the five precepts. While stream-enterers may still commit minor transgressions such as speaking harshly due to anger, they never conceal offenses and immediately confess them and make a strong determination to restrain themselves thereafter. Due to the power of their realization, it is impossible for stream-enterers to commit six great wrongs: the five heinous actions (killing one's mother, father, or an arahant, causing schism in the Saṅgha, and maliciously injuring the Buddha) and regarding anyone other than the Buddha as the supreme spiritual master. Attaining the stage of stream-entry is highly praised for these reasons.

Stream-enterers will never again be born as hell beings, hungry ghosts, animals, or asuras and will take at most seven more rebirths in saṃsāra before attaining arahantship. Stream-enterers with sharp faculties take only one more rebirth; those with middle faculties take two to six rebirths; and those with dull faculties take seven more rebirths.

While they have profound spiritual insight and are firmly on the path to liberation, stream-enterers have overcome only three of the ten fetters, and their minds are not immune to the *eight worldly concerns*—delight with material gain, praise, good reputation, and sensual pleasure and dejection with material loss, blame, notoriety, and unpleasant sensory experiences.

They may still create destructive kamma, although it is not strong enough to bring unfortunate rebirths. In some cases, their external behavior may even resemble that of ordinary beings. They may be attached to their family, enjoy being praised, or compete with others. Sometimes they may even be heedless. Nevertheless, their faith in the Three Jewels is unshakable, and they will definitely continue on the path to arahantship.

Compared to stream-enterers, once-returners have significantly reduced their sensual desire and malice, although they have not yet fully eliminated them. They will be reborn in the desire realm only once more. Nonreturners have abandoned the fetters of sensual desire and malice and will never again take rebirth in the desire realm. If they don't attain nibbāna in that life, they will be reborn in the material (form) realm, often in a pure land, a special group of realms inhabited only by nonreturners or arahants. They will attain nibbāna there.

In the path phase, approachers to arahantship practice the Buddha's teachings with effort and diligence. In the fruit phase, they actualize their goal, become arahants, and are no longer bound by craving. All remaining fetters of desire for existence in the material and immaterial realms, conceit, restlessness, and ignorance are abandoned, and they attain the deathless—the state free from saṃsāra's repeated birth and death—and enjoy the peace of genuine freedom.

Three Jewels: Sanskrit Tradition

Most of what appeared in the foregoing Pāli section is shared by the Sanskrit tradition. The Sanskrit tradition also relies on such treatises as the *Ratnagotravibhāga* (*Uttaratantra Śāstra*) as sources for understanding the excellent qualities of the Three Jewels and their ultimate and conventional aspects. Learning and contemplating these inspire our confidence in them and show us the direction to take in our spiritual practice so that we can become the Three Jewels.

Each of the Three Jewels has ultimate and conventional aspects that encompass the four bodies (*kāya*)[6] of a buddha:

The *ultimate Buddha Jewel* is the dharmakāya, having the nature of perfect abandonment and perfect realization. This is of two types:

1. The *wisdom dharmakāya* (*jñāna dharmakāya*) has three principal qualities: Due to their omniscient *knowledge*, buddhas effortlessly

and perfectly understand the entire variety of phenomena, including the dispositions and capabilities of sentient beings. Due to their *compassionate love* and *abilities*, without any hesitation or self-doubt, they teach appropriate paths according to the different inclinations of sentient beings.

2. The *nature dharmakāya* (*svabhāvika dharmakāya*) is unconditioned and free from arising and disintegration. It is of two types:
   - The *natural stainless purity* is the emptiness of inherent existence of a buddha's mind.
   - The *purity from adventitious defilements* refers to a buddha's true cessation that is free from the afflictive obscurations (*kilesāvaraṇa, kleśāvaraṇa*) binding us in saṃsāra and the cognitive obscurations (*ñeyyāvaraṇa, jñeyāvaraṇa*) hindering knowledge of all phenomena and effortless work for the welfare of sentient beings.

The *conventional Buddha Jewel* is the form bodies (*rūpakāya*) of a buddha, which are of two types:

1. An *enjoyment body* (*saṃbhogakāya*) abides in a pure land and teaches ārya bodhisattvas.
2. *Emanation bodies* (*nirmāṇakāya*) are the appearances of a buddha in a form perceivable by ordinary beings.

Contemplating the four buddha bodies gives us a deeper understanding of Buddha Śākyamuni. The Buddha's physical appearance as a human being such as Gautama Buddha is an emanation body, a form he assumed to suit the spiritual dispositions and needs of ordinary beings. An emanation body derives from a subtler body, an enjoyment body. An enjoyment body emerges from the omniscient mind of a buddha, the wisdom dharmakāya. A wisdom dharmakāya arises within the underlying nature of reality, a buddha's nature dharmakāya.

The *ultimate Dharma Jewel* is the true cessations and true paths in the mindstreams of āryas of all three vehicles—the Śrāvaka, Pratyekabuddha, and Bodhisattva vehicles.

1. *True paths* are consciousnesses informed by the wisdom directly and nonconceptually realizing the subtle selflessness of persons and phenomena. Among them, an *uninterrupted path* is a wisdom directly realizing emptiness that is in the process of eliminating some degree

of defilements. When those particular defilements have been completely abandoned, that wisdom becomes a *liberated path*.

2. A *true cessation* is the purified aspect of the emptiness of a mind that has abandoned a particular degree of obscurations. True cessations have two factors: natural purity and the purity of adventitious defilements, as described above. True cessations are known by oneself in meditative equipoise on emptiness in which all dualistic appearances have vanished.

The *conventional Dharma Jewel* refers to the transmitted Dharma, the 84,000 teachings, the twelve branches of scripture—the Buddha's word taught from his own experience with compassion and skill.

The *ultimate Saṅgha Jewel* is the knowledge (true paths) and liberation (true cessations) in the mindstream of an ārya. True cessations and true paths are both the ultimate Dharma Jewel and the ultimate Saṅgha Jewel.

The *conventional Saṅgha Jewel* is an individual ārya or an assembly of āryas of any of the three vehicles. It includes the eight śrāvaka āryas and bodhisattvas.

The Saṅgha Jewel has inner wisdom that correctly knows reality and knows some portion of the diversity of phenomena. The ārya saṅgha is free from some portion of afflictive obscurations—ignorance, afflictions, their seeds, and polluted karma. Some āryas are also free from some portion of the wish for only personal nirvāṇa that prevents generating bodhicitta. Some ārya bodhisattvas are free from a portion of the cognitive obscurations—the latencies of ignorance and the appearance of inherent existence.

The representation of the Saṅgha Jewel is a community of four or more fully ordained monastics.

Enumerating the excellent qualities of the Three Jewels illustrates why they are valuable and complete sources of refuge. Understanding this, we will repeatedly take refuge in them from the depth of our hearts and deepen our connection with them. In this way, we will always be able to call on their guidance no matter what situations we face in life or at the time of death.

This description of the Three Jewels emphasizes the inner experiential aspect of religion and spirituality. Our objects of refuge—those that we trust completely to lead us to liberation and full awakening—are distinct from religious institutions. While realized beings may be members of religious institutions, these institutions are often operated by ordinary beings.

When taking refuge, being aware of the difference between our actual objects of refuge and religious institutions is important.

Buddha's Awakening, Parinirvāṇa, and Omniscience

The Three Jewels are called "jewels" because they are rare and precious. Like the mythical wish-fulfilling jewel that grants all wishes and needs, they are continuously willing and capable of providing us refuge, protecting us from saṃsāra's duḥkha, and showing us the way to attain lasting, pure, and blissful fulfillment. The Buddha Jewel is the source of sentient beings' virtuous intentions, encouraging us to seek upper rebirth, liberation, and full awakening.

While followers of both the Pāli and Sanskrit traditions take refuge in the Buddha, they may have different perspectives on his awakening, parinirvāṇa, and omniscience. The Pāli tradition says he practiced as a bodhisatta for many previous lifetimes and attained full awakening under the bodhi tree in his life as Siddhattha Gotama. As a buddha, he had no mental pain but experienced physical pain due to having a body produced under the power of craving and kamma. Some say that when he passed away and attained *mahāparinibbāna*, all saṃsāric rebirth ceased, and his consciousness entered nibbāna, an everlasting, stable, unconditioned, peaceful reality that cannot be conceived in terms of time and space. Here *parinibbāna* is a reality that is the opposite of the polluted, impermanent aggregates. Others say that parinibbāna is the cessation of the defilements and the continuation of the aggregates. Here the complete cessation of the aggregates is considered peaceful.

In general, the Sanskrit tradition believes that Gautama Buddha practiced as a bodhisattva for many previous lifetimes and attained full awakening before his life as Siddhartha Gautama. However, by appearing as an unawakened being who attained full awakening in that lifetime, he illustrated the importance of exerting effort and working diligently to train the mind. Through his example, he gave others confidence that they could practice and attain the same awakening he did.

While the Sanskrit tradition agrees that the polluted aggregates do not continue after the causes for saṃsāric rebirth have been extinguished, it says there is no agent or antidote that can totally cease the continuum of the luminous and aware nature of the mind, which remains uninterrupted and endless. When some texts say that the psychophysical aggregates are abandoned at the time of parinirvāṇa, Nāgārjuna explains this refers to their not appearing to an arhat's meditative equipoise on emptiness. At the time of parinirvāṇa, the aggregates in general continue; however they are now purified aggregates. Because the Buddha appeared from the enjoyment body and ultimately from the dharmakāya—both of which are endless—when he passed away, the continuity of his awakened mind remained. While Gautama Buddha no longer exists, the continuum of that omniscient mind continues to fulfill the purpose for which he practiced the Dharma so diligently for so long: to lead all sentient beings to full awakening. To do that, he effortlessly manifests emanation bodies to benefit sentient beings throughout the universe.

From the Buddha's side, he is always ready and capable to help, but because of our lack of merit and spiritual experience, we cannot see him. Just as sunlight radiates everywhere equally, the buddhas' emanations and awakening activities spread everywhere. However, just as an upside-down vessel cannot receive the sunlight, our karmic obscurations and lack of merit curtail the buddhas' ability to help us. When the vessel is turned upright the sun naturally enters; when we purify our minds and accumulate merit, our mind's receptivity to the buddhas' awakening activities increases, and we will be able to understand things such as the four buddha bodies that until then we may have found baffling.

I have heard of some Theravāda monks who are skilled meditators and who say the clear, bright, and aware *citta* (mind), while being superficially tangled up in afflictions, is not subject to complete destruction like saṃsāric phenomena. Afflictions are not inherent in the citta, although it needs to be cleansed of the defilements that obscure it. Deathless and independent of time and space, the citta continues to exist after wisdom has ceased all defilements. One of these monks, Ajahn Mun from the Thai forest tradition, lived in the late nineteenth and early twentieth centuries. He had visions of Buddha Śākyamuni and the arhats, leading him to believe that the mental continua of these realized beings did not cease at the time of death. Such experiences are possible when our defilements have been purified.

Regarding a buddha's omniscience, or all-knowing (*sabbaññutañāṇa*, *sarvākārajñāna*), the Sanskrit tradition says that all existents—past, present, and future—appear to a buddha's mind in every moment. This is possible because the nature of the mind is clear and aware, and once all obscurations are removed, nothing can prevent the mind from knowing objects.

Some passages in the Pāli canon indicate that while the Buddha knows all existents, he does not simultaneously perceive all of them with one consciousness. When the wanderer Vacchagotta directly asks the Buddha if it is true that no matter what he is doing, knowledge of everything is always present in him, the Buddha replies that it is not (MN 71). In general, Pāli commentators take the Buddha's response to mean that while he knows all that is, it does not appear to his mind continuously at all times. Rather, while all knowledge is available to him, he must turn his mind to that topic before it effortlessly appears. Present-day followers of the Pāli tradition have varying thoughts on this.

Some people doubt that the Buddha can see the future, claiming the future would be predetermined. However, one does not entail the other. At any particular moment, the Buddha could see the constellation of causes and conditions that could possibly bring about a certain event in the future, and at the same time know that these causes and conditions change in the next moment. The commentary to the *Visuddhimagga* says that the Buddha knows past and future events by direct perception,[7] and the *Paṭisambhidāmagga* confirms that all past, present, and future phenomena come within the Buddha's faculty of knowledge.

The difference in how the Pāli and Sanskrit traditions describe the Buddha need not confuse us. We don't have to choose one view over the other. Rather, we can see which view inspires us at a particular time. When we feel discouraged, thinking of Siddhartha Gautama as having been an ordinary being who faced the same difficulties on the path as we do is helpful. Just as he diligently practiced the path and attained awakening, so can we.

At other times, seeing Buddha Śākyamuni as one who attained awakening eons ago and appeared in our world as an emanation body is more helpful. This view gives us the feeling of being cared for by many buddhas who are present to guide us.

When I contemplate the Buddha's qualities as depicted in the early Pāli suttas, it seems his abilities as portrayed in the Sanskrit sūtras are a natural extension of those. For example, the Buddha tells Ānanda (DN 16:3.22) that he remembers attending many hundreds of assemblies of *khattiyas* (the ruling caste), where he sat and spoke with them. To do this he adopted their appearance and speech and instructed, inspired, and delighted them with Dhamma discourses. Yet these people did not know who he was and wondered whether he were a *deva* (celestial being) or a man. Having instructed them, he disappeared. The Buddha says the same about his actions in assemblies of brahmans, householders, ascetics, and devas. This passage reminds me of the activities of a buddha's emanation body.

Nowhere in either the Pāli or Sanskrit sūtras is the Buddha seen as either omnipotent or as a creator. He does not seek our worship, and we do not have to propitiate him to gain boons. He does not reward those who follow his teachings and punish those who don't. The Buddha described the path to awakening from his own experience. His intention is only to benefit sentient beings according to their individual inclinations and temperament.

However we think of the Buddha—as already awakened or as attaining awakening during his life on Earth—his life is an example and his attainments an inspiration for us. He had the internal strength to follow his spiritual yearnings, and his confidence in the potential of the human mind was unassailable. With great perseverance he trained in serenity and insight.

When I reflect on the three higher knowledges mentioned in the Pāli suttas, I recognize a correspondence with what the Tibetan sage Tsongkhapa later called the three principal aspects of the path—renunciation, bodhicitta, and correct view. While these are generated before one becomes a buddha, they reach their fulfillment at buddhahood. With the first higher knowledge, the Buddha saw his previous lives—their duḥkha and transience. Knowing all that misery was caused by afflictions and karma, he responded with full *renunciation* of saṃsāra, making the determination to attain liberation. With the second higher knowledge, he saw the passing away and rebirth of sentient beings under the influence of afflictions and karma. His reaction to this horror was impartial love, compassion, and *bodhicitta*. To fulfill this altruistic commitment, he freed his mind of all pollutants and obscurations by realizing the *correct view* of the subtle selflessness of persons and phenomena. Through repeatedly using this wisdom to cleanse his mind, he gained the third knowledge and knew that his mind was totally purified and that he had attained nirvāṇa.

Both Pāli and Sanskrit traditions speak of ours being a fortunate eon in which Gautama Buddha is the fourth wheel-turning buddha to appear and Maitreya will be the fifth. Wheel-turning buddhas are those who give teachings when and where the Dhamma is not otherwise known. According to

Ellora Caves, India

the Pāli tradition, these buddhas are the only buddhas in our world during this eon; other practitioners will become arhats. According to the Sanskrit tradition, every sentient being has the potential to become a buddha, and there are many buddhas in our eon.

Taking Refuge and Maintaining Proper Refuge

I believe there can be different levels of refuge in the Three Jewels, and people may take refuge at a level comfortable and appropriate for them. This helps them on their spiritual path and encourages them to continue learning and practicing the Buddha's teachings. For some people, a comfortable level of refuge involves appreciating the teachings on love and compassion, for others it includes belief in rebirth. What is important is that they trust and respect the Three Jewels.

Within the context of the Buddhist worldview that accepts rebirth, there are several causes for taking refuge. (1) Alarm at the possibility of taking unfortunate rebirth is an immediate cause leading us to seek refuge in the Three Jewels. Alarm at the duḥkha of pervasive conditioning spurs us to seek refuge in them to guide us out of saṃsāra. (2) Understanding the qualities of the Three Jewels and their ability to guide us, we generate faith and confidence in them that is based on knowledge. (3) With compassion, those following the Bodhisattvayāna take refuge in the Three Jewels to attain full awakening so they will be able to alleviate the duḥkha of fellow sentient beings.

It is important to reflect on the qualities of the Three Jewels, the reasons for taking refuge in them, and the meaning of doing so. Having done that, when in our heart we entrust our spiritual guidance to the Three Jewels because we recognize them as reliable sources of refuge, we have found the real meaning of taking refuge and have become Buddhist. However, even without becoming Buddhists, people can practice the teachings that help them in their lives and leave the rest aside for the moment.

Some people wish to affirm their refuge in the Three Jewels by participating in a ceremony in which they recite the refuge formula after a spiritual mentor and take some or all of the five lay precepts (*pañcasīla, pañcaśīla*). These five are to abandon killing, stealing, unwise and unkind sexual behavior, lying, and taking intoxicants.

After taking refuge, people follow guidelines to help them maintain and deepen their refuge. These guidelines include to avoid harming sentient beings, criticizing whatever we dislike, being rough and arrogant, running after desirable objects, engaging in the ten nonvirtues,[8] taking refuge in worldly spirits or gods, and cultivating the friendship of people who criticize the Three Jewels or act in nonvirtuous ways. We also do our best to follow a qualified spiritual mentor, study and put the teachings into practice in our daily life, respect members of the Saṅgha and follow their good examples, be compassionate to other sentient beings, take the eight one-day precepts twice a month, make offerings to the Three Jewels, encourage others to take refuge in the Three Jewels, take refuge three times each morning and evening, offer our food before eating, and respect Buddhist images and Dharma books.

One guideline for maintaining pure refuge is not to turn to other objects of refuge that lack the ability and the qualities to guide us to awakening. Buddha Śākyamuni is our Teacher, and an image of Buddha Śākyamuni should be at the front center of our altar. We entrust our entire spiritual well-being to the Buddha. If we feel remorse for acting harmfully, we confess and purify in the Buddha's presence. We generate virtuous aspirations to become like the Buddha and his Saṅgha in the Buddha's presence.

Most Buddhist traditions speak of Dharma protectors—beings who help practitioners on the path. These Dharma protectors may be supramundane or worldly. Supramundane protectors have directly realized emptiness and are included in the Saṅgha refuge. In the Tibetan context, protectors such as the four great kings and Nechung are worldly beings who have made promises to great masters to protect the Dharma and practitioners. They are not included in the Three Jewels. We may rely on them for temporal help for virtuous purposes in the same way we rely on a powerful person to help us in a time of need. However, we do not seek spiritual refuge in them.

Spirits are saṃsāric beings. Like human beings, some spirits are helpful and others harmful. Some have clairvoyant powers, others do not. Some have virtuous qualities, while others are angry and spiteful. Due to ignorance some people turn to local spirits and spirits such as Dorje Shugden for refuge. Because these beings help only in temporal ways, practitioners' motivations degenerate, and instead of seeking awakening, they seek wealth or power through pleasing the spirit. This corrupts their Dharma practice and runs counter to the Buddha's teachings, in which he clearly stated we are responsible for creating the causes for happiness by abandoning destructive actions and creating constructive ones. Refuge in the Three Jewels and following the law of karma and its effects are the real protection from duḥkha.

Worldly people often look for external things such as amulets, blessed water, and protection strings to protect them from danger. If these things help them to remember the Buddha's teachings and practice them, that is fine. But if they think that these objects possess some inherent power from their own side, they are mistaken. In fact, human beings need to protect the amulets, strings, and so forth because they are easily damaged!

We must always remember that Dharma practice occurs in our minds. True practice entails identifying our afflictions and applying antidotes to them.

3 | Sixteen Attributes of the Four Truths

THE FOUR TRUTHS OF THE ĀRYAS (Pāli: *ariyas*), commonly known as the *four noble truths*, form the framework for understanding all of the Buddha's teachings. Contemplating them deeply motivates us to seek liberation and enables us to understand how the practices we do lead to liberation. Both the Pāli and Sanskrit traditions speak of sixteen attributes of the four truths. Although the list of the sixteen differs in the two traditions and there are differences in their subtle meaning, their overall meaning is similar.

Sanskrit Tradition

Vasubandhu's *Abhidharmakośa* and Dharmakīrti's *Pramāṇavārttika* explain that each of the four truths has four attributes that counteract four distorted conceptions about that truth. The sixteen attributes explain the truths according to their different functions and demonstrate the existence of liberation and the method to attain it.

Four Attributes of True Duḥkha

True duḥkha, or the truth of duḥkha (*dukkha-sacca, duḥkha-satya*), is the polluted aggregates—body, feelings, discriminations, volitional factors (compositional factors), and consciousness. "Polluted" means under the control of afflictions—especially ignorance—and karma. Internal true duḥkha is in the continuum of the person and includes our polluted bodies and minds. External true duḥkha includes the things in our environment that we use and enjoy.

Our physical and mental aggregates are specified as examples of true duḥkha because they are the direct product of afflictions and karma. In addition, they form the basis of designation of the I or self. "Self" has different meanings, depending on the context: (1) The "self" in the fourth attribute refers to the *object of negation* by the wisdom realizing reality. The object of negation may refer to a permanent self or soul, a self-sufficient substantially existent person, or the inherent or independent existence of all phenomena as in "all phenomena are empty of self" or "the selflessness of persons and phenomena." Here "selfless" does not mean the opposite of selfish; it means "not self." (2) "Self" can refer to the conventionally existent person, or I, who walks, meditates, and so forth.

1. The polluted aggregates are impermanent (anicca, anitya) *because they undergo continuous momentary arising and disintegration.*
Understanding this dispels the distortion believing impermanent things are permanent. "Impermanent" here means changing moment by moment. All conditioned phenomena undergo change, disintegrating from what they were and becoming something new. Coarse change occurs when a thing ceases: a person dies, a chair breaks. Subtle change occurs moment by moment—it is a thing's not remaining the same from one instant to the next.

Our senses observe coarse impermanence. However, for something such as our body to be born and cease in this obvious way, there must be a more subtle process of change taking place each moment. Without it, the coarse, observable change from childhood to old age could not occur.

Almost all Buddhists accept that the moment a thing comes into being, it has the nature of disintegrating simply by the fact that it was produced by causes. It is not the case that a cause produces something, that thing remains unchanged for a period of time, and then another condition causes its cessation. Rather, the very factor that causes something to arise also causes it to cease. From the very first moment of a thing's existence, it has the nature of disintegrating. Momentariness indicates that arising and ceasing are not contradictory but are two attributes of the same process.

The present is insubstantial. It is an unfindable threshold between the past (what has already happened) and the future (what is yet to happen). While we spend a great deal of time pondering the past and planning for the future, neither of them is occurring right now. The only time we ever live is in the present, but the present is elusive, changing in each nanosecond. We cannot stop the flow of time to examine a fixed present moment.

Understanding impermanence is a powerful antidote to harmful emotions based on grasping impermanent things—our dear ones, possessions, moods, and problems—as permanent. Do not fall into nihilism thinking that nothing is worthwhile because it will change. Rather, because things are transient, attachment and anger toward them is impractical. Impermanence also means that when we create the causes, our positive qualities such as love, compassion, and altruism will grow.

The Pāli suttas describe impermanence as "arising and passing away." Occasionally, they speak about "knowing things as they arise, as they are present, and as they pass away," outlining three phases: arising, changing while abiding, and disintegrating. The Abhidhamma agrees with this formalization. Meditators focus on the sutta presentation of arising and passing away and, within that, especially on passing away because that forcefully highlights impermanence. Practicing mindfulness, meditators pay close attention to physical and mental processes, coming to see that what appear to be unified objects or events are in fact processes that arise and cease in each moment due to causes and conditions. As mindfulness deepens, subtle impermanence is seen clearly with direct experience.

Seeing arising dispels *annihilation*—the notion that things do not exist at all or that the continuity of the person and of the effects of karma totally stop at death. Seeing disintegration dispels *eternalism*—the notion that people and things have a substantial, permanent, eternal reality.

2. *The polluted aggregates are* unsatisfactory (dukkha, duḥkha) *because they are under the control of afflictions and karma.*

Understanding this counteracts the distorted thought holding things that are by nature unsatisfactory to be blissful. Due to being under the control of afflictions and karma, our aggregates are subject to three types of duḥkha. The *duḥkha of pain* includes painful physical and mental feelings that all sentient beings consider suffering. The *duḥkha of change* includes happy feelings that are polluted because they are unstable, do not last, and leave us dissatisfied. Any pleasurable activity, pursued continuously, eventually becomes uncomfortable. The *duḥkha of pervasive conditioning* is the fact that our aggregates are under the control of afflictions—ignorance in particular—and karma.

While we all want happiness, it eludes us because our body and mind are under the control of afflictions and karma. Understanding that saṃsāric phenomena are unsatisfactory, we turn away from seeing them as the source of lasting bliss and joy, and we release unrealistic expectations of them. Seeing that clinging to saṃsāric things is useless and frustrating, we relinquish clinging in favor of practicing the path and actualizing true cessations.

3. The polluted aggregates are empty (suñña, śūnya) *because of not being a permanent, unitary, and independent self.*
This understanding counteracts the distortion believing the body, which is unclean, has an impeccable possessor.

Theravāda, Yogācāra, and Madhyamaka tenets have some similar and some different ideas about the meaning of the third and fourth attributes. An explanation that all Buddhist schools accept is that "empty" refers to the absence of a permanent, unitary, independent self or soul that is a different entity from the aggregates. In this context "permanent" means eternally unchanging, not produced or destroyed. "Unitary" indicates not depending on parts but being one monolithic whole. "Independent" refers to not depending on causes and conditions.

4. The polluted aggregates are selfless or not-self (anattā, nairātmya) *because they lack a self-sufficient substantially existent self.*
Understanding this opposes the distortion grasping that the aggregates, which lack a self-sufficient substantially existent self, are such a self. The explanation accepted by all Buddhists glosses *selfless* as the absence of a self-sufficient substantially existent person. Such a person would be the same entity as the aggregates, a self that controls the aggregates like a ruler over his subjects. When we say "I" or "my body and mind," we have the impression that there is a self who owns and dominates the aggregates. We feel this self is not merely imputed on the aggregates. Here "merely imputed" means the person cannot be identified without identifying something else such as the aggregates.

In the Pāli tradition, impermanent, dukkha, and not-self are known as the *three characteristics* of things conditioned by ignorance. Meditating on them with insight is the core of the path. In the Sanskrit tradition, impermanent and duḥkha are realized first, then meditators focus on selflessness and emptiness together with bodhicitta.

The Yogācāra school accepts the person as being empty and selfless. It also accepts the selflessness of other phenomena in that they are empty of

Mike Nowak

GAL VIHARA, SRI LANKA

being a different nature from the consciousness perceiving them and are empty of existing by their own characteristics as the referent of a term.

Mādhyamikas follow the meaning of *empty* and *selfless* found in the Prajñāpāramitā sūtras. Here both words refer to the absence of inherent, true, or independent existence and apply to all phenomena. Inherent existence is an essence that should be findable in the basis of designation and should exist without depending on being merely designated by names and concept. A false mode of being, it is refuted on both persons and other phenomena. All phenomena are empty and selfless because they exist dependent on other factors.

To tie these four attributes together, our body and mind change moment by moment; this is their nature. Our aggregates are controlled by their causes, which are ultimately traced to ignorance. Anything caused by ignorance is by nature unsatisfactory; it is the duḥkha of pervasive conditioning. Once we develop this awareness, then no matter how beautiful, pleasurable, and enticing things appear, we know they are not worth clinging to. They are empty and selfless.

Reflecting on these four attributes of true duḥkha is sobering and dramatically alters our perspective on who we are and what will bring us happiness, leading us to renounce craving for polluted aggregates and seek nirvāṇa, true peace. The practice of the four establishments of mindfulness, which will be described later, is a powerful method to realize the four attributes of true duḥkha.

Four Attributes of True Origins

True origins (*samudaya-sacca, samudaya-satya*) of duḥkha are afflictions and polluted karma. Karma, or actions, are driven by afflictions such as attachment and anger, which originate in the fundamental affliction, ignorance. Ignorance prevents us from seeing the aggregates are empty and selfless.

According to the Pāli tradition, ignorance is a state of unknowing and obscuration regarding the truth. This ignorance functions in two ways. As mental darkness, it conceals and obscures the true nature of phenomena. It also creates false appearances or distortions (*vipallāsa, vaparyāsa*)—the four distorted conceptions about true duḥkha mentioned above. Distortions operate on three levels. First we *perceive* things incorrectly. Based on this, we *think* about them in a wrong way. This leads to *understanding* our experience incorrectly. Understanding the three characteristics clears away these distortions. Through learning and reflection we gain a correct conceptual understanding of the three characteristics; through meditation we gain insight into them.

According to Yogācāra and Madhyamaka, ignorance is not simply a state of unknowing but is a wrong knowledge that actively grasps things to exist in a way they do not. According to Prāsaṅgika Mādhyamikas, whereas persons and phenomena do not exist inherently or under their own power, ignorance grasps the opposite of reality and holds them as existing in this way.

Emotions such as attachment and anger are rooted in ignorance. The stronger our grasping an independent I is, the stronger our attachment is to the concerns of this self. We cling to whatever appears important to our self and are hostile toward whatever impedes fulfilling the self's interests. For example, we see a beautiful item in a shop. While it is in the shop, we want to possess it. After we buy it and label it "mine," we become attached to it. Although the article remains the same, our emotional reaction to it changes by labeling it "mine." Behind the label "mine" is the belief in a self whose enjoyment is important. If someone breaks the object, we become angry. Refuting the I as having independent reality eliminates our attachment and anger.

Craving (*taṇhā, tṛṣṇā*), a thirst for the satisfaction of our desires, is a prominent example of afflictions that are the origin of duḥkha. Aside from craving things while we are alive, at the time of death craving stimulates clinging (*upādāna*), ripening the karmic seeds that propel another saṃsāric rebirth.

1. Craving and karma are the causes (hetu) of duḥkha *because they are its root; due to them duḥkha constantly exists.*

Contemplating that duḥkha derives from craving and karma, we gain deep conviction that all sufferings have causes—craving and karma. This refutes the idea that duḥkha occurs randomly or without causes. Rejecting the law of karma and its effects, some materialists do not believe our actions have an ethical dimension and live a hedonistic lifestyle, indulging in sense pleasures with little thought of the long-term effects of their actions on themselves and others.

2. Craving and karma are origins (samudaya) of duḥkha *because they repeatedly produce all the diverse forms of duḥkha.*

Understanding this dispels the idea that duḥkha comes from only one cause, such as a primal substance from which everything originates. If duḥkha rested on one cause, it would not depend on many other factors. If cooperative conditions were not needed for a cause to produce a result, then either that cause would never produce a result or it would never stop producing a result. If a sprout depended only on a seed, nothing else would be necessary for the seed to grow, so it should sprout in the winter. Or, since no other conditions would be necessary for it to sprout, the warmth in spring would not make it grow. Because things arise from many causes, they are not predestined but depend on the coming together of diverse factors.

3. Craving and karma are strong producers (pabhava, prabhava) *because they act forcefully to produce strong duḥkha.*

Understanding this dispels the notion that duḥkha arises from discordant causes, such as an external creator, that could not possibly create the world and the duḥkha in it. Everything sentient beings experience is created by their minds, by the virtuous, nonvirtuous, and neutral intentions and the physical and verbal actions they motivate. All these are karma—intentional actions originating in the minds of sentient beings. These actions influence what we experience.

Afflictions and karma bring intense duḥkha, such as those experienced in the unfortunate realms. Even when ordinary sentient beings act with kindness free from afflictive intentions, their virtuous karma is still polluted by ignorance and brings rebirth in saṃsāra. Secure peace and happiness cannot arise from ignorance or craving.

When we understand that craving and karma are the actual origins of duḥkha, we stop blaming others for our problems and accept responsibility for our actions and experiences. With strong determination to dispel craving and karma, we become empowered to change our situation and create the causes for the happiness we want by learning, reflecting, and meditating on the Dharma.

4. *Craving and karma are* conditions (paccaya, pratyaya) *because they act as the cooperative conditions giving rise to duḥkha.*
Understanding that duḥkha depends on both causes and conditions dispels the notion that the nature of things is fixed. This counteracts the idea that things are fundamentally permanent but temporarily fleeting. If duḥkha were permanent and eternal, it could not be affected by other factors and could not be counteracted. However, when its causes are eliminated, the resultant duḥkha will not occur. Knowing this brings resilience to our Dharma practice.

Contemplation of these four attributes strengthens our determination to abandon true origins of duḥkha.

Four Attributes of True Cessations

True cessations (*nirodha-sacca, nirodha-satya*) are the cessations of various levels of afflictions actualized by progressing through the paths to arhatship and full awakening. Afflictions are of two types: *innate* (*sahaja*) afflictions continue uninterruptedly from one lifetime to another, and *conceptually acquired* (*parikalpita*) afflictions are learned from incorrect philosophies. The final true cessation of an arhat, nirvāṇa—eradication of both acquired and innate afflictions—is the example of true cessations.

1. Nirvāṇa is the cessation (nirodha) of duḥkha *because, being a state in which the origins of duḥkha have been abandoned, it ensures that duḥkha will no longer be produced.*

Understanding that attaining true cessation is possible by eliminating the continuity of afflictions and karma dispels the misconception that afflictions are an inherent part of the mind and liberation is impossible. The knowledge that liberation exists inspires us with optimism and energy to attain it.

2. Nirvāṇa is peace (santa, śānta) *because it is a separation in which afflictions have been eliminated.*

This attribute counteracts the belief that refined yet still polluted states, such as the meditative absorptions of the material and immaterial realms, are cessation. While more tranquil than human life, these states have only temporarily suppressed manifest afflictions and have not abandoned innate afflictions from the root. Not understanding that the cessation of all craving is ultimate peace, some people remain satisfied with such superior states within saṃsāra. People convinced of the harm of craving and karma know that their cessation is lasting peace and joy.

3. Nirvāṇa is magnificent (panita, praṇīta) *because it is the supreme source of benefit and happiness.*

As total freedom from all three types of duḥkha, true cessation is completely nondeceptive. No other state of liberation supersedes it; it is supreme and magnificent. Knowing this prevents thinking that there is some state superior to the cessation of duḥkha and its origins. It also prevents mistaking certain states of temporary or partial cessation as final nirvāṇa. For example, someone in the desire realm with clairvoyance sees the bliss experienced in the material realm. But because his clairvoyance is limited, he does not see the end to that state and mistakes it for lasting liberation.

4. Nirvāṇa is freedom (nissaraṇa, niḥsaraṇa) *because it is total, irreversible release from saṃsāra.*

Liberation is freedom, or definite emergence, because it is an irrevocable release from the misery of saṃsāra. This counters the misconception that liberation is reversible and the ultimate state of peace can degenerate. Because true cessation is the elimination of all afflictions and karma, there no longer exists any cause for rebirth or saṃsāric duḥkha. Once attained, liberation cannot degenerate.

Contemplating these four attributes encourages us not to stop partway but to continue practicing until we attain nirvāṇa.

Four Attributes of True Paths

The Pāli tradition describes true paths as the noble eightfold path. Mādhyamikas say a true path (*maggasacca, mārgasatya*) is an ārya's realization informed by the wisdom directly realizing the emptiness of inherent existence. True paths exist in the mindstreams of āryas of all three vehicles. The wisdom realizing emptiness (selflessness) is the principal true path because it directly contradicts ignorance. While ignorance grasps inherent existence, the wisdom realizing emptiness sees the absence of inherent existence. Thus it is able to completely uproot ignorance and the afflictions stemming from it. When afflictions cease, polluted karma is no longer created. There is no further impetus to be reborn in saṃsāra, and liberation is attained.

1. The wisdom directly realizing selflessness is the path (magga, mārga) *because it is the unmistaken path to liberation.*

This wisdom leads to liberation. Knowing this counters the misconception that there is no path that releases us from saṃsāra and gives us the confidence to practice it. If we believe there is no path, we will not venture to learn and practice it and will thus remain trapped in saṃsāra.

2. The wisdom directly realizing selflessness is suitable (ñāya, nyāya) *because it acts as the direct counterforce to the afflictions.*

The wisdom realizing selflessness is the correct path because it is a powerful antidote that directly counteracts self-grasping and eliminates duḥkha. Understanding this eliminates the misconception that this wisdom is not a path to liberation. With the knowledge that it is the path to liberation, we will be eager to cultivate this wisdom that knows the nature of bondage and release from saṃsāra just as it is.

3. The wisdom directly realizing selflessness is accomplishment (paṭipatti, pratipatti) *because it unmistakenly realizes the nature of the mind.*

Unlike worldly paths that cannot accomplish our ultimate goal, this wisdom leads to unmistaken spiritual attainments because it is an exalted wisdom that directly realizes the final mode of existence of the mind, its emptiness of inherent existence. By doing so, it eradicates afflictions and accomplishes liberation.

Understanding this counteracts the misconception that worldly paths, such as the meditative absorptions of the material and immaterial realms, eradicate duḥkha. Blissful as they may be, these absorptions do not secure true liberation. Similarly, the worldly path of extreme asceticism does not eliminate craving.

4. *The wisdom directly realizing selflessness is* deliverance (niyyānika, nairyāṇika) *because it brings irreversible liberation.*
Phenomena lack inherent existence. Inherent existence and non-inherent existence are mutually exclusive. By realizing the lack of inherent existence, wisdom can conclusively remove the ignorance grasping inherent existence. Definitely eliminating all obscurations, this wisdom does not stop partway but delivers us from saṃsāra completely so that duḥkha can never reappear. This counteracts the misconception that afflictions can regenerate and cannot be totally eradicated. It also counteracts the mistaken notion that while some paths may cease some attributes of duḥkha, no path can cease it completely.

Contemplating these four attributes encourages us to meditate on true paths, destroy duḥkha and its origins, and actualize final, true cessation.

Pāli Tradition

The *Paṭisambhidāmagga*, a work ascribed to Sāriputta in the Sutta Piṭaka, explains the sixteen attributes of the four truths.[9]

Four Attributes of True Dukkha

The five aggregates as well as all conditioned phenomena—our home, friends, possessions, reputation, and so forth—are included in true dukkha. Here "conditioned phenomena" refers to things under the influence of ignorance and kamma. The chief attribute of true dukkha is its being oppressive; the other three attributes demonstrate the way in which the aggregates and other conditioned things are oppressive, stifling, and burdensome.

1. *The aggregates are* oppressive (pīḷana).
Dukkha has the meaning of "oppression by arising and passing away." Given that each of the five aggregates degenerates, not enduring a second moment,

they are unsatisfactory in nature. Wherever we are born in the realms of saṃsāra—from the highest deva realm to the lowest hell—ordinary beings are oppressed by saṃsāric existence, the aggregates, and the environment.

2. *The aggregates are* conditioned (saṅkhata).

The need to create the causes for a fortunate rebirth is one aspect of oppression. To be born as a brahmā-world deva, we must create the cause by attaining jhāna as a human being, which is not easy. Generosity and ethical conduct are the causes to be born as a desire-realm deva. When we practice these two with the aspiration for liberation, the challenges are not experienced as overly burdensome. But when our aim is a fortunate rebirth, the same practices become drudgery, because they bring only another saṃsāric rebirth.

Beings are born in unfortunate realms due to the ten nonvirtues. Acting unwholesomely brings little pleasure now, and we are usually plagued by guilt afterward. Furthermore, in that very life we experience others' reactions to the harm we inflict.

3. *The aggregates are* burning like fire (santāpa).

The aggregates of the unfortunate realms burn with misery with little, if any, moments of respite. Even if we have a favorable rebirth, we are constantly plagued by dissatisfaction. Brahmā-world devas suffer from the conceit "I am," wrong views, and other afflictions. Desire-realm devas burn with passion, self-centeredness, and clinging. Human beings are oppressed by the intensity of their afflictions. Just to stay alive, we have to work hard and, even then, never feel secure. Working sets the stage for engaging in the ten nonvirtues. Our possessions break or are stolen, our body falls ill. We long to be loved, appreciated, and respected, but these are never commensurate to what we do to earn them.

Animals suffer from being eaten by other animals or by human beings. They cannot speak up for themselves when hunted, exterminated, or abused. Hungry ghosts suffer from hunger, thirst, and frustration; hell beings are tortured by physical pain. For those in unfavorable births even a little temporal happiness, let alone Dharma happiness, is difficult to find.

4. *The aggregates are in the* nature of change (vipariṇāma).

Having to die and be reborn repeatedly is wretched for all sentient beings.

Those in fortunate realms leave their comfortable circumstances and are reborn in realms with more suffering, while beings in unfortunate realms face enormous difficulties in creating the causes for a fortunate rebirth. Just having a saṃsāric body ensures loss, death, and more rebirth.

All conditioned things are subject to change; nothing remains a second moment after it arises. With deep mindfulness it is possible to see with wisdom this rapid change occurring. When we do, it almost seems as if nothing is there because whatever arises is gone in the next moment.

Our aggregates, environments, and enjoyments are burdensome because initially we must exert great energy to create the causes to attain them. When we have them, we burn with the afflictions they provoke, and at the end, we must separate from them amid confusion and uncertainty. Through deeply contemplating these four attributes of true dukkha, a strong urge to be free from saṃsāra arises within us.

Four Attributes of True Origin

True origin is responsible for the arising and growth of dukkha. The chief troublemaker, craving, is of three types: *Craving for sensual objects* (*kāma taṇhā*) desires the six sense objects and the pleasant feelings that arise due to contact with them. It leads to involvement in nonvirtuous actions to procure and protect what we desire. *Craving for existence* (*bhava taṇhā*) craves the bliss of the material and immaterial realms and seeks rebirth there. It causes someone to be content with attaining the jhānas and not cultivate the wisdom bringing liberation. *Craving for nonexistence* (*vibhava taṇhā*) believes the cessation of the self at death is peaceful and sublime and craves for this. In a milder form, it craves the cessation of whatever we do not like.

Ignorance and craving work in tandem: ignorance is the first link beginning a set of dependent arising; craving is the active factor creating kamma for a new existence. It also ripens that kamma at the time of death. Both ignorance and craving have no discernible beginning. They were not created by a supreme being, nor did they arise without causes. They are conditioned events that arise due to our having ignorance and craving in previous lifetimes.

1. Craving accumulates the cause (āyūhana) *of dukkha.*

By continually longing for beautiful objects to see, hear, smell, taste, touch, and think about, craving spurs a frantic search to distract the mind, numb ourselves from the world, and medicate our pain. In this way, we never really deal with the heart of our problems.

Usually we think our suffering is due to not getting what we want. In fact, it is due to craving: craving causes dissatisfaction. Not seeing that the problem is within us, we are like a dog with fleas. Unable to get comfortable in one place, the dog moves to another place thinking there are no fleas there. Until we free our mind from craving, misery will follow us around. A mind free from craving is a peaceful mind.

2. *Craving is a constant* source (nidāṇa) *of dukkha.*
Craving doesn't stop when we get what we want. Like drinking saltwater, the more we get what we crave, the more we crave. We get something new and, after enjoying it a short time, are once again bored, dissatisfied, and craving something else. Meanwhile, each moment of craving creates more latencies of craving, which predispose us to crave in the future.

3. *Craving brings* bondage *and* unites (saṃyoga) *us with dukkha.*
Never wanting to separate from the people, possessions, places, ideas, entertainment, and accolades we seek, craving unites us with dukkha. It makes us want to associate with the very things that incite our longing and feelings of insufficiency. Craving recognition, we compete with others. If we prove ourselves better, we fear falling from that status and suffer from the stress of maintaining our position. If the other person comes out on top, we suffer from envy. Craving makes it so there is no peace in any situation.

4. *Craving is an* obstacle and impediment (palibodha) *to freedom from dukkha.*
Craving prevents us from separating from the things we are attached to. Looking deeply at our own experience, we see that even when we fulfill our desires, our mind is not at peace; it is riddled with fear of losing what we like. In this way craving prevents having a peaceful mind and impedes us from practicing Dhamma, the one source of true peace.

While craving is taken as the prime example of the origin of dukkha in both the Pāli and Sanskrit traditions, other impediments exist as well. The Pāli tradition and the Sanskrit *Abhidharmakośa* discuss the ten *fetters* (*saṃyojana*), mental factors binding us to saṃsāra and impeding the attainment of liberation. The five lower fetters are view of a personal identity, deluded doubt, view of rules and practices, sensual desire (*kāmachanda, kāmacchanda*), and malice (*vyāpāda*). The five higher fetters are desire for existence in the material realm (*rūparāga*), desire for existence in the immaterial realm (*arūparāga*), conceit (*māna*), restlessness (*uddhacca, uddhatya*), and ignorance (*avijjā, avidyā*).

The Pāli tradition and the *Abhidharmakośa* outline three *pollutants* (*āsava, āsrava*)—deeply rooted, primordial defilements that have bound us to saṃsāra without respite: the pollutants of sensuality (*kāmāsava, kamāsrava*), of existence (*bhavāsava, bhavāsrava*), and of ignorance (*avijjāsava, avidyāśrava*). Pāli Abhidhamma literature adds a fourth, the pollutant of views (*diṭṭhāsava*).

Pāli scriptures contain a list of afflictions (*kilesa, kleśa*) and auxiliary afflictions (*upakkilesa, upakleśa*) that are offshoots of the root afflictions. There are many overlaps with the list of these two in the Sanskrit tradition.

The Sanskrit tradition usually speaks of the chief impediments to liberation as the six root *afflictions*: attachment to sensuality (*rāga*), anger (*paṭigha, pratigha*), views (*diṭṭhi, dṛṣṭi*), doubt, conceit, and ignorance. With the addition of desire for existence (*bhavarāga*), this corresponds to the list of *underlying tendencies* (*anusaya, anuśaya*) in the Pāli tradition, where they are seen as latent tendencies that enable afflictions to become manifest.

Pāli commentaries clarify that the fetters and other defilements (*sankiḷesa, saṃkleśa*) exist on three levels. As *underlying tendencies*, they are latent potencies in the mind. When *manifest* (*pariyuṭṭhāna*), they actively enslave the mind, and as *motivating forces* (*vītikkama*), they lead to nonvirtuous physical and verbal actions. When afflictions are at the level of underlying tendencies and our mind is relatively calm, we may delude ourselves into thinking we no longer have a problem with a particular affliction. Our mindfulness relaxes, and soon a full-blown affliction overwhelms our mind. Unable to suppress this manifest affliction, it spills over, becoming a motivating force to speak or act in a harmful manner.

Four Attributes of True Cessation

Nibbāna is the true cessation of dukkha and its origins. It is perceived by the four types of ariyas—stream-enterer, once-returner, nonreturner, and arahant—who experience the paths and fruits (*magga-phala*).

1. *True cessation is* freedom *from dukkha.*
Stream-enterers enjoy the peace of freedom from the view of a personal identity, deluded doubt, the view of rules and practices, and other wrong views. While not free from any new defilements, once-returners have reduced their sensual desire and malice. Nonreturners are free from the five lower fetters, and arahants are free from all fetters, defilements, and pollutants. Arahants first attain *nibbāna with remainder* (*saupādisesa, sopadhiśeṣa*), in which the five polluted aggregates received at birth remain, but when they die and those aggregates are forever forsaken, *nibbāna without remainder* (*anupādisesa, anupadhiśeṣa*) is attained.

2. *True cessation is* secluded from disturbance (paviveka).
Unlike ordinary beings who are plagued by defilements and whose rebirths fluctuate from the hells to the immaterial realm, the four ariyas are free from these disturbances. Their minds become progressively more peaceful until liberation is attained.

3. *True cessation is the* deathless (amata).
True cessations do not fade or disappear even though the four ariyas still have the polluted aggregates received at birth. While stream-enterers, once-returners, and nonreturners may die and be reborn, their true cessations are never lost and continue on. Nibbāna is unoriginated and uncreated, free from the vagaries of constant rebirth and death.

4. *True cessation is* unconditioned (asaṅkhata).
Conditioned and impermanent, our unsatisfactory saṃsāric aggregates lead to constant insecurity and fear. Completely free from this conditioning, true cessations are genuine peace. The true cessations of the four ariyas never decline, decay, or cease; they do not need to be generated anew each day or in each meditation session.

Four Attributes of True Path

The noble eightfold path is the true path—a mind directly realizing nibbāna—that brings about all cessations of dukkha and its causes. *Insight wisdom* is generated by meditating on the subtle impermanence of the aggregates and thereby knowing that the aggregates are unreliable and unsatisfactory. Because the aggregates arise and pass away each moment,

Don Farber

ZEN TRAINEES ON ALMSROUND IN JAPAN

they cannot be an independent self. This liberating insight wisdom that sees (*passati, paśyati*) the three characteristics—impermanence, dukkha, and not-self—understands (*pajānāti, prajānāti*) the five aggregates (or six sources, eighteen elements, and so forth) as characterized by the three characteristics. Thus the direct object of insight is the aggregates, sense sources (sense bases), or so forth, and they are apprehended in terms of the three characteristics. As this insight wisdom deepens, a breakthrough to the supramundane occurs, and *path wisdom*, which takes nibbāna as its object, arises.

Each of these eight path factors—right view, intention, speech, action, livelihood, effort, mindfulness, and concentration—has a mundane (*lokiya*) and supramundane (*lokuttara*) aspect. The mundane aspect is together with the pollutants and is practiced by those who are not yet ariyas. It is meritorious and leads to a fortunate rebirth. Possessed by ariyas, supramundane path factors eradicate different levels of fetters and lead to liberation. The path is gradual, and the mundane path factors are cultivated first. When they mature and when serenity and insight are strong, the eight supramundane path factors manifest together during a state of samādhi focused on the unconditioned, nibbāna.

The Buddha explains each path factor as well as its opposite in the *Mahācattārīsaka Sutta* (MN 117).

Wrong views include believing that our actions have no ethical value or do not bring results, that there is no continuity of being and everything ends at the time of death, that other realms of life do not exist, that liberation is impossible, and that defilements inhere in the mind.

Mundane right view is the opposite of these wrong views. It includes knowing that our actions have an ethical dimension and bring results, that there is a continuity of being after death, that other realms exist, that there are holy beings who have actualized the path, and so on.

Supramundane right view is the faculty of wisdom, the power of wisdom, the discrimination-of-phenomena awakening factor, and the path factor of right view in the mindstream of an ariya. Supramundane right view is the direct penetration of the four truths as well as direct knowledge of nibbāna.

Wrong intentions are sensual desire, malice, and cruelty. *Mundane right intentions* are renunciation, benevolence, and compassion. Here renunciation is a balanced mind free from attachment to sense objects. Benevolence encompasses fortitude, forgiveness, and love. Compassion is nonviolence. Right intention spurs us to generate right speech, action, and livelihood and to share our knowledge and understanding with others. For those following the bodhisatta's vehicle, right intention includes bodhicitta.

Supramundane right intention includes coarse and refined engagement, thought, intention, and mental absorption in the mindstream of an ariya. Right view and right intention are included in the higher training in wisdom.

Wrong speech is the four nonvirtues of speech: lying, disharmonious speech, harsh speech, and idle talk. *Mundane right speech* is meritorious speech that abstains from those four. Cultivating right speech requires conscious effort and a strong resolution to speak truthfully, gently, kindly, and at the appropriate time.

Wrong actions are killing sentient beings, stealing, and unwise or unkind sexual behavior. *Mundane right action* involves abandoning these three and using our physical energy to preserve life and protect others' possessions. For lay practitioners, it entails using sexuality wisely and kindly; for monastics it involves celibacy. While taking intoxicants is not included in wrong action, to develop the noble eightfold path abandoning intoxicants is essential. Mindfulness is difficult to cultivate even when the mind is clear, how much more so when the mind is intoxicated.

Wrong livelihood for monastics includes procuring requisites by means of flattery, hinting, coercing, giving a small gift to get a big one, and hypocrisy. It includes inappropriate use of offerings given by people with faith, for example using them for idle pleasure or entertainment. For lay practitioners examples of wrong livelihood are manufacturing or selling weapons; killing livestock; making, selling, or serving intoxicants; publishing or distributing pornography; operating a casino; exterminating insects; overcharging customers and clients; embezzlement; and exploitation of others.

Mundane right livelihood is abandoning the five wrong livelihoods—hinting, flattery, bribery, coercion, and hypocrisy—and procuring requisites truthfully, honestly, and in a nonharmful way. Lay practitioners should engage in work that contributes to the healthy functioning of society and the welfare of others. Right livelihood is also a lifestyle free from the extremes of asceticism and luxury.

Right speech, action, and livelihood pertain to the higher training in ethical conduct. *Mundane right speech* and *right action* are the seven virtuous actions of body and speech that are the opposite of the seven nonvirtuous ones. *Supramundane right speech, action, livelihood* are ariyas' refraining from and abandoning wrong speech, action, and livelihood and their engaging in right speech, action, and livelihood.

Mundane right effort is the four supreme strivings: effort to prevent the arising of nonvirtues, abandon nonvirtues that have arisen, cultivate new virtues, and maintain and enhance virtues that are already present. With right effort we direct our energy away from harmful thoughts into the development of beneficial qualities and try to live in a nonviolent and compassionate way. Right effort enables us to abandon the five hindrances and gain concentration and wisdom. Through right effort, mindfulness and concentration, which constitute the higher training in concentration, are accomplished.

Mundane right mindfulness is the four establishments of mindfulness. In daily life mindfulness enables us to remember our precepts. In meditation it attends to the meditation object, enabling us to discern its distinct characteristics, relationships, and qualities. In a highly concentrated mind, mindfulness leads to insight and wisdom.

Supramundane right effort and mindfulness are these two factors present with other path factors at the time of realizing nibbāna.

Right concentration includes the four jhānas. Concentration directed toward liberation investigates the nature of phenomena with mindfulness. Right concentration for beginners involves gradually developing meditative abilities in daily meditation practice.

Supramundane right concentration is the four jhānas conjoined with wisdom and the other path factors at the time of perceiving nibbāna. The supramundane path is a right concentration. In it, all eight path factors are present simultaneously, each performing its own function. Right concentration leads to right views, knowledge, and liberation. The commentary describes right knowledge as a reviewing knowledge that knows the mind is fully liberated from defilements.

As the first factor, right view focuses on karmic causality and the Buddhist worldview, which are essential for people beginning to practice. Without accepting these at some level, someone may still benefit from practicing the remaining seven factors, but that benefit will not be nearly as great as for a person who has right view.

Each subsequent path factor is connected to the ones before it. Right view and intention provide the proper foundation for practice. Right speech, action, and livelihood, which guide our everyday actions, are practiced first. On that basis, meditation with right effort, mindfulness, and concentration is cultivated. This leads to understanding the right view regarding the nature of reality, which is a deeper level of right view because it focuses on the ultimate nature and nibbāna. The practice of the noble eightfold path is common to followers of all three vehicles.

1. The noble eightfold path leads to release and deliverance (niyyāna).
The noble eightfold path directly counteracts all fetters and defilements, releasing us from these.

2. The noble eightfold path is the cause (hetu) *for attaining all true cessations, especially that of an arahant.*
Due to having practiced the noble eightfold path, from the moment one

becomes an ariya, one enters the stream flowing to liberation. The thirty-seven aids to awakening continue to develop in this person, without declining from one existence to the next, until final nibbāna is attained.

3. *The noble eightfold path* realizes *and* sees (dassana) *the four truths.*
By realizing the four truths as they are in their entirety, ariyas see what ordinary beings are unable to see. They are no longer befuddled, confused, or indecisive about what to practice and abandon.

4. *The noble eightfold path* overcomes *all varieties of craving and* gives mastery (ādhipateyya).
Ariyas never fear losing their attainments; they know insight wisdom and path wisdom remain firmly in their mindstreams. By practicing the three higher trainings, ariyas have become masters of themselves. Through having seen nibbāna, if only for some moments, they have full confidence in the Dhamma and the attainments of the Buddha and Saṅgha.

When someone fully sees with correct wisdom (*sammāpaññāya*) the three characteristics or the four attributes of true dukkha, he or she automatically understands the other twelve attributes of the four truths.

4 | The Higher Training in Ethical Conduct

THE FOUR TRUTHS establish the reason and framework for Dharma practice. To attain nirvāṇa we must cultivate the three higher trainings in ethical conduct, concentration, and wisdom (DN 10:1.6). The three *higher* trainings differ from the three trainings because their goals are higher. The mere three trainings are done to fulfill aims in saṃsāra, such as having a fortunate rebirth, while the three higher trainings are directed toward liberation and full awakening.

The Importance of Ethical Conduct

Buddhists accept that human life has a deeper purpose and that good rebirths, liberation, and full awakening are valuable aims. Since afflictions prevent us from actualizing our virtuous aims, we try to reduce and eventually eradicate them. The various ethical codes are designed to do this by helping us to subdue our physical, verbal, and mental actions.

According to the Sanskrit tradition, the wisdom realizing selflessness eliminates obscurations from the root. For wisdom to function properly, it must be accompanied by single-pointed concentration. To gain deep concentration, firm mindfulness and introspective awareness (*sampajañña, samprajanya*) are needed to subdue the subtle internal hindrances. These are initially cultivated through restraining the coarse external hindrances of nonvirtuous physical and verbal actions through practicing ethical conduct.

Ethical conduct means to restrain from doing harm and applies to both monastics and lay followers. Tibetan Buddhism contains three levels of ethical restraints: prātimokṣa (Pāli, *pāṭimokkha*), bodhisattva, and tantric. The prātimokṣa ethical restraint focuses on abandoning harmful physical and verbal actions. The bodhisattva ethical restraint emphasizes abandoning self-centered thoughts, words, and deeds. The tantric ethical restraint aims to overcome subtle mental obscurations. Because their focus is progressively more subtle, the three sets of ethical restraints are taken gradually and in that order.

Keeping the commitments and precepts we have taken is essential to attain realizations. Some people are brave when taking precepts and commitments but are cowardly when it comes to keeping them. We should be the opposite, thinking well before taking ethical restraints, humbly requesting them from our teachers, and afterward keeping them properly and joyfully.

Whether someone practices principally the Śrāvaka Vehicle or the Bodhisattva Vehicle, ethical conduct is the foundation of the practice. The prātimokṣa precepts help us regulate physical and verbal actions, and in doing so, we must work with the mind that motivates these actions.

Although all Buddhists try to abandon the ten nonvirtues, taking precepts involves special commitment and thus brings special benefit. Living in precepts prevents destructive karma and purifies harmful habits. It also brings rapid and strong accumulation of merit, because every moment we are not breaking a precept, we are actively abandoning that destructive action, thus enriching our mind with merit from acting constructively. Ethical conduct cools the fires of afflictions, prepares the mind to attain higher states of meditative absorption, is the path leading to the awakenings of all three vehicles, and brings about the fulfillment of our wishes. Keeping ethical conduct prevents guilt, remorse, and anxiety. It averts fear and reproach from others and is the basis for self-esteem. Our ethical conduct contributes to world peace, for others trust and feel safe around a person who abandons the wish to harm others. Good ethical conduct cannot be stolen or embezzled; it is the basis for having a fortunate rebirth, which is necessary to continue practicing the Dharma. Living in precepts creates the cause to encounter favorable circumstances and be able to continue practicing in future lives. Because we will already be habituated in our future lives to releasing attachment and practicing the path, we will attain awakening swiftly.

Prātimokṣa Ethical Restraints

The principal motivation to receive any of the eight types of prātimokṣa ethical restraints is the determination to be free from saṃsāra. Five types of prātimokṣa ethical restraint are for monastics: (1–2) fully ordained monks (*bhikkhu*, *bhikṣu*) and fully ordained nuns (*bhikkhunī*, *bhikṣuṇī*), (3) training nuns (*sikkhamānā*, *śikṣamāṇā*), and (4–5) novice monks (*sāmaṇera*, *śrāmaṇera*) and novice nuns (*sāmaṇerī*, *śrāmaṇerikā*). Three are for lay followers: (6–7) laymen (*upāsaka*) and laywomen (*upāsikā*), and (8) one-day precept holders (*upavāsa*).

Lay followers take the five lay precepts for the duration of their lives, abandoning killing, stealing, unwise and unkind sexual behavior, lying, and taking intoxicants (alcohol, recreational drugs, and misuse of prescription medicines). When taking the eight one-day precepts, lay followers additionally abandon sexual activity; sitting on high or luxurious seats or beds; singing, dancing, and playing music; wearing perfumes, ornaments, or cosmetics; and eating at improper times (between midday and dawn of the following morning).

People have different abilities and interests, so you can choose the type of prātimokṣa ethical restraint best suited to you. Whichever one you choose, practice the precepts with a good motivation. The wish to escape debts or avoid caring for children or aged parents are not good reasons for taking monastic vows; neither is the wish to have a place to live or free food.

Some people think that because monastic precepts restrain physical and verbal misdeeds, purity in vinaya involves only external appearances—acting and speaking in a refined manner. However, to actually subdue our outward behavior requires subduing the mind, because all physical and verbal activities flow from a mental intention.

For those who choose to become monastics, the practice of vinaya helps increase contentment. Because we voluntarily put limits on what we do, we practice being satisfied with what we have and let go of our desirous impulses. A monastic may eat only during certain times and may not demand specific food; whatever he receives, he must accept. Buddhist monastics are not required to be vegetarian, although Chinese monastics who hold the bodhisattva ethical restraint are. Monastics are limited to having one set of robes that we consider our own. Monastics cannot wear expensive robes and are limited to having a small number of personal items. Anything else should be considered as property of the monastic community or as property shared with other monastics. This reduces the dissatisfied mind seeking "more and better."

Monastics limit relations with family in order to avoid emotional dependency and involvement in activities that take us away from Dharma practice. Using our ordination name signifies leaving behind our old identity as others' relative or friend and adopting the life of a monastic.

The practice of vinaya develops mindfulness and introspective awareness. If we are about to do certain actions, we train to immediately think, "I am a monastic and have chosen not to do this." By cultivating such mindfulness and checking if our behavior is proper when we are awake, our mindfulness becomes stronger and will also arise in our dreams.

The practice of vinaya also helps to develop fortitude (*khanti, kṣānti*). The *Prātimokṣa Sūtra* says:

> Fortitude is the first and foremost path.
> The Buddha declared it as the supreme way to attain nirvāṇa.
> One who has left the home life yet harms or injures others
> is not called a renunciate.

To refine their virtue, the Buddha instructed monastics to practice fortitude in four situations: (1) If others are angry with you, do not react with anger but with fortitude. (2) If others hit you, do not retaliate. (3) If others criticize you, do not criticize them in return. (4) And if others embarrass or insult you, do not respond by embarrassing or insulting them. These are real ascetic practices that will increase your fortitude, bring harmony to your relationships and to society in general, and lead to awakening.

Some people think of precepts as nonnegotiable rules propounded by an absolute authority. Naturally, this makes them uncomfortable. But the prātimokṣa precepts are not like this. They are helpful trainings that lead to good results. For example, if we want to be healthy, we voluntarily adopt new eating habits and avoid activities that weaken our bodies. Similarly, when we want to abandon ignorance, anger, and attachment, we voluntarily curtail actions motivated by them and avoid objects that trigger them. Thus precepts are not forced on us by an external authority; they are trainings we voluntarily uphold because we want to fulfill our spiritual aims.

For the first twelve years, the saṅgha did not have any precepts. But when some monks misbehaved, it was reported to the Buddha, who established a precept to abandon that action. Later, when different conditions were present, he made exceptions or gave other guidelines. Thus precepts are not absolute rules.

Some precepts concern etiquette. Since etiquette differs from one cul-

Losel Chuah

OFFERING FOOD TO THE SAṄGHA, MALAYSIA

ture to another, we must adapt our behavior to whatever is suitable in a particular place.

Prātimokṣa ethical restraints are common to practitioners of all three vehicles. Those engaging in bodhisattva or tantric practice cannot ignore or belittle their prātimokṣa precepts. In fact, being negligent with respect to prātimokṣa precepts is explicitly forbidden in the bodhisattva and tantric ethical codes, and doing so is a serious downfall. We must try to maintain all our precepts as best as we can.

WHY CELIBACY?

Since modern society extols sexual pleasure, some people wonder why monastics have a precept of celibacy. This has to do with our spiritual aims.

On the first level of Buddhist practice, we work within human nature, which comes from having this saṃsāric body. Here subduing the coarse level of afflictions and avoiding the ten nonvirtues are emphasized. People are encouraged to subdue extreme sexual lust and abandon unwise or unkind sexual behavior that creates pain and confusion for themselves or others. However, proper use of sexuality is fine for lay practitioners. Thich Nhat Hanh, a renowned Vietnamese monk, considers sexual activity without love and commitment to be unwise sexual behavior. Although this is not mentioned in the scriptures, I think it is true. Love for one's partner and a sense of responsibility are important for the stability and longevity of a relationship.

On the second level of practice, we no longer seek saṃsāric pleasures but want to go beyond saṃsāra. Since craving is one of the principal causes of saṃsāra, freeing ourselves from attachment to objects of the five senses is important to attain liberation. Of all forms of attachment, sexual desire is the most intense and complex because it involves all five senses plus the mind. Thus the Buddha advised that those seeking freedom from craving refrain from sexual desire.

At this point of the path, we must confront and go against tendencies that may even normally be considered human nature and part of our biological makeup, including sexual desire. Our aim now is liberation, and attachment to sexual relations prevents this. Although sexual desire arises naturally in our body, we can control it. Thus monastic ordination is taken with the determination to be free from saṃsāra and includes a precept of strict celibacy.

Skilled athletes with high goals eagerly abandon activities that impede their training or ability to attain their goals. They willingly refrain from certain foods and a grand social life and spend their time in consistent training. Their restraint is not unhealthy suppression but is necessary and conducive to realize their desired goals. Similarly, monastics willingly give up sexual relations and immersion in sensual pleasures because these hinder attaining their spiritual goals.

Many factors are at work in choosing how to or whether to use one's sexuality, and these need to be carefully considered by each individual. The Buddha did not say that everyone must give up sexual activity. It is one's own choice. However, if someone becomes a monastic, he or she must be celibate. There is no such thing as "a monastic with a spouse"!

The Vinaya Schools

All vinaya schools are included in the Śrāvakayāna. There is no such thing as a Mahāyāna vinaya monastic ordination, although many people who practice the Bodhisattva Vehicle become monastics and practice vinaya. The three extant vinaya lineages stem from the original eighteen schools of early Buddhism:

- The Theravāda (T. *gnas brtan pa*, C. *shangzuo-bu*) vinaya is in Pāli and is practiced predominantly in South and Southeast Asia. It comes from the vinaya lineage brought to Sri Lanka by Aśoka's daughter and son in the third century B.C.E.
- The Dharmaguptaka (T. *chos sbas pa*, C. *fazang-bu*) vinaya was translated into Chinese in 410–12 by Buddhayaśas, and in 709 the emperor Zhongzong decreed it was to be the only vinaya used in China. It is followed principally in China, Taiwan, Korea, and Vietnam.
- The Mūlasarvāstivāda vinaya (T. *gzhi thams cad yod par smra ba*, C. *genben shuoyiqieyou-bu*) was brought to Tibet by the Nālandā master Śāntarakṣita and is followed in Tibet, Mongolia, and the Himalayan regions.

The literature of these vinaya schools was passed down orally for many centuries before being written down, and the geographical distance between them is considerable. Thus the remarkable similarity in their presentation of monastic life is striking. They all follow essentially the same precepts and perform the same saṅgha transactions (*saṅghakamma, saṅghakarma*).

The **Theravāda vinaya** is divided into three sections:

1. The *Suttavibhaṅga* contains the pāṭimokkha precepts. Each precept is explained in four parts: the background story that caused the Buddha to establish it, the precept itself, the word-by-word explanation of the precept from the *Padabhājaniya*, the old commentary, and more stories to show exceptional situations pertaining to this precept and how to deal with them.
2. The *Khandhaka* consists of two volumes:

   The *Mahāvagga* deals with topics such as ordination, fortnightly confession and restoration of precepts (*uposatha, poṣadha*), rains retreat (*vassa, varṣā*), invitation for feedback (*pavāraṇā, pravāraṇa*), footwear, medicine, *kaṭhina* robe offering, garments, formal acts, and schism.

   The *Cullavagga* describes disciplinary transactions; penance, probation, and their imposition; settling issues; lodgings; schism; protocols; cancelling the pāṭimokkha; bhikkhunīs; and the first two councils.
3. The *Parivāra* is an appendix of nineteen chapters covering material from the *Suttavibhaṅga* and the Khandhakas. It seems to be a later addition, written or compiled by a Sri Lankan elder.

Buddhaghosa wrote an authoritative commentary, *Samantapāsādikā*, on the pāṭimokkha in the fifth century, and Dhammapāla wrote one a century later. Both Buddhaghosa and Dhammapāla relied heavily on very old commentaries written at the Mahāvihāra Monastery in Sri Lanka. Several more vinaya commentaries were written after these.

The **Dharmaguptaka vinaya** is also called the *Four-Part Vinaya* because it consists of sixty volumes placed in four sections. It is also divided into three categories:

1. The *Sūtravibhaṅga* contains the bhikṣu and bhikṣuṇī prātimokṣas.
2. The *Skandha* explains various practices the monastic community should perform and consists of twenty *vastus*, or "bases." Its contents are similar to the Khandhakas.
3. The *Parivāra* is an appendix compiled around the third century B.C.E. It supplements the *Sūtravibhaṅga* and the *Skandha* and discusses the compilation of the vinaya and the first and second councils. It clarifies doubts, delineates extraordinary circumstances pertaining to the precepts, and deals with other pertinent topics.

The **Mūlasarvāstivāda vinaya**, with four vinaya-āgama sections, was translated from Sanskrit into Tibetan.

1. The *Vinayavastu* corresponds to the *Khandhaka* and consists of seventeen bases (*vastu*) of ethical training: ordination, fortnightly confession and restoration of precepts, invitation for feedback, rains retreat, hides and skins, medicine, garments, kaṭhina, the dispute at Kausambi, formal acts, disciplinary measures, persons, changing locations, exclusion, house and bed, disputes, and schism.
2. The *Vinayavibhaṅga* gives the origin stories for the bhikṣu and bhikṣuṇī precepts, a detailed explanation of each precept, and exceptions. It corresponds to the Pāli *Suttavibhaṅga*.
3. The *Vinayakṣudrakavastu* discusses minor points of the bhikṣu and bhikṣuṇī prātimokṣas.
4. The *Vinayottaragrantha* clarifies the profound and difficult points of the above three.

Tibetans follow the vinaya commentaries of the Indian masters Guṇaprabha and Śākyaprabha. Guṇaprabha was an Indian scholar well versed in

Number of Precepts in Each Tradition

Vinaya	*Bhikṣu precepts*	*Bhikṣuṇī precepts*
Theravāda	227	311
Dharmaguptaka	250	348
Mūlasarvāstivāda	253	364

Number of Bhikṣu Precepts by Category

Category of precepts	*Theravāda*	*Dharma-guptaka*	*Mūlasar-vāstivāda*
defeats (*pārājika*), the most serious infractions	4	4	4
remainders (*saṅghādisesa*, *saṅghāvaśeṣa*), offenses entailing a meeting of the saṅgha	13	13	13
undetermined rules (*aniyata*, *aniyata*)	2	2	2
lapses with forfeiture (*nissaggiya-pācittiya*, *naiḥsargika-pāyattika*)	30	30	30
lapses expiable by confession (*pācittiya*, *śuddha-pāyattika*)	92	90	90
acknowledgment confessions (*pāṭidesanīya*, *pratideśanīya*)	4	4	4
training rules (*sekhiya*, *śaikṣa*)	75	100	112
rules for settling disputes (*adhikaraṇasamatha*, *adhikaraṇaśamatha*)	7	7	7

the sūtras, vinaya, and commentaries. His commentaries, the *Vinaya Sūtra* and *Ekottarakarmaśataka*, are used to study the monastic code.

The number and meaning of the precepts in the three vinayas are very similar, and the differences are minor. For example, seven precepts concerning how to wear the lower garment in the Mūlasarvāstivāda are subsumed into one precept in the Theravāda.

The Value of the Monastic Community

In the Sanskrit tradition, the Saṅgha Jewel we take refuge in is any person, monastic or lay, who has directly realized emptiness. *Saṅgha* also refers to a monastic community of at least four fully ordained monastics. The monastic saṅgha represents the Saṅgha Jewel, although not everyone who is a monastic has directly realized emptiness. To be a fully functioning saṅgha, they must do the three main monastic practices—fortnightly confession, rains retreat, and invitation for feedback. The Buddha also spoke of the "fourfold assembly" (*catuparisā, caturparṣadāḥ*)—the broad community of his followers that consists of fully ordained monks and nuns and of laymen and laywomen who have taken refuge and the five precepts. Calling a group of lay followers at a Dharma center "saṅgha" is confusing, especially if people mistakenly think that this group is the Saṅgha Jewel that is an object of refuge. For this reason, using the word *saṅgha* in the traditional sense to refer to the monastic community is clearer and avoids misunderstanding.

The reason the saṅgha has been important, respected, and valued throughout history is that its members practice the higher training in ethical conduct through taking and observing the bhikṣu and bhikṣuṇī precepts. Because saṅgha members live a simple lifestyle and are free from family concerns and the necessity to work to provide for a family, they have more time for Dharma study and practice. Thus the saṅgha has been chiefly responsible for preserving the Buddha's teachings throughout the millennia by memorizing, studying, contemplating, and meditating on them, and by teaching them to others. Lay practitioners are fully capable of doing this too; however, the home of a lay family serves a different function than a monastery. Monasteries act as physical locations for the full-time practice and preservation of the teachings. When people think of monastics living together for the purpose of studying and practicing the Dharma, they feel inspired. They have a sense of optimism and hope and look forward to going to the monastery, temple, or Dharma center to practice together with the saṅgha.

Upholding the doctrine so that it exists for future generations is important. The *transmitted doctrine* is upheld when people study and explain the Buddhadharma. The *realized doctrine* is upheld when people practice and actualize the meaning of those teachings in their own minds. In this connection, the saṅgha is important, for they extensively practice and realize the higher training of ethical conduct, which is the foundation for cultivating concentration and wisdom.

According to scripture, whether the Buddhist doctrine flourishes in a place is determined by the presence of the fourfold assembly, which makes a place a "central land." The existence of the monastic community practicing the vinaya—specifically by performing the three main monastic practices—is crucial for making Buddhism a living tradition in a society. Although an individual may practice well and be highly realized, this does not constitute the flourishing of the doctrine in a place.

Stable interest in becoming a monastic develops naturally from deep reflection on the basic Buddhist teachings. As a result of contemplating compassion and dependent arising, one becomes interested in the nature of the mind, which leads to an appreciation of emptiness, rebirth, and karma. This leads to understanding the possibility of attaining liberation. When one is convinced of this possibility, one will naturally be drawn to living a life according to ethical precepts, which could lead to taking monastic ordination. The Buddha explained the proper motivation to ordain (MN 29:2):

> Here some clansman goes forth out of faith from the home life into homelessness considering, "I am a victim of birth, aging, and death, of sorrow, lamentation, pain, grief, and despair. I am a victim of dukkha, a prey to dukkha. Surely an ending of this whole mass of dukkha can be known."

The Buddha established the monastic community for a purpose. To overcome afflictions, we need correct wisdom, and to maintain such a view, single-pointedness of mind is essential. To concentrate, mindfulness and introspective awareness are required, and these are cultivated through training in ethical conduct. The ethical conduct of monastics is stricter than that of lay followers and thus is more effective in subduing the mind. Whereas the life of a householder may be more colorful, monastic life is more stable. Although it is difficult and requires giving up sexual relations and so on, there are benefits even in this lifetime. The monastic way of life is praised because it has direct relevance in developing the three higher trainings.

This latter point is important, lest people think that the monastic life is outdated or irrelevant in modern times. Our Teacher Buddha Śākyamuni was a monk. The Buddha lived as a monk from the time he left the palace until his passing away—over fifty years. His ethical restraint and monastic lifestyle were natural expressions of the purity of his mind. So many great Buddhist masters also lived this way, and the examples of their lives convey to us the importance and benefit of monastic life.

However, monastic life is not suitable for everyone. People must choose the lifestyle most appropriate for themselves and have confidence in their ability to practice. A lay practitioner who practices diligently can attain high realizations. Marpa and his disciple Milarepa were highly realized lay practitioners, yogis, and teachers.

Fulfilling the Purpose of Monastic Life

The Buddha describes how one lives as a monastic (DN 2:42):

> Having gone forth [from the householder life to the homeless life of a monastic], he dwells restrained by the restraint of the precepts, persisting in right behavior, seeing danger in the slightest faults, observing the commitments he has taken regarding body, deed, and word, devoted to the skilled and purified life, perfected in ethical conduct, with the sense doors guarded, skilled in mindful awareness, and content.

To receive monastic precepts, a person must be motivated by renunciation—the aspiration to be free from saṃsāra and attain liberation. Nevertheless, some people ordain with more worldly motivations. As a result some monastics are genuine practitioners while others are not. It is better if those who misbehave return to lay life and be good lay practitioners. I believe more emphasis on the quality rather than the quantity of monastics is necessary. One step would be to screen candidates more carefully and ensure they

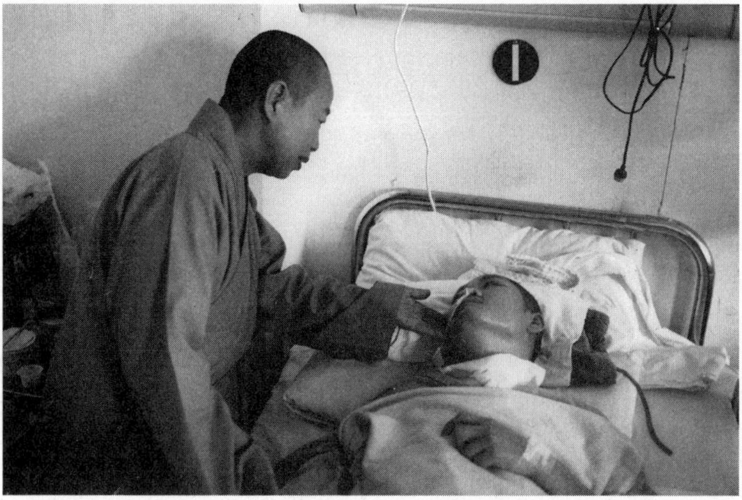
Don Farber

NURSE WHO IS A BUDDHIST NUN COMFORTS A PATIENT AT TZU CHI HOSPITAL IN HUALIEN, TAIWAN

receive proper training and guidance from wise elder monastics after they ordain.

Wearing robes and shaving your head are not sufficient to be a monastic. One must keep the precepts well. Accepting offerings but not keeping the precepts well creates destructive karma that will ripen in an unfortunate rebirth. The commentary to the Numerical Discourses explains four ways of enjoying or using requisites (food, clothing, shelter, and medicine). *Enjoyment with theft* is when a monastic transgresses precepts, has poor conduct, yet uses requisites offered with faith. This is likened to stealing because the requisites were offered to those who practice well. *Enjoyment with debt* is when a monastic with correct conduct enjoys offerings without reflecting on the kindness, generosity, and merit of the donor and without dedicating for the donor's welfare. This person consumes the requisites but has not fulfilled his or her commitment to the donor. *Enjoyment like an inheritance* is when training ariyas enjoy offerings. Since they are on their way to become arahants, it is as if they are using the inheritance that will later become theirs. *Enjoyment as an owner* is arahants' use of requisites. Since they have eradicated all pollutants and fulfilled the aim of the path, the offerings are theirs to use.

As the Buddha pointed out (MN 29:2), some people may begin their life as a monastic with a sincere motivation but later be sabotaged by the eight worldly concerns. They become attached to offerings and respect, which leads them to praise themselves and disparage others. Intoxicated with their material gain and renown, they grow complacent and negligent, living in suffering now and creating the causes for future suffering.

Other people practice ethical conduct well but are arrogant, praising themselves for upholding the precepts and disparaging others for being sloppy. Such arrogance makes them become self-satisfied and negligent in developing further virtues. Similarly, monastics may attain serenity or experience temporary liberation in deep concentration. Lacking introspective awareness, they become attached to and conceited about their attainment and thus lose energy, become complacent, and do not fulfill their spiritual goals. Thus it is important always to remain humble and focused on the ultimate attainments of liberation and full awakening.

Monastics must constantly strengthen their motivation to renounce the eight worldly concerns and duḥkha and to attain liberation. As monastics, our task is to learn, think, and meditate on the vast and profound teachings as much as possible. Having done that, we should teach, translate, write, and lead others in practice so that the Dharma will long exist in our world.

Monastics are not perfect, and we may see a monastic behaving in an inappropriate manner. At this time, we should do our best to help this person correct his behavior. But we must not let the bad behavior of one individual cause us to lose faith in the entire saṅgha. We should avoid criticizing all monastics based on the poor behavior of one.

Monastics, Priests, and Lay Teachers

In Tibet, two communities of practitioners evolved, the "white" and the "saffron/maroon." The white refers to lay practitioners, because they wear white clothing common to lay Buddhists. While they do not observe the external forms of ordained life, such as shaving the head, they follow the five lay precepts as well as the bodhisattva and tantric ethical restraints. The saffron are celibate and follow the monastic ethical restraint. Externally, they wear the saffron monastic robes.

In Tibet, both communities practiced with clarity and direction. However, today we find people who are neither in one camp nor the other. We find monastics who put on lay clothes and lay practitioners who wear clothes that look like monastic robes. The public is confused and question, "This person looks like a monk but has a wife and wears jewelry. How is that?" Even I am confused when I see these people!

This is a problem in the international Buddhist community as well. Many people become confused when they cannot clearly determine someone's status: is this person a monastic, a lay teacher, a priest? What can I expect of these different practitioners if I cannot differentiate among them?

Names are one point of confusion. Since prātimokṣa ordination does not exist in Japan, Japanese clergy are usually married. I recommend that married teachers from all Buddhist traditions are called priests. I heard that the World Fellowship of Buddhists refers to those with vinaya ordination as "venerable" and those who are married priests as "reverend." This is very helpful.

In terms of dress it is better if monastics, priests, and lay practitioners wear their own distinctive clothing. On many occasions I have asked lay teachers in the Tibetan tradition to wear either Tibetan or Western lay clothes or a lower white robe and an upper shawl that is white with a few maroon stripes. In this way, people will know that they are not monastics and will be able to relate to them accordingly. However, many of these people continue to wear clothing that looks like monastic robes. There is nothing I can do about this.

Monastics should wear their robes, unless there is some danger in doing so—for example, if they are doing manual work.

Tibetan Monastics and Monastic Institutions

Some monastics in the Theravāda, Dharmaguptaka, and Mūlasarvāstivāda traditions do not eat after noon, and many Theravāda monastics go on almsround and do not handle money. This is wonderful. Due to the large percentage of the Tibetan population that is ordained, practical constraints prevent everyone from strictly following some of these practices.

Prior to 1959, approximately one quarter of the male population in Tibet was monks. In Tibet and now in India, some monasteries have thousands of monks and are the size of small towns. These large monasteries are also schools with a full study program that lasts about twenty years and includes teachings, memorization, debate, vinaya ceremonies, personal study, and group ceremonies. Many young boys join the monasteries, and with so many children and young adults who are memorizing and studying, these monasteries are filled with activity. Older monks go to remote places to meditate without disturbance.

The tradition of debate originated in ancient India. The Buddha himself debated philosophical principles with the śramaṇas and brahmans of his time. In later centuries, large Indian monastic universities used debate as a learning tool and to establish the validity of the Buddha's teachings when challenged by non-Buddhist scholars. Tibetan Buddhism has continued this tradition.

A key element in debate is having a large number of monastics who share their diverse ideas. Given the large population at these major monasteries, local villagers cannot afford to give alms on a daily basis, and the streets would be jammed with thousands of monastics on almsround! While lay people donate food to the monasteries, it is difficult to cook for thousands, so many monks prepare meals in their group houses within the monastery. This necessitates buying and cooking their own food, which requires handling money.

Nevertheless, in Tibet and in the early years of our exile in India, some monks continued their studies and practice with their belly only half full on a regular basis. I know some excellent monks who are now Dharma teachers who lived like this.

Challenges for Western Monastics

The situation for Western monastics in the Tibetan tradition is especially difficult because few monasteries are established in the West, and living in India brings difficulties with visas, health, and language. Some teachers do not adequately screen and prepare Western candidates before ordination or provide proper training for them afterward, and some Western monastics face financial difficulties. During a conference with Western Buddhist teachers in 1993, some Western monastics told me of the difficulties they face, and I couldn't help but weep.

We must think how to remedy this situation and then act to do so. The best solution is for Western monastics to establish monasteries and develop their own training programs. We Tibetans will help from our side.

I appreciate the gradual approach in many monasteries where candidates pass through many stages before receiving full precepts. This gives them time to think about monastic life and evaluate whether it is suitable for them. Similarly, the monastic community has the opportunity to assess the suitability of candidates. I encourage Westerners considering monastic ordination to live in a monastery as lay practitioners for some time so they can experience living and practicing in this way. If it agrees with them, they can slowly take the progressive levels of precepts and be able to adjust to each level before deepening their commitment.

Living with other monastics—be they our teachers, peers, or students—is valuable. Although monasteries are rare in the West at present, hopefully more will be established in the future. Monastics who do not live in a community should cultivate friendships with spiritual friends with similar precepts, views, and aspirations and keep in contact with monastics who live in other places. They can then discuss the Dharma and challenges they face with these Dharma companions.

Full Ordination for Women

Over the years I have spoken many times about bhikṣuṇī ordination and expressed my wish and hope that this ordination will be given in our Mūlasarvāstivāda vinaya tradition. When Śāntarakṣita brought the bhikṣu ordination lineage to Tibet in the eighth century, he unfortunately did not bring bhikṣuṇīs too, and thus the bhikṣuṇī ordination never took root in Tibet. However, our Teacher, the Buddha himself, established the bhikṣuṇī order during his lifetime, and at the same time he affirmed women's ability to attain both liberation and full awakening. He also expressed his wish for the fourfold assembly to exist and said that these four groups harmoniously practicing the Buddhadharma will make his teachings last a long time in this world. For all these reasons, it is important that bhikṣuṇīs exist in our Tibetan community. This is especially true now, when the quality of the nuns' education has vastly improved. We now see many nuns becoming good scholars; some nuns are now receiving their *geshema* degrees, signifying their mastery of Buddhist philosophy.

Wherever I go in the world, I see multitudes of women devotees; in many places they outnumber the men. Therefore it is only right that women have access to the responsibilities and privileges that full ordination brings. As one individual, I do not have the authority to institute bhikṣuṇī ordination in the Tibetan community. This is an issue that the saṅgha as a group must decide. For many years now I have suggested there be an international meeting of the saṅgha to decide this issue. In preparation for that, it would be good if Tibetan bhikṣus could agree on a way to give the Mūlasarvāstivāda bhikṣuṇī ordination. I am pleased to see the support for this from many heads of Tibetan lineages. I have also shared some vinaya material with Laotian and Burmese Buddhist leaders. We will have a serious discussion, and I am quite sure some agreement will be achieved eventually.

We Tibetans were very fortunate that after persecution by King Langdarma in the ninth century we were able to restore the bhikṣu lineage, which was on the verge of extinction in Tibet. As a result, so many men have been able to listen, reflect, and meditate on the Dharma as fully ordained monks, and this has benefited Tibetan society as well as the world. Therefore, let us do our best to research this issue and find a way to establish the bhikṣuṇī saṅgha as well. In countries that currently have bhikṣuṇī ordination, such as Taiwan, Korea, and Vietnam, bhikṣuṇīs benefit the Dharma and society in many ways. Recently Theravāda bhikkhunī ordination has been restored in Sri Lanka—there are nearly one thousand bhikkhunīs as of 2014—and there are now even some bhikkhunīs in Thailand.

Equal opportunity regarding ordination is important. Citing passages in the vinaya, some Tibetan vinaya masters suggest that under special circumstances, a bhikṣuṇī ordination performed by the bhikṣu saṅgha alone is valid. These special circumstances include a place where bhikṣuṇīs are not available to give the ordination because no bhikṣuṇīs reside in that area or because it is too dangerous for bhikṣuṇīs to travel to that place. Previous and contemporary vinaya masters in the Chinese community agree with this.

In the meantime, several women who practice Tibetan Buddhism have received bhikṣuṇī ordination in the Dharmaguptaka vinaya from Chinese, Vietnamese, or Korean saṅghas. We recognize them as bhikṣuṇīs. I encourage them to do the three main saṅgha activities together.

In addition to introducing bhikṣuṇī ordination, bhikṣuṇīs must also become objects of reverence. Therefore, we must examine passages in Buddhist texts as well as attitudes and practices in our communities that are biased against women. The Buddha wanted his saṅgha to conform with many of the cultural attitudes of the time. As the saṅgha, we must do this in the twenty-first century as well. Since modern societies, as well as the

United Nations, stress the importance of gender equality and respect for women, we Buddhists must do so as well.

Advice for Monastics

I would now like to address those of you who are monastics. Since we have obtained a precious human life with all conditions conducive for practicing the Dharma, now is the time to stop the suffering of saṃsāra. Having the time and opportunity for Dharma practice that monastic life provides, we must do our best to abandon unnecessary activities and cultivate contentment. As a monastic, our foremost practice is to abandon afflictions.

Monastic life is more than abiding in precepts. To keep the precepts, we must examine our minds and confront and avert the afflictions. To do this the Buddha recommends living in seclusion. Seclusion does not mean simply living alone in a remote place. The deeper meaning of seclusion is being separated from afflictions, destructive actions, and the eight worldly concerns. Seclusion from self-centeredness and ignorance are the best. Such seclusion entails developing mindfulness and introspective awareness and training our minds patiently and diligently over time.

We take precepts because we are imperfect beings who are trying to subdue our minds. It is natural that we make mistakes, but doing so should not be treated lightly. When we transgress a precept, we must reveal it and use the methods taught in the vinaya to purify both the destructive karma and the infraction of the precepts. Transgressing the root precepts results in losing the ordination, so we must be especially conscientious to avoid that.

While it is up to each person to decide whether to become a monastic, once we are ordained, we must practice sincerely. If we wear the robes of a monastic but our behavior is not good, the lay community will lose respect for the saṅgha. That would be very sad. Monastics must practice well and make themselves objects worthy of respect.

Monastics help each other to grow in the Dharma by giving and receiving admonishment. When a monastic misbehaves but does not acknowledge his error, with a compassionate motivation we should admonish him so that he can correct his ways. When we receive admonishment, we must listen respectfully and contemplate what those who are senior in ordination or wiser in the precepts advise. Being obstinate and insolent regarding either the Buddha's advice or the admonition of the saṅgha creates many hindrances for our practice, whereas receiving admonition with humility and appreciation enables us to grow in the Dharma.

Whether or not we are ordained, it is important to appreciate the simplicity of a monastic life lived with precepts. Appreciating the monastic way of life will leave latencies so we can be ordained in future lives.

The Joy of Monastic Discipline

To express in a brief way my respect for monastic discipline, I would like to share with you some verses I wrote in 1973, "The Joy of Prātimokṣa Discipline."

We fortunate ones who follow
our supreme teacher, the Impeccable One:
it is becoming for us to engage with pure faith
in uncompromised ethical conduct.

Externally pure, internally pure,
beneficial and joyful, both here and beyond,
medicine for both self and others,
marvelous! We have met the Buddha's Way!

Though difficult, we have encountered it this once;
those who seize it are even fewer.
With firm determination in our hearts,
observe pure conduct by all means possible.

Beyond doubt, this discipline subdues
the extremely coarse afflictions;
even the duḥkha natural to householders' lives—
what need to mention that this discipline eases that, too?

The supreme mind of bodhicitta—
the lifeline of the bodhisattva path—
concentrations such as the union of serenity and insight,
and so forth:
what escapes being produced by this discipline?

The wondrous and marvelous
profound path of tantra,
the method to realize selflessness with the subtlest level of mind:
that, too, is founded on this discipline.

The state of a buddha,
the inseparable union of compassion and emptiness,
emaho! the swiftest path leading to it.
That, too, relies on this discipline for its cause.

Therefore, O intelligent friends,
do not disparage or treat as trivial
the prātimokṣa ethical discipline,
which originates in the śrāvaka's scriptures.

Know that the discipline is praised
as the basis and root of the doctrine.
Strive to follow it well, supported by study and analysis,
with mindfulness, introspective awareness, and conscientiousness.

Guard well with utmost striving,
with personal integrity and due respect;
do not give in to indifference and indolence,
lest you should squander the very root of steadfast well-being.

Bodhisattva and Tantric Ethical Restraints

Those practicing the Bodhisattva Vehicle take the bodhisattva ethical restraints with the wish to attain full awakening to benefit all sentient beings. The bodhisattva precepts focus on subduing self-centeredness, the main obstacle to generating bodhicitta and engaging in the bodhisattvas' practice. Different versions of the bodhisattva ethical restraints are found in Tibetan, Chinese, and Japanese Buddhism.

The tantric ethical restraint is undertaken with a more intense bodhicitta motivation, wishing to attain full awakening quickly to be capable of benefiting sentient beings sooner. It consists of fourteen root precepts, eight heavy infractions, and other precepts as well. Their main purpose is to help diminish dualistic view, but they also strengthen all forms of ethical conduct by prohibiting contentious criticism of the prātimokṣa and bodhisattva precepts, scorning the Dharma teachings, and relinquishing love and bodhicitta.

Unlike the prātimokṣa precepts that focus on physical and verbal actions, bodhisattva and tantric precepts emphasize ethical conduct on the mental level. Here motivation is foremost. This means that if our motivation is pure, we can transform all actions into the Dharma. However, this does not give us license to rationalize selfish and nonvirtuous actions by saying "My motivation was compassion."

Vinaya practice emphasizes decreasing attachment, so monastics are not allowed to touch gold or precious things. The bodhisattva precepts, which presuppose having some control over attachment and emphasize the welfare of others, specify that if the donor would be hurt by our refusing her monetary gift, we should accept it and then use it to benefit others. Although these actions superficially seem contradictory, they are both ethical precepts that apply to one person at different times in her training.

Practitioners who observe the tantric restraints and commitments should also observe vinaya precepts, which are easier to keep and are good preparation for taking the bodhisattva and tantric precepts. Practicing tantra should not be used as an excuse to neglect the vinaya. Quite the opposite, we should be more strict in practicing vinaya because if we aren't, how can we expect to observe the tantric restraints, which are more difficult to follow?

5 | The Higher Training in Concentration

The Importance of Concentration

The benefits of concentration (*samādhi*) and serenity (*samatha*, *śamatha*) are many. Serenity united with insight (*vipassanā*, *vipaśyanā*) into selflessness uproots the causes of saṃsāra. It enables us to develop virtuous qualities, integrate Dharma understanding with our minds, and attain the superknowledges, which are essential to benefit others most effectively. If we are serious about actualizing the paths, the practice of samādhi is a must.

While it is useful to be able to focus the mind single-pointedly, we should first focus on developing a broad understanding of the Dharma and cultivating a proper motivation for Dharma practice, such as renunciation or bodhicitta. If we develop samādhi with the motivation to have supernormal powers, be famous, or remain in a blissful meditative state, we are doing ourselves a disservice. The effort we put into developing concentration will bring little benefit compared to the results when concentration is cultivated with a motivation aspiring for liberation or awakening.

The meaning of *concentration* depends on the context. The mental factor of concentration is already present in our minds, although it is underdeveloped. While artists, students, athletes, and mechanics need concentration, the concentration in the noble eightfold path is different: it refers particularly to single-pointed concentration that leads to the four meditative stabilizations (*jhāna*, *dhyāna*). *Concentration* is a powerful state of mind able to control mental activity and the arising of afflictions. *Serenity* is concentration supported by the bliss of pliancy (*passaddhi*, *praśrabdhi*) that is able to keep the mind in equipoise on its object. "Concentrations" also refers to special meditations enabling a practitioner to engage in specific activities.

Concentration unifies the primary mind and its associated mental factors on the meditation object in a balanced way. It ensures uninterrupted attention and mindfulness on the object and produces mental tranquility. Free from manifest afflictions, it is like a mirror clearly reflecting objects. When combined with wisdom, such a mind brings deep realizations. This is very different from our usual distracted mind that sees only superficially and is often afflictive.

It is important to train in samādhi under the guidance of a qualified teacher. Working with the mind is a delicate venture, and without proper guidance we may go astray. A good meditation master who understands the various experiences that may arise in meditation is able to steer us skillfully and correctly and confirm our progress, preventing worry and unnecessary detours on the path.

The Buddha himself emphasized the attainment of samādhi and the jhānas. In the Pāli tradition, detailed meditation instructions are found in the commentaries and the *Visuddhimagga*. In the Sanskrit tradition, commentaries by Maitreya, Asaṅga, and Kamalaśīla discuss serenity and concentration in depth.

Realms of Existence and Spheres of Consciousness

Some familiarity with realms (levels or planes of existence; *bhūmi*) and spheres of consciousness (*avacara*), as presented in the Pāli abhidhamma, is helpful before training to gain samādhi. Saṃsāra consists of three realms: the desire, material, and immaterial realms. Corresponding to these are the three spheres of consciousness: the desire- or sense-sphere consciousness (*kāmāvacaracitta*), the material-sphere consciousness (*rūpāvacaracitta*), and the immaterial-sphere consciousness (*arūpāvacaracitta*) (CMA pp. 29–31). There also exists supramundane consciousness (*lokuttaracitta*). *Spheres of consciousness* are mental states, while *realms* are planes of existence into which sentient beings are born.

The three spheres of consciousness are mundane states of consciousness; they are included within saṃsāra and true dukkha. While occurring most often in its corresponding realm, a particular sphere of consciousness is not limited to that realm. For example, the material-sphere consciousness occurs most frequently in beings born in the material realm. How-

Don Farber

THERAVĀDA MONKS ON ALMSROUND, THAILAND

ever, a human being in the desire realm may cultivate deep concentration such that when he goes into meditative absorption, his mind becomes a material-sphere consciousness. According to the depth of his concentration, he attains the first, second, third, or fourth jhāna. If his concentration is even more subtle, his mind becomes an immaterial-sphere consciousness, but when he emerges from meditation, his mind is again a desire-sphere consciousness.

If a human being attains a specific level of meditative absorption and maintains it through the rest of her life, she creates the karma to be born in that realm after death. For example, a meditator who has attained the sphere of consciousness called the *base of nothingness* of the immaterial realm creates the kamma to be born in the realm of the base of nothingness after death.

Pāli Tradition

The Pāli commentarial tradition formalized in the *Visuddhimagga* recognizes forty objects of meditation with which serenity may be cultivated. A meditation teacher usually prescribes one of the following objects for the disciple depending on the disciple's temperament:

- The ten *kasiṇas* (totalities): earth, water, fire, air, blue, yellow, red, white, limited space, and light
- The ten foul objects (*asubha*): corpses in various states of decay
- The ten recollections (*anussati, anusmṛti*): mindfulness of the Buddha, Dhamma, Saṅgha, ethical conduct, generosity, deities (the divine qualities of celestial beings), death, the parts of the body, breathing, and nibbāna
- The four divine abidings (*brahmavihāra*) or four immeasurables (*appamañña, apramāṇa*): love (*mettā, maitrī*), compassion (*karuṇā*), joy (*muditā*), and equanimity (*upekkhā, upekṣā*)
- The meditation objects of the four immaterial states, in ascending order: the bases of infinite space, infinite consciousness, nothingness, and neither-discrimination-nor-nondiscrimination
- The one discrimination (*ekasaññā*): discerning the repulsiveness of food
- The one analysis (*dhātuvavaṭṭhāna*): defining the four elements

Not all of the forty meditation objects are unique to Buddhism. The kasiṇas and the four immaterial-state objects are used by meditators of other faiths. Meditation on many of the forty objects will bring the four material and four immaterial absorptions (*appanā samādhi*). However, meditation on ten of the objects leads only to access concentration (*upacāra samādhi*); these are eight of the recollections (omitting mindfulness of the parts of the body and mindfulness of breathing), discerning the repulsiveness of food, and defining the four elements. Meditation on all the other objects can bring full absorption. Any of the kasiṇas is a condition for cultivating the first five superknowledges.

People with certain temperaments are better suited for particular objects. Someone with strong attachment focuses on the ten foul objects and the parts of the body; someone suffering from anger uses one of the four divine abidings or four color kasiṇas. An easily scattered mind meditates on the breath. Someone inclined toward faith finds the first six recollections riveting. The intelligent focus on death, nibbāna, analysis of the four elements, and the repulsiveness of food. The remaining kasiṇas and the four immaterial-state objects can be used by everyone.

Before going to a quiet place to practice, think that you give your life to the Buddha. Doing this strengthens the mind. A good motivation and a strong determination to confront and work with afflictions are also important. Request your teacher for a meditation object and receive instructions on how to develop samādhi by using it.

At the beginning of a meditation session, review the disadvantages of sensual desires and cultivate the wish to be free from them. Recollect the qualities of the Three Jewels, feel joyful that you are entering the path of renunciation that all ariyas have followed, and be confident that you will gain the bliss of nibbāna.

Three signs are cultivated in the process of developing samādhi: the preliminary work sign (*parikamma nimitta*), the learning or acquired sign (*uggaha nimitta*), and the counterpart sign (*paṭibhāga nimitta*). Using the example of an earth kasiṇa, a meditator makes the kasiṇa disk—a round disk of clean clay about four fingers wide that is placed on a board in front of the meditator. With her eyes open, she looks at it, thinking "earth, earth." When the image of earth is firm in her mind, she closes her eyes and continues to focus "earth, earth." The actual object of meditation now is the image of earth, which is an object of mental consciousness, not visual consciousness. This is the *preliminary work sign*. If the image fades, she opens her eyes and looks at the earth kasiṇa to refresh her visualization and again lowers her eyes and meditates on the image of earth appearing to her mental consciousness. In this way she "develops this sign," forming the image in her mind sometimes with open eyes and sometimes with them closed. At this initial stage of practice her concentration is called *preliminary concentration* (*parikamma samādhi*), and most of her effort goes toward being mindful of the object, noticing when a distraction or other hindrance has arisen, applying the antidote, and bringing the mind back to the meditation object.

She continues to develop the preliminary work sign until the *learning sign* arises. This subtler object replaces the preliminary work sign and arises when the meditator sees the mental image just as clearly when her eyes are closed as when she is looking at the kasiṇa. Now she stops looking at the external kasiṇa and focuses exclusively on the mental object, the learning sign. However, if her apprehension of the learning sign fades, she again looks at the physical earth kasiṇa with her eyes. Coarse engagement (*vitakka*) is important at this point to establish familiarity with the learning sign.

As she continues meditating, the five hindrances (see below) are gradually suppressed by the five absorption factors (*jhānaṅga*). Here "suppression" means manifest hindrances do not appear. Suppression of the five hindrances leads to greater clarity and ability to discern the functioning of the mind. The mind and body are at ease; the mind is virtuous, and one feels either pleasure or equanimity.

Untroubled by manifest afflictions and the five hindrances, the mind becomes more concentrated. The *counterpart sign* arises and access concentration is attained. While imperfections are seen in the learning sign, the counterpart sign is brighter and more purified. Luminous, beautiful, and vivid, it has no physical color or shape and is an object only of mental consciousness. It lacks the three characteristics of impermanence and so forth. Stabilizing the counterpart sign is difficult, so the meditator must guard it carefully and continue practice to attain full absorption.

Serenity begins with the state of access concentration prior to the first jhāna. Whereas access concentration, also called the stage of *suppression abandonment* (*vikkhambhana-pahāna*), is marked by the suppression of the five hindrances, the first jhāna is *full absorption* and is marked by full, stable development of the five absorption factors. While the absorption factors are present in access concentration, they are not firm, and a meditator can lose access concentration easily. But in full jhāna the absorption factors are stable and strong, and a shift in the sphere of consciousness occurs. The mind in full absorption does not perceive sensory objects but functions like a material sphere of consciousness. The person is in seated meditation at this time.

Many meditation masters suggest using the breath as the meditation object because focusing on it slows the thought processes and clears the mind of scattered thoughts. In this case, one begins by observing the physical sensations of the breath at the nostrils and upper lip, as it enters and exits. The learning sign is an image arisen from this physical sensation. When it arises, the meditator turns her attention to the *nimitta*—a colored luminous sphere or a radiant light—and that becomes her object of meditation.

Five Hindrances and Five Absorption Factors

Spoken about in both the Pāli and Sanskrit traditions, the five main hindrances (*nīvaraṇa*) and their antidotes need to be overcome with skill and effort from the beginning.

Sensual desire (*kāmacchanda*) produces craving and clinging. While the experience of sensual pleasure itself is not "bad," attachment to it diverts our mind from spiritual practice. Remembering impermanence and the unsatisfactory nature of sensual pleasure helps to calm the mind. Sexual desire is the strongest desire human beings have, and it can be very distracting.

Mentally analyzing the parts of the body and seeing their unattractiveness is an effective method for counteracting it.

Malice (*vyāpāda*) may arise toward a person, physical or mental pain, loneliness, certain ideas, sounds, thoughts, and so forth. Meditation on love or fortitude is the antidote.

Dullness and drowsiness (*thīnamiddha, styānamiddha*) manifest physically and mentally. *Dullness* is a heaviness of mind. The mind lacks energy, is bored, or is in a fog. *Drowsiness* is sleepiness, but it is not related to lacking sleep or being physically tired. Thinking about the qualities of the Three Jewels, the preciousness of our human life, our opportunity to cultivate wonderful spiritual qualities, and so on energizes the mind. Imagining brilliant sunlight filling us and dispelling mental darkness is also helpful.

Restlessness (excitement) and remorse (*uddhaccakukkucca, uddhatyakaukṛtya*) take the mind into the past or the future. *Restlessness* is an agitated mental state that includes anxiety, fear, apprehension, and worry. *Remorse* is an uncomfortable emotion that we did something we should not have done or did not do something we should have done. Focusing on the breath or any other object that soothes and pacifies the mind is effective to calm restlessness and worry. Bringing our attention back to the present is also useful: we are sitting in a safe place, cultivating virtue, and focusing on our meditation object.

Doubt (*vicikicchā, vicikitsā*) involves doubting our abilities, the teachings, or the possibility of actualizing our spiritual goals. After identifying a mental state as deluded doubt, bring your mind back to the meditation object. Deluded doubt differs from a virtuous mind that is curious and wants to learn. When we have doubts because we don't understand a topic well, we should go to a teacher and request clarification.

The Buddha taught five methods for training the mind when it loses its meditation object (MN 20). When a hindrance is not so strong, simply returning the mind to the meditation object is sufficient. But when that doesn't work, we must temporarily leave the meditation object and reflect on another topic to actively counteract the hindrance and bring the mind back to a balanced perspective. Antidotes to apply in sequence are: (1) Give attention to another object that is virtuous. Contemplate the opposite of the distracting thought or emotion. (2) Examine the danger and disadvantages of those thoughts. (3) Do not give attention to those thoughts and do something else. (4) Give attention to stilling the thoughts; for example, ask yourself, "What are all the factors that led to this thought or emotion coming into my mind?" Watch the thoughts flow by from a detached standpoint until they gradually quiet down. (5) Crush a nonvirtuous mental state with a virtuous one.

By employing these counterforces consistently and properly, hindrances decrease, and we are able to return to our meditation object. Over time the mind will become quiet, single-pointed, and concentrated.

The five absorption factors are cultivated in the process of attaining serenity. Their full development marks entrance into the first jhāna. *Coarse engagement* (*vitakka, vitarka*) repeatedly directs and applies the mind to the meditation object, which at this point is the counterpart sign. *Refined engagement* (*vicāra*) is sustained awareness on the meditation object. It examines and knows the object, keeping the mind on it. Coarse engagement is compared to ringing a bell and refined engagement to the resonance of the sound.

Rapture (*pīti, prīti*) is delight and satisfaction due to being interested in the object. It arises when the mind settles down and becomes peaceful due to coarse and refined engagement and lightness of body and mind. *Bliss* (*sukha*) is the pleasant, joyful, happy feeling accompanying concentration due to the depth of stillness in the mind. Rapture and bliss arise sequentially after coarse and refined engagement become more refined and concentration deepens. Rapture is tinged with exuberance and elation and is coarse compared to bliss, which is tranquil and satisfied.

One-pointedness (*ekaggatā, ekāgratā*) unifies the mind and its accompanying mental factors on the object. It is a stillness of mind that allows the mind to stay in a relaxed manner on the meditation object.

As the meditator approaches jhāna, the strengthening of the five factors happens sequentially. When all five factors are present and work together to plunge the mind into the object so that it becomes completely absorbed in the object, the first jhāna is attained.

These five factors have to be patiently cultivated. We cannot will ourselves to attain access concentration or to go from access to full concentration. If we cultivate the factors with consistent and relaxed effort, when they are mature and strong the mind will enter full absorption by itself.

A mind with full concentration is like a room with only one chair. When the chair is occupied, a guest coming into the room leaves immediately because there is no place for him to sit. Similarly, when samādhi is focused one-pointedly on the meditation object, other thoughts cannot stay in the mind.

Concentration does not eliminate the hindrances and afflictions completely; it suppresses their manifest forms. Only the wisdom developed by unifying serenity and insight can eradicate them completely.

Four Jhānas

A meditator in the human realm can attain the four material absorptions and four immaterial absorptions. In each successive state of absorption, concentration deepens. However, the immaterial absorptions are not useful for cultivating wisdom because the mind is too absorbed.

In the Pāli suttas, the Buddha describes right concentration in terms of the four jhānas, which are distinguished by their component factors. While the sutta presentation and the Abhidhamma analysis may differ superficially, they come to the same point. The table on the following page shows both presentations.

Jhānic concentration is sharp, focused, and free from tension. It is arrived at through balanced effort that is firm but not tight. The mind is totally withdrawn from sense objects, although there is some difference of opinion whether there is recognition of sound. But even if there is, it does not disturb the mind. The mind is secluded from nonvirtuous states, and the five hindrances have been suppressed.

Some people mistakenly believe that Buddhism requires us to give up pleasure. Here we see this is not the case. We actively cultivate rapture and bliss that pervade the entire body in the first jhāna (MN 39:15). Rapture and bliss help stop the mind's obsession with sensual pleasure, thus halting the creation of destructive karma involved with procuring and protecting sense objects.

Just as stability in access concentration is needed before attaining the first jhāna, mastery of the first jhāna is needed before going on to the second, and so forth. This involves perfecting our skill in the lower jhāna so that we can enter, abide, and emerge from it without difficulty. We can stay in that jhāna for as long as we wish, and when we emerge the mind is clear, not confused about where we are or what is happening around us. After coming out

Progressing through the Four Jhānas

Jhāna	*Abhidhamma Analysis*	*Sutta Exposition*
First	*Present:* 1. coarse engagement 2. refined engagement 3. rapture 4. bliss 5. one-pointedness	*Absent:* 1. sensual pleasures 2. nonvirtuous states of mind *Present:* 1. coarse engagement 2. refined engagement 3. rapture 4. bliss born of seclusion (from the five hindrances)
Second	*Present:* 1. rapture 2. bliss 3. one-pointedness	*Absent:* 1. coarse engagement 2. refined engagement *Present:* 1. internal stillness 2. one-pointedness of mind 3. rapture 4. bliss born of concentration
Third	*Present:* 1. bliss 2. one-pointedness	*Absent:* 1. rapture *Present:* 1. equanimity 2. mindfulness 3. introspective awareness 4. physical bliss
Fourth	*Present:* 1. neutral feeling 2. one-pointedness	*Absent:* 1. physical bliss and pain 2. joy and grief *Present:* 1. neutral feeling 2. purity of mindfulness 3. equanimity 4. mind that is purified, bright, unblemished, rid of imperfection, malleable, wieldy, steady, and attained to imperturbability

of the jhāna, we can review the experience, noting the process by which we entered, abided, and emerged from it and analyze it clearly knowing each absorption factor that was present.

Meditators must develop several meditative skills in one jhāna before going on to the next (SN 34): knowing the absorption factors that jhāna has; entering jhāna easily; steadying the mind in jhāna; being able to emerge from the jhāna at the time we have determined before entering it; relaxing the mind and making it flexible; knowing and being comfortable with the object; knowing whether a sign or one of the three characteristics is the object;[10] resolving to elevate the mind to the next, higher jhāna; acting with care to enter jhāna; maintaining continuity in the practice; and fulfilling the necessary and beneficial qualities for concentration.

As we develop these skills and become familiar with the first jhāna, we begin to reflect that while the first jhāna is wonderful and definitely better than pleasures of the desire realm, it also has some faults. It isn't far removed from the desire-realm mind with its five hindrances and manifest defilements, and coarse and refined engagement are comparatively coarse factors. We recall that the Buddha spoke of another meditative absorption even more excellent and peaceful in which coarse and refined engagement are absent. Having repeatedly reflected on the defects of the first jhāna and the benefits of the second, we make a determination to attain the second jhāna. According to the Pāli commentaries, this analysis occurs after we have left the first jhāna and resumed normal consciousness, because there is no thought or deliberations while absorbed in the jhānas.

In the break times, we receive the four requisites—food, shelter, clothing, and medicine—with right livelihood, alternate walking and sitting meditations, and sleep in moderation in the middle part of the night. Then during meditation sessions, after continuing to focus on the meditation object and strengthening our faculty of concentration, we enter access concentration and go directly into the second jhāna without passing through the first jhāna.

To attain the first jhāna, coarse and refined engagement were necessary to direct the mind to the meditation object and hold it there. Now other factors perform those functions, so those two factors are released. Due to this, inner stillness and clarity of mind become more prominent. Rapture and bliss are still present, and the one-pointed unification of mind is stronger, so the depth of concentration increases. Whereas previously rapture and bliss arose due to being separated from the five hindrances, now they are present due to the power of samādhi itself.

As before, we familiarize and train in this jhāna, developing the skills mentioned above. Although we initially experience the second jhāna as much superior to the first, after some time we see its faults: as concentration deepens, rapture makes the mind too exhilarated. Aware of a deeper level of concentration, we resolve to attain it. With the intention to abandon rapture, we renew our practice with the meditation object, strengthening the faculty of concentration until rapture subsides. When it does, the third jhāna dawns. Bliss and one-pointedness are still present. Mindfulness, introspective awareness, and equanimity now come to prominence. Our body is blissful and we have a pleasant abiding. Free from rapture, bliss drenches and pervades our entire body. Cultivating skill in the various aspects of the third jhāna, we train and develop mastery in it.

After mastering the third jhāna, we see that it too is faulty because the feeling of bliss is comparatively coarse and subtle attachment to it may arise. A neutral feeling would be the best support for equanimity. Knowing there is a superior state of concentration, we resolve to attain the fourth jhāna and practice in order to release the bliss. When our faculties are strong enough, the bliss fades away, and we enter the fourth jhāna. Pleasure and pain vanish, and equanimity, which is far more peaceful than bliss, comes to the forefront. The firmness of equanimity fully purifies mindfulness, and one-pointed unification of mind is strong. Now the meditator "sits pervading this body with a pure bright mind, so that there is no part of his whole body not pervaded by the pure bright mind" (MN 39:18). This radiant mind abides in equanimity, undisturbed even by bliss.

The jhānas are higher levels of the mundane mind; they are more focused, flexible, and have greater ability to perceive clearly than the confused, obscured mental states of the desire realm. People who have attained any of the four jhānas see sensual pleasure as pointless and boring. They would much rather partake in jhāna meditation, where they can remain for days and emerge refreshed and invigorated, unlike people who go on vacation and return exhausted.

Some meditation masters encourage their disciples to use insight to analyze the jhāna states after emerging from them. Examining states of samādhi in this way, practitioners see that even these blissful states are composed of various factors, arise due to causes and conditions, and are impermanent,

The Jogye Order of Korean Buddhism

KOREAN MONKS MEDITATING DURING A THREE-MONTH-LONG WINTER RETREAT

impersonal, and not to be grasped at. Such analysis prevents meditators from craving and longing for these meditative experiences for their own sake. It also prevents them from generating the erroneous view that these states are a self or an encounter with a supreme being. Furthermore, such analysis prevents the temptation of conceit to arise. Instead, they see once again that everything lacks self.

Four Immaterial Absorptions

Beyond the four jhānas are the four immaterial states, deeper states of concentration in which mental peace remains undisturbed. While advancing from one jhāna to the next involves refining the mind by successively abandoning coarse mental factors, sequentially progressing through the four immaterial states entails refining the object of meditation. Taking their names from their meditation objects, the four immaterial states are called base of infinite space (*ākāsānañcāyatana, ākāśānantyāyatana*), base of infinite consciousness (*viññāṇañcāyatana, vijñānānantyāyatana*), base of nothingness (*ākiñcaññāyatana, ākiñcanyāyatana*), and base of neither-discrimination-nor-nondiscrimination (*n'evasaññānāsaññāyatana, naivasañjñānāsañjñāyatana*). This last state is also called the *peak of saṃsāra* due to being the most refined mental state within saṃsāra.

To go into the immaterial absorptions, we focus on a luminous sphere or radiant light—blue, for example—which is the counterpart sign of our jhānic meditation, and expand it until it is as vast as space. Undivided, seamless, and pervading all space, blue is the only thing in our field of awareness. We absorb in this vast blueness with the mind of the fourth jhāna. To enter the absorption of infinite space, we consider that while the fourth jhāna is peaceful, it is nevertheless faulty because its object is a form, and a meditative absorption without form would be superior and more peaceful. We resolve to attain the base of infinite space, and resolving "Let this form vanish," we mentally remove the blue pervading all space. When our mind is properly prepared, the blue light vanishes, and all that remains as an object of awareness is the infinite space where the bright light had been. The mind now immerses in this infinite expanse of space, with no perception of a sign at all. We thus enter and dwell in the base of infinite space, the first immaterial absorption.

When we are accustomed to infinite space, we reflect that consciousness is aware of infinite space; it is as if consciousness pervades that infinite space. Shifting our attention from infinite space to the infinity of consciousness pervading it, we make a determination to attain the absorption on infinite consciousness. By means of this determination and repeated practice, the perception of space falls away and there is just consciousness extending infinitely. We enter the second immaterial state.

When we master the absorption on infinite consciousness, we reflect that it lacks obstruction and impediment. We now focus on the unimpeded nature of infinite consciousness until the awareness of consciousness falls away and there remains only the awareness of nothingness. Focusing on the nonexistence of the consciousness of infinite space, we enter the absorption on the base of nothingness.

After becoming familiar with this, we turn our attention to the consciousness that is aware of nothingness. That consciousness is very subtle, and when we focus on it, we enter the fourth immaterial state that has as its object the consciousness that is aware of nothingness. This absorption is so subtle and refined that when in it, we cannot say whether discrimination is present or not. Neither-discrimination-nor-nondiscrimination is the object of that absorption.

Beings born in the immaterial realms due to having attained these states of meditative absorption when they were human beings stay in these states of samādhi for eons. When the kamma to abide in them is exhausted, those beings take rebirth in other saṃsāric realms. When the Buddha was still a bodhisattva, he trained with two meditation teachers and mastered the absorption on neither-discrimination-nor-nondiscrimination. Realizing that his mind was still not completely free from defilements, he respectfully departed. Under the bodhi tree, he perfected wisdom and insight, attaining full awakening.

Eight Meditative Liberations

The Buddha spoke of eight meditative liberations (*vimokkha*, *vimokṣa*), deep states of concentration bringing temporary liberation from defilements (MN 77:22): the four jhānas using (1) an internal form, interpreted by the commentary as a color in one's own body, (2) an external form, interpreted as a colored kasiṇa or a color in another's body, (3) "the beautiful," interpreted as a pure, beautiful colored kasiṇa or the four brahmavihāras, (4–7) the four immaterial absorptions, and (8) cessation of discrimination and feeling (*saññāvedayitanirodha, saṃjñāveditanirodha*), also called the attainment of cessation (*nirodhasamāpatti*). The last, the temporary suspension of all manifest activity of the six consciousnesses, requires both concentration and insight. Unlike the first seven meditative liberations, which can be attained by ordinary beings, it can be attained only by nonreturners and arahants who have mastered the four jhānas and four immaterial absorptions.

Maitreya's *Abhisamayālaṃkāra* in the Sanskrit tradition also explains the eight meditative liberations and defines them as "exalted knowers not polluted by the afflictions of their own level." The first three are called the "three paths of emanation" because by abandoning attachment to forms, bodhisattvas eliminate obstacles to emanating many forms that fulfill the needs of sentient beings. Here they (1) emanate many forms while their own bodies remain visible to others, (2) emanate many forms while their bodies are not visible to others, and (3) counteract their like and dislike for emanating beautiful and unattractive forms respectively. Bodhisattvas practice the eight meditative liberations and nine meditative absorptions for the benefit of others.

Superknowledges

While the most important aim of the Buddha's teachings is ceasing rebirth under the influence of ignorance and kamma and attaining nibbāna, the suttas praise other spiritual accomplishments as well. One is mastery over dimensions of the mind—the jhānas and four immaterial absorptions, which are praised for their peace and ease. Another is mastery over nature and external phenomena, gained by actualizing the first five superknowledges (*abhiññā, abhijñā*). A byproduct of samādhi, these five give meditators supernormal physical and mental powers, enabling them to perform feats that cannot be explained by available scientific means. While some non-Buddhists see these as the purpose of the path, the Buddha emphasized that only nibbāna is actual liberation from dukkha. Thus when cultivating the superknowledges, it is essential to have a good motivation and to take care not to fall prey to conceit and clinging. Compassionately using these powers to benefit others and spread the Buddha's teachings is meaningful. The superknowledges are:

1) *Supernormal powers* (*iddhi, ṛddhi*) are cultivated based on the powerful concentration of the fourth jhāna. They enable us to defy ordinary scientific laws by gaining mastery over nature. With them we can make our body into many bodies and then absorb these bodies back into a single body. We can become invisible, appearing and vanishing at will, pass through walls and mountains with ease, go under the earth, walk on water, and fly in space.

Chapter 12 of the *Visuddhimagga* describes the rigorous training necessary to do this, attaining each jhāna using various kasiṇas, progressing through all eight absorptions in forward and reverse order, alternating various absorptions, entering and emerging from absorptions very quickly, and so forth. With this extraordinary mental power, we then direct our mind to the exercise of the supernormal powers. Through the force of intention, and based upon this profound acuity and agility in samādhi, we gain the supernormal powers described above.

2) *Divine ear*, or clairaudience, is the ability to hear sounds in the human world, heavenly realms, and other realms and directions where sentient beings dwell. We can hear these faraway sounds as easily as if they were nearby.

3) *Understanding the minds of others* is the ability to know the mental states of others. We know minds affected and unaffected by attachment, anger, and confusion; exalted and unexalted minds, concentrated and unconcentrated minds, liberated and unliberated minds. Others' mental states are known as clearly as seeing a spot on our own face reflected in a clean, bright mirror.

4) *Recollection of past lives* is the ability to know the particular details of our own lives for eons in the past.

5) With the *divine eye* we can see beings dying and reappearing in their next life according to their kamma. We know what actions sentient beings did to cause rebirth in particular realms and can see events in faraway places and other dimensions in the universe. Dhamma teachers with this ability may use it to know the kamma of sentient beings and thus who they will be able to benefit and which beings are ripe to enter the Dhamma path. Then with supernormal powers, they will go to these places to teach them.

6) Unlike other superknowledges, *knowing the destruction of all pollutants* does not require the full power of samādhi as a prerequisite. We can attain it on the basis of any of the four jhānas or, according to the commentary, with access concentration. This superknowledge realizes the "liberation of mind liberation by wisdom" (*cetovimuttipaññāvimutti, cittavimuktiprajñāvimukti*), nibbāna, which is totally free from all defilements.

While the Buddha taught the three spiritual accomplishments of nibbāna, meditative absorptions, and superknowledges, he did not expect all his disciples to accomplish the latter two. He knew his followers had different aptitudes and interests. Someone who attains nibbāna but not the other two abilities is "one liberated by wisdom" (*paññāvimutta, prajñāvimukta*). This person may attain jhāna or he may attain liberation without jhāna, developing wisdom and eradicating defilements on the basis of access concentration. Those who attain nibbāna as well as the various meditative absorptions have mastery of a wide range of mental states and are called "those liberated in both ways" (*ubhatobhāgavimutta, ubhayatobhāgavimukta*). Śrāvakas who attain nibbāna as well as mastery over mental states and the superknowledges that follow from them are called "arahants having the six superknowledges" (*chalabhiññā arahant, ṣaḍabhijña arhat*). In Theravāda countries we find all three persons to this day.

I heard about an Indian laywoman named Dipa Ma who was renowned as a stream-enterer; she passed away a little over twenty years ago. At the request of her meditation teacher, she mastered all eight meditative absorptions and the five superknowledges. She would resolve to sit in a particular absorption for a specific amount of time and emerge from it exactly at that time. Her teacher attested to her powers: one day he saw her floating in the sky above the treetops outside his window and at another time watched her dive into the ground and emerge from it. One day her teacher and a professor arranged for someone to be with her in one location, but she arrived for an appointment with the professor ten miles away at the same time. There are many such stories about her, yet she always remained a humble and sincere Dharma practitioner. She died in an interesting manner: she bowed to the Buddha and passed away before she could stand up.

The first five superknowledges are mundane powers attained through the fourth jhāna; the knowledge of the destruction of all pollutants is supramundane. While non-Buddhists may actualize the first five, only Buddhists will develop the insight and wisdom necessary to attain the sixth, an arahant's liberation. The last three superknowledges—recollection of past lives, knowledge of the passing away and rebirth of beings according to their kamma and destruction of the pollutants—are the *three higher knowledges* the Buddha gained under the bodhi tree.

Sometimes two other powers—insight knowledge and mind-made body—are included at the beginning of the list of superknowledges, bringing the total to eight. *Insight knowledge* (*vipassanā ñāṇa*, *vipaśyanā jñāna*) knows "this body of mine, made of material form, consisting of the four great elements, procreated by a mother and father, and built up out of boiled rice and porridge, is subject to impermanence...and this consciousness of mine is supported by it and bound up with it" (MN 77:29).

Due to the ability of jhāna, we can create a *mind-made body* (*manomayakāya*)—a physical body with limbs and sense sources that is an exact replica of our own body. Once the mind-made body is extracted from the physical body—like a reed extracted from a sheath—we mentally control it because it has no mind of its own, even though to others it looks like a normal body moved by its own consciousness. The mind-made body can travel to distant places while we remain at the monastery. It can appear to teach Dhamma elsewhere, and when it has served its purpose, we absorb it back into our own body.

According to the Sanskrit tradition, cultivating the first five superknowledges is essential for bodhisattvas to be of great benefit to sentient beings and to accumulate the extensive merit necessary to attain full awakening. Bodhisattvas go to pure lands where they listen to Dharma teachings directly from the Buddha and create enormous merit by emanating abundant and magnificent offerings for the holy beings there.

By means of clairaudience, bodhisattvas listen to teachings given in other places. Understanding all languages, they hear a wide range of teachings and can speak to students in their own language. Through knowledge of others' mind, bodhisattvas directly know others' interests and dispositions as well as their emotional patterns and habitual thoughts so they can teach them skillfully. By knowing their past lives, bodhisattvas can seek out the spiritual mentors, Dharma practices, and spiritual friends they knew in previous lives, enabling them to progress rapidly on the path.

The divine eye enables bodhisattvas to know others' karmic tendencies and their receptivity to the Dharma, so they can interact with them accordingly. They also know the karmic results of actions people are creating now, enabling them to guide disciples more effectively. They can locate their previous disciples and, because of their karmic connection, help them in their present life forms. Knowledge of the destruction of pollutants is knowledge of their own level of spiritual attainments and the paths they have attained.

While the Buddha possessed the superknowledges, he did not display them to show off and prohibited his followers from doing so. To ensure that monastics remain humble, one of our precepts is not to publicly proclaim one is an arhat or has these special abilities. Throughout the ages, the Buddha's disciples with these abilities have used them discreetly, without drawing attention to themselves, working in unobtrusive ways to benefit others and spread the Dharma.

Attaining these powers through samādhi without having the correct motivation can be dangerous. If someone has not cultivated compassion, he may use these powers to gain power, respect, or material gain, which are very far from the goal of the Buddhist path—liberation and full awakening.

A few ordinary people have some clairvoyance by the power of karma; they may know a future event or someone's thoughts. These karmic abilities are limited in scope, are lost at death, and what they perceive may not be completely accurate. Possessing them does not indicate that person has spiritual realizations.

Sanskrit Tradition

Many of the instructions to cultivate serenity in the Pāli and Sanskrit traditions are the same, so only points that have not been previously explained or that are slightly different are explained below.

Regarding meditation in general, we can talk about two processes—serenity and insight—and two types of meditation—stabilizing and analytical. Stabilizing meditation is predominantly used to develop serenity and analytical meditation to develop insight. The difference between serenity and insight lies not in their meditation object but in the way the mind engages with the object. Serenity focuses on the object single-pointedly, while insight analyzes it deeply.

External factors—altitude, temperature, time of day, and physical health—influence our ability to meditate. Without good conditions, we may be able to develop some concentration but not full serenity. Therefore we should seek appropriate internal and external environments for meditation. Asaṅga and Kamalaśīla encourage us to have the following conditions when doing retreat to develop serenity and as many of them as possible during daily meditation practice. First, live in a calm, quiet, safe place with clean water and air where you can secure food, clothing, and shelter easily. Be near other meditators, teachers, or Dharma friends who can help if questions or hindrances arise. Prior to beginning retreat, develop a clear, correct understanding of how to do the practice and to overcome difficulties that may arise. In addition, be free from coarse desires and be satisfied and content. Avoid involvement in worldly activities and commotion. Finally, observe pure ethical conduct, keeping whatever precepts you have received and abandoning at least the ten nonvirtues.

The real meaning of "living in seclusion" has to do with renouncing the glitter of saṃsāra: abandoning thoughts of the past and future and relinquishing sensual desire for present objects (MN 21:10). Without this, our arrogance could increase by living in an isolated place and thinking, "Others should praise me and give me offerings because I am a great meditator doing what others cannot do." We may have given up good food but be nourishing our arrogance instead!

It is important to practice in a consistent manner and avoid grandiose expectations of quick results. Short meditation sessions are recommended; pushing ourselves to do long sessions makes the mind tight, causing resistance to meditation. As the mind becomes more stable, sessions are gradually lengthened. Mindfully engaging in appropriate activities during break times between sessions helps the mind to be settled during the next session.

Meditation Position and Meditation Objects

The seven-point meditation position of Vairocana straightens the subtle energy channels in our bodies, allowing the wind-energies (*pāṇa, prāṇa*) to flow smoothly, making the mind clearer and calmer.

1. Sit on a cushion with your legs in the vajra position: the left foot on the right thigh and the right foot on the left thigh. Other cross-legged positions that do not strain the knees are also fine. If you cannot sit cross-legged, you may also sit on a small bench or in a straight-backed chair with your feet flat on the floor.
2. Put your right hand on top of the left, palms up. Touch the thumbs together lightly and put your hands in your lap near your navel. Some meditation masters advise putting the hands palms down on the knees.
3. Keep your shoulders level.
4. Straighten the back.
5. Slightly incline your head, but do not let it droop.
6. Keep your lips and teeth natural. Your tongue should be on the upper palate to prevent thirst as well as excess saliva.
7. Direct your eyes toward the tip of your nose. If this is difficult, direct your gaze downward, but don't focus on anything.

Keeping your eyes a little bit open when you meditate prevents drowsiness. The position of the eyes may vary according to the practice you do. Your physical position should be firm but also relaxed.

Begin the meditation session by taking refuge in the Three Jewels and cultivating a bodhicitta motivation. Recite inspiring verses and make requests to your spiritual mentor and the Three Jewels to uplift the mind. At the completion of the session, dedicate the merit for the welfare of all sentient beings.

While any object, internal or external, may initially be used to cultivate serenity, the final or actual object has to be one perceived by the mental consciousness. This is because concentration is developed with the mental consciousness not the sense consciousnesses. Although we may initially gain familiarity with the object by looking at it, we meditate on it with our mental consciousness.

Because sentient beings have different tendencies and dispositions, the Buddha described four general categories of objects for serenity meditation:

Extensive objects are so called because they are used for the development of both serenity and insight.

Objects for purifying behavior correspond with our temperament and help us counteract habituation with a particular affliction. Those with great desire concentrate on the ugly aspect of their object of attachment. Someone with strong anger meditates on the four immeasurables. Someone suffering from confusion contemplates dependent arising, while a conceited person reflects on the five mental and physical aggregates, the twelve sources, and the eighteen constituents. Doing this illustrates there is no independent self that is special. Someone with many distracting thoughts meditates on the breath to calm the mind.

Objects of skillful observation are so called because becoming skilled in or knowledgeable about them helps us realize emptiness. These objects are the five aggregates, eighteen constituents, twelve sources, twelve links of dependent arising, and appropriate and inappropriate results of various karmic causes.

Objects for purifying afflictions help to purify coarse and subtle afflictions of the three realms by temporarily suppressing them—this occurs by seeing the lower dhyānas as coarse and the higher dhyānas as peaceful—or by cutting their root through meditating on the sixteen attributes of the four truths.

In addition to these four objects, several other objects may also be used to cultivate serenity.

The conventional nature of the mind is the clear and aware nature of the mind. "Focusing the mind on mind" means one moment of mind focuses on the moment of mind immediately preceding it. To do this, we need to know what the mind is and be able to identify it. When the mind is distracted toward external objects and internal conceptualizations, its own clear and aware nature is obscured. When it can be seen alone, its qualities of *clarity* (which reflects objects by arising in their aspect) and *awareness* (which knows objects) become evident.

To identify the mind, gaze at an object with a muted, uniform color, and focus on the mind that is perceiving it. Immediately identify any distractions that may arise and return your attention to the clear and aware

Keith Adams (Woking, Surrey)

MOGAO CAVES, DUNHUANG, CHINA

nature of the mind. As you do this, gradually these distractions will cease, and you will perceive a stable, lucid state of mind.

When the mind is able to remain in the present, undisturbed by thoughts of the past and future, we may experience a vacuum because we have removed our mind from its familiar focus on external objects. After some time of increasing the duration of this experience, we will glimpse the clear and aware nature of the mind. This is the mind that is the meditation object for developing serenity on the conventional nature of the mind. The practices of *mahāmudrā* and *dzogchen* both emphasize meditating on the mind itself to cultivate serenity.

The challenge with using the mind as the focal object is that because it is formless, we can easily slip into meditating on a mere conception of the lack of materiality or fall into blank-minded meditation on nothingness. In both instances we have lost the object of meditation.

Emptiness as the object for cultivating serenity is only for those of exceptionally astute aptitude who have realized emptiness inferentially. Temporarily forsaking analysis, they concentrate on emptiness that has been conceptually understood. Here, there is some danger that if they lack clear ascertainment of emptiness, they will meditate on nothingness instead.

The Buddha as the object for cultivating serenity is recommended by many masters due to its many advantages. It helps us recollect the Buddha's qualities, inspires the mind, accumulates much merit, and facilitates other practices that involve visualizing the Buddha.

Begin by looking at an image of the Buddha or reflect on an eloquent description of him. Lower your eyes and, in the space in front of you, visualize the Buddha as a three-dimensional living being with a body made of brilliant golden light. Imagining a small figure makes the mind more alert; visualizing a bright figure counteracts laxity (*laya*); imagining it to be heavy prevents excitement and scattering.

Mentally go over the features of the Buddha's body, then focus single-pointedly on his body as a whole. If the image fades, review the various features again and then sustain your concentration on the entire form. If one part of the Buddha's body appears clearly, focus on that, and when it fades, return your attention to the entire body. Do not insist on trying to visualize every detail clearly before concentrating on the image.

The breath is a good meditation object. By focusing on it for a long time, the mind becomes still and settled, bringing respite from the afflictions.

Before being able to seriously cultivate serenity, we need to subdue whichever affliction is strongest, so it does not intrude when we meditate. By following this advice, our mind will be more malleable when meditating, and our ethical conduct and psychological well-being will also improve. A more stable mind provides the opportunity for concentration, bodhicitta, and wisdom to grow.

While cultivating serenity, we should use one meditation object without changing it in each meditation session. During a retreat to gain serenity, it is advisable to do mainly stabilizing meditation, with little analytical meditation, because analysis may disturb concentration. After serenity is attained, a meditator does analysis to combine serenity and insight, and at this time analysis does not disturb concentration.

Five Faults and Eight Antidotes

Maitreya's *Madhyāntavibhāga* speaks of five faults that interfere with developing serenity and eight antidotes that eliminate them.

1) *Laziness* (*kosajja, kausīdya*) may be of three types: sleeping and lying around, busyness doing useless saṃsāric activities, and discouragement. The

actual antidote to laziness is *mental pliancy*, but since it takes a while to strengthen this mental factor, we begin by cultivating three other antidotes. *Faith* in the benefits of serenity appreciates the excellence of meditation. Depending on it, *aspiration* (*chanda*), which takes interest in and wants to derive the benefits of cultivating serenity, easily arises. Aspiration leads to *effort*, a mental factor taking delight in practicing concentration. By practicing, we eliminate excitement and laxity and develop *pliancy*, a mental factor free from mental and physical inflexibility, heaviness, and feelings of hardship. With physical and mental pliancy, our body feels light and flexible, and we are able to keep our mind on whatever virtuous object we choose without difficulty.

2) *Forgetting the instruction* means losing the meditation object. The mind strays from the object and goes to objects of attachment, anger, and so forth. This fault occurs mainly on the first four stages of sustained attention explained below. The antidote is *mindfulness*, a mental factor that is familiar with the meditation object and holds the mind on it in such a way that it impedes distraction and forgetfulness. To develop strong mindfulness in meditation, cultivating mindfulness in all aspects of life is important.

3) Since *excitement and laxity* have the same antidote, *introspective awareness*, they are grouped together as the third fault. Single-pointedness of mind has two characteristics, stability and clarity. *Stability* is the ability to stay on the meditation object. Excitement is the chief obstacle to stability because it distracts the mind to objects of attachment. With coarse excitement we lose the meditation object completely; with subtle excitement the meditation object isn't entirely lost, but we are unable to engage it completely because an object of attachment is about to pop into our mind.

Clarity is the clarity of the mind apprehending the meditation object; its chief obstacle is laxity, which decreases the intensity of the clarity so that the mind's mode of apprehending the object becomes loose. Laxity differs from *lethargy* (*thīna, styāna*)—a heaviness of body and mind that is close to sleep and makes us lose both stability and clarity. With coarse laxity there is some stability on the object, but the clarity has decreased and the object no longer appears clearly. The mind lacks force and remains in a vague state with an agreeable sensation, although it isn't distracted to another object.

Subtle laxity is especially dangerous and difficult to recognize because it is similar to samādhi in that both have stability and clarity, and the mind is peaceful and experiences a pleasurable sensation. Although clarity remains and the mind may abide single-pointedly on the object, the mind is too relaxed, its grip on the object too loose. A meditator's breath may stop, and she may sit in meditation for days believing she has attained serenity, when in fact subtle laxity has set in.

Mindfulness and introspective awareness work together to eliminate faults. Mindfulness holds and remembers the object of meditation, and introspective awareness assesses whether excitement or laxity has arisen to interrupt concentration. Although introspective awareness is said to be the antidote to excitement and laxity, it is not the actual antidote; it lets us know we need to apply the antidote. Here introspective awareness is like a spy, occasionally checking to see if faults to concentration have arisen. If not, continue meditating. If so, apply the specific antidote to that fault. For coarse excitement, the antidote is to make the mind more sober by contemplating impermanence, death, or the sufferings of saṃsāra. The remedy for subtle excitement is to relax the intensity of concentration slightly, but not so much that we lose the object. The antidote to coarse laxity is to enlarge the scope of the object, making it brighter and elaborating on the details. If coarse laxity persists, temporarily leave the meditation object and, to uplift the mind, contemplate a topic such as precious human life, the good qualities of concentration, benefits of bodhicitta, or qualities of the Three Jewels. When subtle laxity is present, hold the meditation object more firmly in the mind.

4) *Non-application* (*anabhisaṃskāra*) means we do not apply the antidotes when we know excitement or laxity is present. The antidote is to *apply the appropriate antidote* to whichever fault has arisen and exert effort to eliminate it.

5) *Over-application* applies antidotes to excitement and laxity when they haven't occurred or when they have already been eliminated. Its antidote is *equanimity*, where effort is slightly relaxed.

Being able to identify in our own experience the mental factors interrupting concentration and those supporting it is essential. It takes time and introspective awareness to observe how our mind operates, but as we do, Dharma will come alive for us.

Nine Stages of Sustained Attention

Maitreya outlined *nine stages of sustained attention* that are accomplished sequentially to attain serenity. Certain faults are prominent in each stage, so specific antidotes are emphasized in each. To progress through these stages, we develop *six powers* (*bala*) and *four mental engagements* (*manaskāra*).

1) *Placing the mind* (*cittasthāpana*). Here our goal is to find the meditation object and place the mind on it, even though the mind cannot remain there for long. This stage is accomplished by the *power of hearing* (*śruti*), for we learn about the cultivation of serenity and place the mind on the object as instructed by our teacher. *Effortful engagement* (*balavāhana*) is used because great effort is required to make the mind stay on the object.

2) *Continual placement* (*pravāhasaṃsthāpa*). The *power of reflecting* (*āśaya*) on the object collects the mind and binds it to the object at least for a short while. Effortful engagement is still necessary to keep the mind on the object, but now the mind is not immediately distracted and can stay on the object with some continuity.

3) *Repeated placement* (*pratiharaṇa*). Distractions are fewer, and when they arise we are able to recognize them quickly and bring the mind back to the object. Due to developing the *power of mindfulness* during the previous two stages, the mind easily returns to the meditation object. *Interrupted engagement* (*sacchidravāhana*) is present on the third through seventh stages because concentration is not continuous.

4) *Close placement* (*upasthāpana*). Mindfulness is generated at the beginning of a session, and attention remains on the object more easily and distractions are fewer. Coarse excitement and laxity are present, so engagement with the meditation object is still interrupted.

5) *Taming* (*damana*). The mind is tamed—it can stay on the object almost continuously without wandering. Coarse laxity and coarse excitement are no longer problems. Now the mind becomes too absorbed in the object, and subtle laxity occurs. Engagement is interrupted by subtle laxity and subtle excitement, but concentration is easily restored by the *power of introspective awareness*, which sees the faults of distraction to sense objects, discursive thoughts, and auxiliary afflictions and prevents the mind from going toward them.

6) *Pacifying* (*śamana*). Through the power of introspective awareness, all resistance to single-pointed meditation is gone. During the fifth stage, concentration was tightened to eliminate laxity. Now concentration may be too tight, causing subtle excitement. Subtle laxity may still arise from time to time, so both of these make for interrupted engagement with the object. The power of introspective awareness can now sometimes identify excitement and laxity before they arise and deal with them.

7) *Thoroughly pacifying* (*vyupaśamana*). Even if subtle thoughts or disturbing emotions manifest, they are easily pacified. Subtle laxity and subtle excitement arise occasionally—so engagement is still interrupted—but the *power of effort* easily and quickly stops them. Mindfulness, introspective awareness, and effort are well developed, but non-application of the antidotes may still occur.

8) *Making single-pointed* (*ekotīkaraṇa*). Only a little effort is needed at the beginning of the session to discern the details of the object and guard against laxity and excitement. After that, the mind can stay on the object through the power of effort, so *uninterrupted engagement* (*niśchidravāhana*) is present. Single-pointed concentration lasts longer.

9) *Placement in equipoise* (*samādhāna*). Due to the *power of familiarity* (*paricaya*) with the previous powers, the mind spontaneously remains in samādhi. Effort to maintain mindfulness and introspective awareness is no longer required. Once mindfulness is placed on the object and the mind has entered meditative equipoise, it effortlessly remains single-pointed. *Spontaneous engagement* (*anābhogavāhana*) is present, and single-pointed meditation automatically continues for a long time. The sense consciousnesses are totally absorbed and no longer respond to external stimuli during meditation. This is the highest concentration attainable with a desire-sphere mind. It is a similitude of serenity; fully qualified serenity has not yet been attained.

As we progress through these stages of samādhi, the strength of mind and the power of meditation increase in dependence upon each other, and correspondingly clarity and stability increase, resulting in peace and happiness. Our complexion becomes youthful and radiant; we feel light and vigorous, and our dependence on coarse food decreases.

Serenity and Further Meditative Absorptions

After attaining the ninth stage, we must still attain mental and physical pliancy, and the bliss of physical and mental pliancy. Some people are able to do this quickly; others must meditate for weeks before attaining serenity.

Asaṅga (LRCM 3:82) defines *pliancy* as "a serviceability of the body and mind due to the cessation of the continuum of physical and mental dysfunctions. It has the function of dispelling all obstructions." *Physical dysfunctions* are related to wind-energies and make the body heavy and uncomfortable when engaging in virtue. *Mental dysfunctions* prevent us from enjoying eradicating afflictions.

Increased familiarity with concentration overcomes physical dysfunctions. At this time a sense of bliss and a pleasant tingling sensation occur on the head because dysfunctional wind-energies are exiting from the crown. Immediately afterward, dysfunctional mental states are overcome and *special mental pliancy* is attained. This is a serviceability of mind—lightness and clarity coupled with the ability to set the mind on whatever virtuous object we wish.

Special mental pliancy induces serviceability of the wind-energies flowing through the body as the wind-energies that power the afflictions subside. A wind-energy of physical pliancy pervades the whole body, and the body's lack of serviceability for meditation is overcome. *Physical pliancy* is a lightness, buoyancy, and serviceability of body that enables it to be used for whatever virtuous purpose we wish, without pain or hardship. This leads to the experience of the *bliss of physical pliancy*, a very blissful tactile sensation.

As samādhi continues, we have the sense that the body has melted into the meditation object. At this point, the *bliss of mental pliancy* is experienced. The mind is very joyous, pliant, and confident in concentration. Following this, there is a sensation similar to placing a cool hand atop a freshly shaven head. The mental bliss decreases a little, and when it becomes stable, *unchangeable bliss of concentration* and *unchangeable mental pliancy* are experienced. At this point serenity and access concentration have been attained. As human beings, we are desire-realm beings, but while meditating our mind of access concentration is a material-sphere consciousness.

After attaining serenity, a practitioner may follow a mundane path to gain the five superknowledges and rebirth in material and immaterial realms. This involves *mundane insight*, where during seven preparatory stages one contemplates the faults of the lower absorption and the benefits of the higher absorption and then suppresses the level of afflictions interfering with attaining the higher one. Both Buddhists and non-Buddhists may do this.

Alternatively, Buddhists may, after attaining serenity, follow a supramundane path, in which serenity is used as the basis for cultivating insight into selflessness and emptiness. Doing this is necessary for attaining nirvāṇa and is unique to Buddhism.

It is not necessary to gain all eight meditative absorptions of the material-sphere and immaterial-sphere consciousnesses to cultivate insight realizing emptiness. Tsongkhapa says that union of serenity and insight as well as liberation can be attained by cultivating insight based on serenity—that is, by depending on access concentration (LRCM 3:95). However, unlike śrāvakas, who can attain their path of seeing with access concentration, bodhisattvas have their first direct perception of emptiness and enter the bodhisattva path of seeing while meditating in the fourth jhāna. At some time in their training, bodhisattvas will develop all eight meditative absorptions of the material and immaterial realms to enhance the flexibility of their concentration.

When human beings have attained access concentration or above, their single-pointed concentration does not vanish completely during the break times between meditation sessions. It is not manifest, however, and when they go about their daily activities, their five senses function. Their afflictions are weaker due to the powerful influence of samādhi, but afflictions may still arise, so practitioners must maintain mindfulness and introspective awareness in all activities.

Serenity becomes a Buddhist practice when supported by refuge in the Three Jewels. When coupled with the determination to be free and the wisdom realizing emptiness, serenity brings liberation. And when conjoined with bodhicitta and the wisdom realizing emptiness, serenity leads to full awakening. To ensure our practice of serenity brings liberation or full awakening, beginners should not seek meditative concentration to the exclusion of other practices. They should be sure to meditate on the defects of saṃsāra and the possibility of attaining liberation to cultivate a proper motivation and have a firm foundation for practicing insight.

The way of generating serenity is the same for śrāvakas, pratyekabuddhas, and bodhisattvas. Those following the Sūtrayāna and those practicing the first three classes of tantra develop serenity in a similar manner and first attain serenity, then insight. Highest yoga tantra contains special techniques involving concentration on subtle objects. This makes the mind more subtle as well. A tantric practitioner who is already very familiar with meditation on emptiness through analytical meditation can attain serenity and insight simultaneously.

The depth of concentration needed to uproot cognitive obscurations is much greater than that needed to overcome afflictive obscurations. For that reason, bodhisattvas cultivate amazing states of concentration. Seventh

Dekyi Wong

SHWEDAGON PAGODA, BURMA

ground bodhisattvas are able to enter and leave nondual concentration on emptiness in a split second. Their mental pliancy is so great that they can switch from single-pointedness on one meditation object to the same depth of concentration on another object in a moment. Other practitioners are not capable of doing this as quickly or with such ease.

CHINESE BUDDHISM

While many great meditation masters in China have written about the cultivation of serenity and of concentration in general, the Tiantai master Zhiyi (538–97) authored some of the clearest and most important texts. His writings are particularly important because they appeared early in the history of Chinese Buddhism, when proper meditation instruction was available to sincere monastic practitioners but not to general Buddhist practitioners. Rooted in the classic Indian texts, Zhiyi's comprehensive and clear instructions were a great boost to practitioners of his time and have been practiced by meditators in many Chinese schools to the present day. Presenting serenity and insight in accord with Maitreya and Asaṅga's texts, Zhiyi emphasized practicing them in a balanced fashion.

Zhiyi's *Essentials for Practicing Serenity, Insight, and Dhyāna* (*Xiuxi zhiguan zuo chan fa yao*) is a comprehensive guide to the cultivation of concentration. He speaks of the prerequisite internal and external conditions for the cultivation of serenity, emphasizing the importance of confession, purification, and renouncing desire for objects of the five senses. He also discusses sitting in the proper position, overcoming the five hindrances, adjusting the breath and the mind when entering meditation; adjusting the body, breath, and mind when abiding in meditation; and adjusting them when concluding a meditation session. His text also covers relating with sense stimuli and practicing in the break times when sitting, lying down, walking, and standing. Regarding meditation objects, he speaks specifically of the breath, foulness of the body, love, dependent arising, and the Buddha. He describes true and false signs of dhyāna absorption and how to resolve physical disorders and imbalances and hindrances from spirits. He concludes the book with realization of the fruits for śrāvakas and bodhisattvas.

Zhiyi's *Six Gates to the Sublime* (*Liu miao fa men*) speaks of a sixfold meditation explained in Kātyāyaniputra's *Abhidharma Vibhāṣā* (about 200 B.C.E.), Vasumitra's *Mahāvibhāṣā* (150 C.E.), and Vasubandhu's *Abhidharmakośabhāṣya* (fourth century). Buddhaghosa transforms this into an eightfold formula in the *Visuddhimagga* (8:189–225). The "six gates" are counting the breath, following the breath, stabilizing, analyzing, transforming, and purifying. This same meditation is taught in the Tibetan tradition as well.

6 | The Higher Training in Wisdom: Thirty-Seven Aids to Awakening

BUILT ON THE foundation of the higher trainings in ethical conduct and concentration, the higher training in wisdom involves the practice of the thirty-seven *aids to awakening* (*bodhipakkhiyā-dhamma*, *bodhipakṣya-dharma*) and leads to insight. While not all thirty-seven aids are considered higher training in wisdom, they all directly or indirectly contribute to the cultivation of the wisdom that understands selflessness and the four truths correctly and thus leads to liberation.

The thirty-seven aids are explained in both Pāli and Sanskrit sūtras and are valued practices in all three vehicles. In the Sanskrit tradition, they are explained in detail in both the *Abhidharmakośa* and *Abhisamayālaṃkāra*. Candrakīrti's *Madhyamakāvatāra* also speaks of them. In the Pāli canon, their chief source is the *Mahāvagga* in the Saṃyutta Nikāya. The passages on the thirty-seven aids here are almost word for word the same as in the Sanskrit *Daśabhūmika Sūtra*. The main differences in how the thirty-seven aids are practiced in the Śrāvaka and Bodhisattva vehicles is that bodhisattvas do them with a bodhicitta motivation and apply them to all sentient beings. For example, when establishing mindfulness of the body, bodhisattvas meditate on the impermanence and foulness of both their own and others' bodies. From the Madhyamaka perspective, practitioners of all three vehicles meditate on the thirty-seven aids with the view of their being empty of inherent existence. Tibetan monastics study the thirty-seven aids in their curriculum, and I encourage them to do more meditation on these, especially the four establishments of mindfulness.

The thirty-seven aids are divided into seven sets, and in the Sanskrit tradition, these are correlated with the five paths. This does not mean that practitioners on either the previous or subsequent paths do not practice them. Rather, the practice of a particular set becomes full-fledged and fully qualified at a certain level of the path.

Cultivating the four establishments of mindfulness and reflecting on their specific and common characteristics enables us to understand the four seals that determine a teaching to be the Buddha's doctrine. These are mentioned in the *Samādhirāja Sūtra* in the Sanskrit tradition: (1) all conditioned phenomena are impermanent, (2) all polluted phenomena are unsatisfactory, (3) all phenomena are empty and selfless, and (4) nirvāṇa is true peace.

Once we understand these, especially that nirvāṇa is peace, we will want to engage in the practice to attain nirvāṇa. This leads to practicing the four supreme strivings, which are the nature of joyous effort. Through putting forth effort, we develop concentration, which involves the four bases of supernormal power. If we have not previously attained serenity, we do so now.

We then put special attention on the five faculties and five powers to overcome all unfavorable conditions and attain the union of serenity and insight on selflessness. The seven awakening factors and the noble eightfold path are then cultivated to actualize nirvāṇa.

Here these seven sets are spoken of as qualities attained by those on the first four of the five paths, not with regard to an ordinary person who has yet to enter a path. However, some scriptures explain the thirty-seven aids for those who haven't entered a path, giving us clear directions on how to practice in our daily lives. The explanation is taken from both the Pāli and Sanskrit traditions. Each emphasizes certain points that complement the perspective of the other.

Four Establishments of Mindfulness

The four *establishments of mindfulness* (*satipaṭṭhāna*, *smṛtyupasthāna*) focus on the body (*kāya*), feelings (*vedanā*), mind (*citta*), and phenomena (*dhamma*, *dharma*). To "establish mindfulness" means to place our mindfulness on an object comprehended by wisdom. *Body* refers to three kinds of body: (1) the internal (five cognitive faculties), (2) the external (five sense objects), and (3) both internal and external (coarse physical sense organs). *Feelings* refers to pleasant, unpleasant, and neutral feelings, both those accompanying sense consciousnesses and those accompanying our thoughts and other mental states. *Mind* refers to the six primary consciousnesses, and *phenomena* includes mental objects (*dhammāyatana*, *dharmāyatana*)—all other impermanent and permanent phenomena that are not included in body, feelings, and mind.

These four objects are selected as objects of mindfulness to help us ordinary beings understand the errors of: (1) conceiving our body to be the place where the self resides—"I am here, inside my body," (2) conceiving our feelings to be what the self enjoys and experiences—"I feel happy, I feel miserable, I feel indifferent," (3) conceiving our mind to be a real self—"I am what thinks and perceives," (4) conceiving phenomena, in particular our attitudes and emotions, as what make the self afflicted or worthwhile—"I have so many problems with anger and jealousy," or "My confidence makes me a good person." In each instance, the self is erroneously conceived as a solid personal identity. We see our self as standing alone, independent from other factors, and view everything else—our body, feelings, mind, and phenomena—as arranged around that self.

When we analyze the nature of the body, feelings, mind, and phenomena to attain insight, we do so in two ways: by meditating on the characteristics common to all of them—impermanent, unsatisfactory, empty, and selfless—and by meditating on their specific characteristics. Regarding the latter, cultivating each object with mindfulness counteracts a particular misconception, enhances an understanding, and deepens our understanding of one of the four truths, as shown in the table below.

The Pāli tradition explains that the purpose of the four establishments of mindfulness is to gain direct insight into the *three characteristics* of our body and mind—impermanence, dukkha, and not-self—and to use this insight to eliminate the mental defilements binding us in saṃsāra.

To practice the four establishments of mindfulness successfully, the guidance of a qualified spiritual mentor experienced in these meditations is necessary. We also need to study well the suttas teaching these practices, especially the *Mahāsatipaṭṭhāna Sutta* (DN 22), *Satipaṭṭhāna Sutta* (MN 10), *Ānāpānasati Sutta* (MN 118), and *Kāyagatāsati Sutta* (MN 119). Buddhaghosa wrote two commentaries on the *Satipaṭṭhāna Sutta*, and Dhammapāla wrote a subcommentary that further clarifies many points.

Nowadays, some Theravādin masters teach the four establishments of mindfulness—especially mindfulness of the breath—to develop serenity, while others teach them to cultivate insight. Training the mind to be

The Four Establishments of Mindfulness overcoming Misconceptions related to the Four Truths

Object of Mindfulness	*Misconception*	*Understanding*	*Truth*
Body	Holding the unclean as clean	The body is unclean in nature.	Truth of duḥkha
Feelings	Holding what is unsatisfactory (*duḥkha*) as pleasurable	Feelings are unsatisfactory in nature.	Truth of the origin of duḥkha
Mind	Holding what is momentary as permanent	The mind arises and passes away each moment.	Truth of cessation
Phenomena	Holding what lacks a self as having a self	Phenomena are not the self. Some phenomena are to be practiced and others abandoned.	Truth of the path

continually mindful of the meditation object stabilizes and calms the mind, increasing concentration. Mindfulness also knows its object along with its characteristics and attributes well, leading to insight.

Mindfulness of the Body

To establish mindfulness of the body, we reflect on the cause, nature, and result of the body. Through this, we see the body is unclean and unsatisfactory in nature, which decreases our attachment, anxiety, and obsession about the body. The causes of the body are the sperm and egg as well as ignorance, craving, and karma. Its nature is unclean; this is evident when we examine the inside of the body. The result of our body is a corpse. While we are alive, our body is the basis for illness and injury and a source of pain, worry, fear, and aggravation. We have to work hard to earn the money to feed, clothe, shelter, and protect this body. This stimulates greed and anger and leads to wars and extortion. In short, the body and the need to take care of it are the basis of so many troubles—economic problems, environmental pollution, war, crime, overpopulation, and social injustice. Contemplating this, it becomes evident that the body is unsatisfactory in nature.

Nevertheless, the body is the physical basis that supports our human intelligence, which, if used properly, enables us to practice Dharma and attain awakening. From this perspective, our body is considered valuable, and we treasure our precious human life. Therefore, while we see our body for what it is, we should not despise it. We keep it healthy, clean, and somewhat comfortable so that we can utilize it for Dharma practice.

When explaining mindfulness of the body (MN 10), the Buddha detailed mindfulness of breathing (*ānāpānasati*, *ānāpānasmṛti*), four physical postures, foulness of the body, the four elements, and nine charnel-ground contemplations. Mindfulness of the breath, in brief, involves observing the breath according to sixteen steps. Broken into sets of four, these apply to the body, feelings, mind, and phenomena, and by contemplating them in terms of the three characteristics, wisdom understanding the body steadily increases.

Most commentaries recommend attending to the breath at the nostrils and upper lip. It seems that this point is more conducive for generating the *nimitta* or "sign" spoken of in serenity meditation. Some meditation teachers recommend observing the breath at any point in the body where it can be experienced distinctly, such as the abdomen or the chest. For some people, these points may be more conducive for cultivating insight.

Establishing mindfulness with the *four postures*—walking, sitting, standing, and lying down—entails being mindful of what we are doing and why, no matter what position our body is in. We are fully present in the moment, not thinking about the past or future. Being mindful during break times supports mindfulness in meditation sessions.

Establishing mindfulness on the parts of the body makes its *foulness* apparent. The Buddha mentioned thirty-one parts of the body to be mindful of—the brain was later added to make thirty-two. These are broken into six groups: (1) the skin quintet—head hair, body hair, nails, teeth, skin; (2) the kidney quintet—muscles, tendons, bones, marrow, kidney; (3) the lung quintet—heart, liver, connective tissue, spleen, lungs; (4) the brain quintet—intestines, mesentery, stomach, feces, brain; (5) the fat sextet—bile, phlegm, pus, blood, sweat, fat; and (6) the urine sextet—tears, grease (on skin), spit, snot, oil of the joints, urine.

Beginning with the skin quintet, we focus on each part individually, observing its color, shape, texture, location in the body, and surrounding organs. After contemplating the skin, we go backward through the group, contemplating each part again until we reach the head hair. Then we go forward once again, contemplating each member of the skin quintet and continuing on to the kidney quintet. The forward-backward-forward cycle is repeated for each group. In this way, we become familiar with each part of the body, seeing it clearly for what it is. It soon becomes apparent that what we call "my body" is just a collection of unclean parts. Seeing this reduces our craving to take another saṃsāric body. Meditating on the body of another person in this way lessens sexual desire. Meditation on the parts of the body by focusing single-pointedly on their unclean nature is serenity meditation. Mindfulness of the body parts performed by investigating the various elements composing the body and by seeing the parts in terms of the three characteristics is insight meditation.

Contemplation of the body also includes reflecting on the *four great elements* (elemental properties) that compose it—earth (solidity), water (cohesion), fire (heat), and air (mobility). A person of sharp faculties does this by scanning the body, focusing on the characteristics of each element, and taking all instances of it together as being that element. The expanded meditation is done by seeing which parts have a predominance of each element—for example, in bones, teeth, and internal organs the property of solidity is dominant. Another way of meditating in an expanded manner is to scan the body and experience each element. Through this we understand that the body is an inseparable combination of the four elements. At this time, the mere collection of elements is apparent, and the perception of a person or self is lost.

The *charnel-ground contemplations* are done by comparing our present body to corpses in various stages of decomposition. Our body is the same nature as these corpses, is not exempt from death, and will become like those corpses under suitable conditions. This reduces our identification with and attachment to this body. As with all meditations, it is important to understand its purpose and do it with a balanced mind and without generating superstitious or fearful thoughts.

In brief, mindfulness of the body investigates what this body is, seeing that it is not beautiful, permanent, something providing real happiness, or a self. Through consistent meditation on the body as having the three characteristics, concentration and wisdom arise.

Mindfulness of Feelings

Through mindfulness of feelings we understand how craving arises in response to various feelings, thus perpetuating saṃsāra. Feelings arise through contact with objects of the five senses. We become attached to pleasant feelings, have aversion for unpleasant ones, and are apathetic toward neutral feelings. We strongly grasp the I that experiences these feelings. Afflictions become more powerful, karma is created, and saṃsāra continues. In this way, mindfulness of feelings makes us aware of the true origins of duḥkha.

To establish mindfulness of feelings, we contemplate our feelings, examining what we feel now, what we felt in the past, and what we expect to feel in the future. The three feelings are correlated with the three types of duḥkha: painful feelings with the duḥkha of pain; pleasant feelings with the duḥkha of change; and neutral feelings with the duḥkha of pervasive conditioning. We observe that the experience of pleasant feelings eventually changes into the experience of painful ones. Because neutral feelings are unstable and polluted by ignorance, they contain the seed for manifest suffering; the suffering of pain is always ready to flare up. In this way, we see all these feelings as unsatisfactory, and aspiration for liberation grows in us.

Our feelings continuously change with pain, pleasure, and neutral feelings following in quick succession. Because feelings are transient, there is no sense in being attached to pleasant ones or upset by unpleasant ones.

Observing the *causes* of feelings, we understand how the interdependence of object, cognitive faculty, and consciousness produce contact and thus feeling. Observing the *results* of feelings helps us to understand craving and clinging and how these perpetuate saṃsāra.

Responding to feelings with mindfulness instead of craving and clinging stops feelings from instigating afflictions. When a painful or pleasant feeling arises, we turn our mindfulness to observe it. Investigating its *nature*, we see it isn't one solid entity. It is a flowing process, a series of moments of pain or pleasure. Each moment differs slightly from the preceding and following moments. In the case of pain, what appeared to be an unchanging, unified, painful feeling is now seen as a mental construct projected on a series of moments that have a similar quality. Furthermore, we observe there are different kinds of pain—throbbing, prickling, stabbing, aching, and so on. When we make painful feelings the object of mindfulness, we no longer feel weighed down or tormented by them. Interestingly, many doctors have found that mindfulness meditation is a great aid for people suffering from chronic pain.

The Pāli scriptures say pleasant, painful, and neutral feelings each have two subdivisions: worldly and spiritual.

Worldly happiness arises from acquiring desirable sense objects; spiritual happiness arises from having positive mental factors such as concentration, faith, and love.

Worldly pain is triggered by contact with undesirable sense objects or from not acquiring what we want. Spiritual pain may arise when we aspire for states of concentration or for attainments that we have not yet actualized. It may also arise from regret regarding harmful actions we have done. Here spiritual pain can motivate us to engage in virtuous actions to actualize our spiritual goals.

Worldly neutral feelings arise when we are oblivious to the results of our actions, leaving us apathetic, complacent, and lazy. Spiritual neutral feelings are, for example, the equanimity of the fourth jhāna.

Worldly pleasant, painful, and neutral feelings are the source of afflictions if they are not observed with mindfulness, while spiritual pleasant, unpleasant, and equanimous feelings are beneficial and can lead us to further our practice of virtue.

At a certain point when establishing mindfulness of feelings, we stop focusing on feelings as being pleasant, unpleasant, or neutral and stop observing their arising and passing away. Instead we become mindful simply that there is feeling so as to cultivate bare knowledge and constant mindfulness. Here feelings are experienced as impersonal phenomena. We do not identify with them and cease to grasp them as I, mine, or my self.

Mindfulness of the Mind

To meditate on the impermanent nature of the mind, we contemplate the mind of the past, which is now gone, and the mind of the future, which has yet to come. Only the present mind remains, but this, too, is ever-changing and does not stay for a moment. Each moment of mind arises, abides, and disintegrates simultaneously.

Mindfulness of the mind's subtle impermanent nature brings two understandings: (1) although a moment of mind does not remain for a second moment, the continuity of mind is indestructible, and (2) the I is imputed in dependence on the mind. Understanding these reduces fear at the time of death of becoming totally nonexistent, which triggers craving and clinging. Relaxing that fear gives more opportunity to meditate and gain deep realizations at the time of death.

Establishing mindfulness on the mind also entails gaining a direct experience of this formless mind that is aware and knows objects. Like a mirror, it reflects things, but precisely identifying its clear and aware nature is difficult.

In our daily lives, our five senses are very active, and the experiences of our mental consciousness usually concern what our five senses have contacted. Most of our lives are controlled by these external experiences and our reactions to them; we do not have the opportunity to experience the real nature of mind.

To allow the actual conventional nature of our mind to arise, we must let go of thoughts about external events and internal experiences and thoughts of the past and future. Initially we may feel the mind is nothing, void, thoughtless. When we are able to prolong this time of not thinking of the past or future, we might get a glimpse of voidness. This voidness is not the emptiness of inherent existence of the mind; rather, we have created a gap by intentionally stopping mental elaborations and manifestations of the coarser level of mind. An experience of stillness arises because the senses are not active. There is just the experience of the present, of a void. As we sustain this gap, we might get a glimpse of the mere clear and aware nature of mind. Only then have we found the object of meditation for practicing mindfulness of the mind. Becoming familiar with this, we will experience the momentariness of the mind.

As we continue meditating, we become aware: (1) The natural state of our mind is free from both destructive and constructive emotions. Emotions arise due to causes and conditions; they are adventitious and do not exist in the clear and aware nature of the mind. Seeing this neutral nature of the mind, we know it is possible to put an end to the mental defilements. (2) The mind is momentary. Thus thoughts are also transient. This, too, enables us to understand that putting an end to mental defilements and actualizing true cessations are possible. In this way, mindfulness of the mind leads to understanding true cessations, the third truth of the āryas.

Mindfulness of the mind also leads to the realization of the selflessness of the person. We usually think of the person as related to or identified with the psychophysical aggregates. Sometimes we feel the I exists on the body; other times it seems the I exists on the mind. When we meditate with mindfulness on the body, we feel "I am meditating on the body." The I appears to be inside the body, yet separate from it. When we meditate on mindfulness of feelings, we feel there is an I who experiences pain and pleasure. This I, too, seems to be separate from the feelings; it is the experiencer or owner of the feelings.

Meditating on the mind, we initially believe that our mind could be us. But later on, we discover a neutral, subtle mind that is the object to investigate with mindfulness. At that time, we may wonder, "Where is the I now?" We may get the feeling that the I is merely designated in dependence on the collection of mind and body. There is no independent I that owns the body and the mind. In this way, meditation on the mind leads to understanding the selflessness of person and true cessations.

Mindfulness of the mind and its impermanent nature also leads to understanding the selflessness of phenomena, phenomena's emptiness of inherent existence. Inherent existence is synonymous with independent existence. If something existed independently, it would not depend on anything else, including causes and conditions, and would thus be permanent and unchanging. However, since the mind arises and passes away in each moment, it is not permanent. It thus depends on causes and conditions and does not exist independently of all other factors. Thus the mind is empty of inherent existence.

In the Pāli tradition, *mindfulness of mind* refers to mindfulness of mental states—states of mind colored by the mental factors accompanying the primary consciousness. Just as water mixed with orange syrup becomes an orange drink, the mind accompanied by anger becomes an angry mind, and a mind accompanied by concentration becomes a concentrated mind. Mindfulness of the mind develops naturally from mindfulness of feelings because due to the three types of feelings, the three poisonous mental states arise.

We begin the meditation session by observing the breath to settle the mind and then turn our mindfulness to the mind itself, observing whatever mental state is present without clinging or pushing it away. In doing so, we learn to discern virtuous and nonvirtuous mental states.

We also contemplate the arising of the mind—that various mental states

Mike Nowak

GANDHAKUṬI IN JETAVANA MONASTERY, WHERE THE BUDDHA TAUGHT MANY SŪTRAS, SHRAVASTI, INDIA

arise due to their own unique conditions—and the vanishing of the mind—that these mental states do not last in the next moment and pass away as soon as they arise. We then contemplate both their arising and passing away, the momentary nature of all mental processes.

When familiarity with the characteristics of various mental states is established and we are able to identify them quickly and easily, we can observe the mental process itself with mindfulness. Through this we dwell without clinging.

Mindfulness of Phenomena

Tsongkhapa explains the phenomena contemplated in the fourth mindfulness as the factors to adopt and discard on the path. Here "phenomena" refers to both the pure class of phenomena—beneficial phenomena to cultivate—and the impure class—afflictive phenomena to abandon. By reflecting on these, we enter the practice of the fourth truth of the āryas, true paths, the essence of which is the realization of emptiness and selflessness.

Mental factors are the most important phenomena to consider in mindfulness of phenomena. We identify the afflictive mental factors within our own mind and investigate their causes, characteristics, and effects. When afflictive mental factors accompany the primary consciousness, they disturb the mind, making it unclear and unmanageable. Purified mental factors make it clear, manageable, and tranquil. With mindfulness, we observe this in our own experience.

We also observe that disturbing mental factors lack a valid basis, depend on ignorance, and can be uprooted by wisdom. Beneficial mental factors are supported by reasoning and are capable of counteracting disturbing ones. Moreover, positive attitudes and emotions can be increased limitlessly.

None of these mental factors is the person. Yet a conventionally existent self—one that is merely designated in dependence on the aggregates—exists. This realization that persons and phenomena are empty of inherent existence yet exist as imputations is the true path leading to true cessation.

In the Pāli *Mahāsatipaṭṭhāna Sutta*, five sets of phenomena serve as the objects of mindfulness of phenomena: the five hindrances, five aggregates, six sources (sense bases), seven awakening factors, and four truths.

The sequence of the five sets is itself a map. Mindfulness of the five hindrances comes first because they are the major impediments to development of the mind, specifically to cultivating serenity and insight. Overcoming them is an essential first step, enabling us to explore the field of our experience using the framework of the five aggregates and six sources. As insight develops, the seven awakening factors become prominent, and as they mature, penetrative understanding of the four truths arises. This leads to understanding the ultimate truth of the Dhamma.

Mindfulness of the five hindrances requires us to (1) be aware of the presence of each hindrance when it is manifest and its absence after it has subsided, (2) know the factors causing each hindrance to arise, (3) understand how to temporarily suppress each hindrance, and (4) understand how to eliminate each hindrance completely.

In mindfulness of the five aggregates, we understand the characteristics of each aggregate. Then we focus on knowing its origin and disappearance by investigating the conditions through which each aggregate arises and its nature of impermanence. Mindfulness of the six sources involves seeing their role in causing the fetters to arise. We then learn how to temporarily suppress the fetters and hindrances and how to eliminate them through insight into their actual nature.

Mindfulness of each of the seven awakening factors entails understanding (1) when it is present and absent in our minds, (2) the causes for its arising, and (3) how to bring it to fulfillment once it has arisen. With mindfulness of the four truths we clearly know how dukkha arises due to its causes and the possibility of attaining cessation by cultivating the path.

When our insight wisdom is very familiar with the three characteristics, the mind will momentarily break through the conditioned world and have a glimpse of the unconditioned. It now sees and understands "This is the cessation of dukkha." However, the mind cannot yet hold this realization for long and falls back to the conditioned world. But now we know with certainty that the five aggregates, six sources, and so forth are dukkha. Seeing the evolution of saṃsāra from ignorance and craving, we know the origin of dukkha. Through our own experience we know the noble eightfold path is the true path leading to the cessation of dukkha. This first breakthrough experience, during which we have direct and full knowledge of the unconditioned, establishes us as a stream-enterer. By repeatedly developing insight, we will attain full realization of the unconditioned.

The four establishments of mindfulness are not mutually exclusive practices. One can be the framework in which the others are contemplated. For example, if mindfulness of breath is our primary practice, when a strong feeling or emotion arises, we contemplate it temporarily. When it subsides, we return to contemplating the breath.

Four Establishments of Mindfulness for Bodhisattvas

According to Mādhyamikas, bodhisattvas practice the four establishments of mindfulness with the motivation of bodhicitta, and they cultivate the wisdom realizing the subtle selflessness of both persons and phenomena—their emptiness of inherent existence. This wisdom realizes that the body, feelings, mind, and phenomena are empty of "existing from their own side" or "under their own power." Bodhisattvas also meditate on the four establishments of mindfulness by seeing the body, feelings, mind, and phenomena as existing by being merely designated by term and concept. They see the body is like an illusion, feelings like a dream, the mind like space, and phenomena like fleeting clouds. In this way, bodhisattvas do both space-like and illusion-like meditation on emptiness in relation to these four objects.

Bodhisattvas also meditate on the impurity and impermanence of others' bodies to realize that sentient beings suffer in cyclic existence. Seeing sentient beings bound to bodies polluted by ignorance, bodhisattvas generate great compassion and bodhicitta.

Four Supreme Strivings

Having meditated on the four establishments of mindfulness, especially mindfulness of phenomena, we aspire to develop positive qualities and remove afflictions. The four supreme strivings (*sammappadhāna*)[11] enable us to do this. We arouse aspiration and apply effort to: (1) prevent nonvirtues—afflictions and destructive actions—from arising, for example by restraining our senses, (2) abandon nonvirtues already generated by applying their antidotes, (3) generate new virtues, for example by cultivating the four establishments of mindfulness and the seven awakening factors, (4) enhance virtues that have been generated, especially by sustaining favorable meditation objects to attain full samādhi.

In addition to counteracting laxity and excitement—two faults impeding serenity—the four supreme strivings balance and enhance serenity and insight. If one or the other is too strong, we strive to strengthen the other.

Four Bases of Supernormal Power

With the four supreme strivings, we make effort to reduce and eliminate afflictions and destructive actions, strengthen positive qualities, and refine serenity and insight. Now we practice meditative concentrations that give rise to supernormal powers. The four bases of supernormal power (*iddhipāda, ṛddhipāda*) are single-pointed concentrations of aspiration, effort, intention, and investigation. Through practicing them, practitioners develop special power to emanate and transform things. The objects emanated or transformed by supernormal powers—such as making one's body very large, emanating several bodies, and transforming an ugly place into a beautiful one—are the objects of these four bases of supernormal power. With these powers, bodhisattvas may visit many buddha lands and accumulate vast merit by making offerings to a multitude of buddhas.

The four establishments of mindfulness are the mental factors of wisdom and mindfulness, the four supreme strivings are types of effort, and the four bases of supernormal power are concentrations associated with the mental factors of aspiration and so forth. Aspiration, effort, intention, and investigation are the means to refine our concentration in order to develop powerful meditative abilities.

Supernormal powers are gained through mental development, specifically deep concentration. Worldly supernormal powers include making manifestations of one's body, flying in space, walking on water, passing through walls or mountains, and going under the earth. However, the highest supernormal power is unpolluted liberation of the mind, nibbāna.

The suttas explain two factors contributing to concentration. The first, determined striving, is common to all four concentrations. The second is unique to each concentration: (1) *Aspiration* (*chanda*) is a deep desire or wish to attain supernormal powers that fuels our efforts to attain samādhi. (2) *Effort* (*viriya*, *vīrya*) spurs the cultivation of concentration leading to supernormal powers. (3) By means of *intention* (*citta*), one calms the mind, making it tranquil, pure, and radiant. Through the resulting clarity of mind, we gain concentration that is a basis for supernormal attainments. (4) *Investigation* (*vīmaṃsā*, *mīmāṃsā*) examines the mind and the factors promoting and hindering its development. Fueled by a wish to investigate and realize nibbāna, we strive to attain concentration. These four concentrations can be combined with wisdom to attain liberation.

Five Faculties and Five Powers

The five faculties (*indriya*) and the five powers (*bala*) have the same names and are the same qualities, but the five powers are the stronger and fuller development of the five faculties. With the five faculties we are still unable to remedy opposing factors—non-faith, laziness, forgetfulness, distraction, and faulty wisdom—which may still occasionally arise. When the five faculties are strong enough not to be dislodged by their opposites, they become the five powers. With the five powers, we have mastery over the opposing factors and are able to override, though not yet fully abandon them. Although the five qualities are spoken of individually, in practice they function harmoniously together. All five may simultaneously accompany a single primary consciousness. The five faculties and five powers reach fulfillment in nibbāna.

As the Sanskrit tradition describes the five: (1) *Faith* refers to believing faith that has confidence in the path of practice and in the resultant liberation or, for bodhisattvas, full awakening. This faith arises from investigation, so it is naturally combined with wisdom and has conviction in the four truths. (2) *Effort* overcomes the laziness interrupting meditation on the four truths and enables us to quickly realize them. For bodhisattvas, this effort also includes enthusiasm for engaging in the six perfections. (3) *Mindfulness* ensures that we do not forget the objects and aspects of the four truths. For bodhisattvas, this mindfulness is conjoined with bodhicitta seeking others' welfare. (4) *Concentration* eliminates the five faults preventing perfect concentration on the four truths and focuses single-pointedly on them. It also realizes the emptiness of true existence of all phenomena. (5) *Wisdom* overcomes wrong conceptions about the four truths and individually discriminates their features and qualities as well as their ultimate mode of existence. Bodhisattvas cultivate wisdom realizing all aspects of all phenomena.

The Pāli tradition says: (1) *Faith* has trust and confidence in the Three Jewels, especially in the Buddha's awakening and the Dharma teachings as the path leading to it. It directs us to the path and keeps us on it even when we go through bouts of questioning. The power of this kind of faith cannot be overcome by doubt, skepticism, or disbelief. (2) *Effort* is an energetic mind. It combats laziness, heedlessness, and unconscientiousness and facilitates the practice of the four supreme strivings. The power of effort is not affected by laziness, procrastination, and discouragement. (3) *Mindfulness* keeps us aware and cognizant of what we are doing and of what to practice and abandon in daily life. In meditation it remembers the object of meditation and keeps the mind focused on it. It combats forgetfulness, oblivion, and wandering, and the power of mindfulness cannot be harmed by these obstacles. (4) *Concentration* keeps the mind focused one-pointedly on its chosen object and thus prevents distraction. (5) *Wisdom* correctly understands its object. Combating ignorance and wrong views and analyzing conditioned phenomena to understand their nature, wisdom knows the three characteristics, correctly understands the four truths, and penetrates nibbāna. The power of wisdom cannot be harmed by ignorance.

Seven Awakening Factors

The seven awakening factors (*bojjhaṅga, bodhyaṅga*) are called "correct" because they have been transformed into the ārya path. "Factors" indicates they are causes of awakening. (1) *Mindfulness* enables the mind to retain the meditation object in mind without forgetfulness and to subdue afflictions. (2) *Discrimination of phenomena* (*dhammavicaya, dharmavicaya*) is a wisdom that clearly knows what to practice and what to abandon. It understands selflessness with wisdom and thus destroys obscurations. (3) *Effort* stabilizes renunciation, enabling us to attain awakening quickly. (4) *Rapture* makes the mind continually happy, benefiting the body and mind. (5) *Pliancy* removes all mental and physical discomfort and unserviceability, making the body and mind flexible, blissful, and capable of engaging in virtue. (6) *Concentration* abides single-pointedly on a chosen object of meditation, enabling us to fulfill all our wishes by developing awakened qualities. (7) *Equanimity* enables us to adopt what is to be practiced and avoid what is to be abandoned. This mental factor of equanimity is free from the faults impeding serenity and is the opposite of the unbalanced mind of afflictions.

The Buddha explains how the cultivation of the four establishments of mindfulness fulfills the seven awakening factors (MN 118). When we contemplate the body as a body, we arouse strong (1) *mindfulness*, develop it, and bring it to fulfillment. Based on this, we investigate and examine bodily phenomena and their impermanence by means of (2) *discrimination of phenomena*. Probing with discrimination boosts our (3) *effort* because discrimination brings understanding, which inspires deeper practice. Effort leads to (4) *rapture* flooding the body from head to toe. Because the ecstasy of rapture can be agitating, it must be refined and brought to fulfillment. Doing so leads to (5) *pliancy*, tranquility of body and mind. As pliancy develops and is brought to fulfillment, bliss increases. Bliss and pliancy together enable the mind to settle on the object with more stillness, thus deepening (6) *concentration*. Once concentration is firm, the mind naturally abides in (7) *equanimity*.

We then employ the seven awakening factors to attain true knowledge (*vijjā, vidyā*) of the four truths and liberation. Within equanimity, we strengthen discrimination of phenomena so that it becomes wisdom supported by single-pointed concentration. By investigating the nature of phenomena, especially the three characteristics, we eventually break through and perceive nibbāna, at which time all seven awakening factors are present.

The Noble Eightfold Path

The eight parts of the noble eightfold path are āryas' paths. In the Sanskrit tradition, they can be divided into four branches.[12]

Right view refers to realizing, during post-meditation periods, the correct understanding of the four truths that was realized in meditative equipoise. It constitutes the first of the four branches, the *branch of affirmation*, because it affirms the realization of emptiness that occurred during meditative equipoise.

Right intention is the motivating intention wishing to correctly explain to others the view of selflessness realized in meditation. It is thus included in the *branch of promoting understanding in others*.

Right speech is speech explaining to others the right view we have realized. *Right action* refers to refraining from physical acts harmful to self or others. *Right livelihood* consists of procuring food, shelter, clothing, and medicine without recourse to the five wrong livelihoods. These three are included in the *branch that develops trust and respect in others* because others see that we keep pure ethical conduct.

Right effort exerts energy to develop the antidotes eliminating the objects to be abandoned on the path of meditation, enabling us to advance to higher paths. *Right mindfulness* does not forget the object of meditation, thus preventing and eliminating hindrances to single-pointedness. *Right concentration* is the antidote to obstructions to mental absorption—unserviceability of the mind that hinders the development of concentration. Through *right concentration*, we are able to cultivate the superknowledges and focus on the meaning of the four truths single-pointedly. These three constitute the *branch of antidotes to opposing factors* because they overcome and purify obstructions.

Many mental factors such as mindfulness, effort, concentration, and wisdom appear repeatedly in the thirty-seven aids, emphasizing the vital role they play in the path to liberation. The fact that they are found in different contexts illustrates not only the various situations in which they are needed but also that their capacity and potency increase as a practitioner advances.

Conventional and Ultimate Natures of the Thirty-Seven Aids

The Sanskrit tradition emphasizes cultivating the thirty-seven aids to awakening in the context of both their conventional and ultimate natures. Their conventional nature concerns how they arise and function on the path. For example, the four establishments of mindfulness see the body as unclean, feelings as unsatisfactory, the mind as impermanent, and certain phenomena to practice and others to abandon.

In the context of ultimate nature, we investigate the ultimate mode of existence of the thirty-seven aids. Śāntideva (BCA 9.78–105) discusses the four establishments of mindfulness from the perspective of ultimate reality, examining the body, feelings, mind, and phenomena to determine their ultimate nature—their emptiness of inherent existence. Understanding their emptiness prevents us from attributing a self to the very paths designed to liberate us.

7 | Selflessness and Emptiness

Correct understanding of selflessness (not-self) is essential in both the Pāli and Sanskrit traditions. In the Pāli tradition insight wisdom correctly understanding selflessness is a mundane mind because it examines mundane objects—the polluted aggregates—seeing them as impermanent, unsatisfactory, and not-self. This insight is a precursor to the realization of nibbāna, a supramundane mind that makes one an ariya. In the Sanskrit tradition when insight wisdom directly realizes subtle selflessness, it becomes an ārya's supramundane mind capable of eradicating afflictions. Both traditions employ reasoning to arrive at the correct understanding of selflessness and translate this understanding into experience through meditating with the union of serenity and insight.

In the Pāli suttas, the Buddha examines not-self using many schemas. The schema of the three characteristics is used to cultivate insight wisdom knowing the aggregates are not the self. The schema of the four truths is employed to examine saṃsāric phenomena's specific nature, the conditions for their arising and cessation, and the noble eightfold path as the path to that cessation. The Buddha also investigates saṃsāric phenomena in terms of gratification (*assāda, āsvada*), danger (*ādīnava*), and freedom (*nissaraṇa, niḥsaraṇa*) or in terms of disenchantment (*nibbidā, nirvida*), dispassion (*virāga*), and deliverance (*vimutti, vimukti*) (MN 22:28–29). Using these different schemas, meditators investigate the five aggregates, eighteen constituents, six elements, six sources and their six objects, six consciousnesses, and so forth to determine that they are "not mine, not I, and not my self" (MN 22:26, SN 22–34).

While the Sanskrit tradition presents the views of selflessness of several tenet systems, here we deal specifically with the Madhyamaka view, and within that, the view of the Prāsaṅgika Mādhyamikas according to Tsongkhapa's presentation. This is the view indicated by the word "Madhyamaka" in the following chapters.

This chapter looks at some schemas shared by both the Pāli tradition and the Madhyamaka school: examination of the relation between the self and the aggregates, the six elements, and the four possible modes of arising. In the next chapter, we will look at dependent arising, a signature feature of the Buddha's teachings found in all Buddhist traditions and schools.

Pāli Tradition: The Self and the Aggregates

The word *self* has various meanings. One is reflexive, as when the Buddha says, "You must train yourself." Another indicates the person; because the aggregates are present, the person exists, and we say, "I walk, I think." These two meanings of self are acceptable. However, to assert a self that is a substantial personal identity, an enduring subject at the core of the aggregates, is mistaken.

The ancient Indian conception of self (*atta*, *ātman*) is of a permanent, eternal, and intrinsically blissful self. This self is the master of the aggregates and is able to accomplish its wishes without depending on anything else.

Apart from philosophy, our ordinary ingrained view of ourselves either identifies the body or mind as self or thinks a self stands in some relation to the aggregates. This self appears to be an unchanging entity enduring through time; it is one indivisible whole that lacks parts; it is self-sufficient, existing by its own power, independent of causes and conditions; it is in control of and has mastery over the aggregates.

Such a self is an illusion. If it existed, there should be no conflict between what we want ourselves to be and what we are. Furthermore, what can be identified as such a self? The polluted aggregates, appropriated due to ignorance and craving, are impermanent and unsatisfactory in nature. They are clearly not suitable to be regarded as "this is mine; this I am, this is my self."

Dhammadinnā Bhikkhunī explains how the view of personal identity arises in relation to the aggregates (MN 44):

> An untaught ordinary person...regards form as self, or self as possessed of form, or form as in self, or self as in form. He regards feelings...discrimination...volitional factors...consciousness as self, or self as possessed of consciousness, or consciousness as in self, or self as in consciousness.

A TIBETAN MONK STUDYING THE SŪTRAS, INDIA

Since there are four positions with respect to each of the five aggregates, there are twenty wrong views of self. The commentaries use the relationship between the self and the body (form) to explain these. (1) Regarding the body as self is like regarding the flame of an oil lamp as identical to the color of that flame. (2) Regarding the self as possessing the body is like regarding a tree as possessing its shadow. (3) Regarding the body as being in the self is like regarding the scent as being in the flower. (4) Regarding the self as being in the body is like regarding a jewel in a box.[13] A fifth possible relationship between the self and the aggregates is that the self is entirely different from and unrelated to the aggregates. Dhammadinnā does not mention this because she is speaking to a lay Buddhist who already understands there is no self distinct from the aggregates.

These five positions are condensed into two: the self is the same as the aggregates or some aspect of the body-mind complex, or the self and the aggregates are different and unrelated. In the latter case, the self would be findable as a separate entity either inside the collection of aggregates, behind them, or as their invisible owner.

If the aggregates were the self, one or all of them would have the four attributes of a real self. (1) That self should be permanent, but the aggregates are impermanent. (2) The self should be an indivisible whole, but there are five aggregates, each of which consists of many components. (3) The self should be self-sufficient and independent of causes and conditions, yet the aggregates are conditioned and dependent on causes. (4) The self should be in control, but the aggregates cannot be controlled and are simply processes with no supervisor managing them. A controlling self should be able to stop the body from aging and stop the mind from experiencing painful feelings.

The aggregates have none of the characteristics of a true self and, in fact, have opposite characteristics: the body is like a ball of foam, lacking any substance. Feelings are like bubbles, arising and breaking up quickly. Discriminations are like a mirage, appearing but not found when searched for. Volitional factors are like the hollow trunk of a plantain tree. Consciousness is like a magical illusion, appearing but lacking any substance. There is no core in any of the aggregates. They are empty of any independent, substantial essence (SN 22:95).

The Buddha analyzed the six internal sources, six external sources, six consciousnesses, six contacts, six feelings, and six cravings (MN 148). All of these arise and cease. If they were the self, the self would have to rise and cease as well, but a substantial self cannot do that. Nāgārjuna uses a similar refutation (MMK 18.1ab):

> If the aggregates were the self,
> then the self would be subject to arising and disintegration.

He then explains that if any of the aggregates were the self, the self would begin at conception and end at death, just as the aggregates of this life do. In that case, memory of previous lives and the experiencing of karmic effects in a later life would be impossible.

The Buddha clearly refutes a self that controls the aggregates (MN 35:15–19). When the non-Buddhist wanderer Aggivessana says the five aggregates are the self, the Buddha challenges him, asking if a king exercises power in his realm to punish people who deserve punishment. Aggivessana responds positively. The Buddha then asks him if he can exercise power over any of his five aggregates, such that he can make them be what he wants. Aggivessana remains silent. He understands that if a controller self existed, it should be able to make the aggregates be and do what it wished. Clearly, this is not the case, for we cannot prevent our body from aging or subdue our emotions by wishing them away.

The Buddha explains why none of the aggregates are the self (SN 22:59).

First, since the aggregates lead to affliction, they are in the nature of dukkha. Something in the nature of dukkha is not suitable to be a permanent, eternal, blissful self. Second, similar to the previous refutation, if one of the aggregates were the self, we should be able to control that aggregate and make it do or be what we want. But we cannot tell ourselves what to feel; feelings arise dependent on their own conditions. Although we may believe there is a self that is a commander of the aggregates, in fact no controlling self exists.

Although there is no independent self that controls the aggregates, accomplished meditators are able to control and direct their minds. They do so dependent on causes and conditions. Training their minds through diligent practice, they create the causes for virtuous mental states to arise and for mental factors such as mindfulness, concentration, and wisdom to be strong. While there is no controlling self that can will us to attain awakening, nurturing constructive thoughts and emotions and applying antidotes to destructive ones will bring this result.

If the self were distinct from the aggregates, it would be a separate entity lying behind the aggregates. However, when we identify anything that the self does, such as walking or thinking, we see only the aggregates doing those actions. No separate, substantial self can be identified.

In short no inner nucleus of selfhood can be found within or distinct from the conventional person made up of the five aggregates. Rebirth and the results of kamma occur without an enduring self. Each moment of experience, each moment of body and mind, is connected with its predecessors and successors through a causal process. We identify ourselves as the "same" person from birth to death and beyond because there is a causal continuity, not because there is a substantial self that holds everything together.

Madhyamaka: The Object of Negation

The subtlest *object of negation* is the self—i.e., inherent existence—that does not exist in either persons or phenomena. Nevertheless ignorance and the view of a personal identity believe this exists. If we want to catch a thief, we have to know what he looks like. Similarly, to refute inherent existence, we need to properly identify the object of negation by having an idea of what inherent existence would be like. Candrakīrti says, "Here what we call *self* refers to any nature or state that objects could have in which they rely on nothing else. The nonexistence of this is what we call *selfless*." Tsongkhapa defines inherent existence this way: "What exists objectively, in terms of its own essence, without being posited through the power of a subjective mind is called *self* or *inherent nature*" (LRCM 3:213).

To understand this subtlest object of negation, it is helpful first to identify the three levels of erroneous conceptions—each with its own object of negation—regarding the person. From the coarsest to the subtlest: (1) misconceiving the person to be permanent, unitary, and independent from its causes, (2) grasping the I as self-sufficient substantially existent, and (3) grasping the I as inherently existent. All of these superimpose a false mode of existence—an object of negation—on the I. Disproving them is like peeling away layers of an onion until there is nothing left, until only their absence—phenomena's emptiness of existing in those erroneous ways—remains.

The belief in a *permanent, unitary, independent self* is the conception of the ātman accepted by non-Buddhists. As explained above, the core of the person is seen as permanent, while the aggregates are considered impermanent and disposable. The relationship of the self and the aggregates is like a porter and a load: in each life the self picks up and discards aggregates. Some people believe this permanent self or soul goes from life to life appropriating new aggregates each lifetime. Others believe it becomes nonexistent after death. This view does not arise in our minds innately; it is acquired by studying erroneous philosophies.

The view of a *self-sufficient substantially existent self* sees the I as the controller and the aggregates as the controlled. The I appears to be self-sufficient in that it can stand on its own and substantially existent in that it can be identified without one or more of the aggregates appearing to the mind. This grasping has innate and acquired forms.

Grasping the person as *inherently existent* sees the I as mixed in with the aggregates yet able to stand on its own. The I appears to exist from its own side, under its own power, with its own essence, without being posited by mind. It exists truly, ultimately, and independently. Here "independent" means it does not depend on other factors such as its basis of designation (the aggregates) and the mind that conceives and designates it. This is the view of a personal identity *grasping I* and has both acquired and innate forms, the latter being the root of saṃsāra.

The view of a personal identity *grasping mine* arises in relation to things that belong to us, especially the aggregates. It focuses only on the sense of mine—the feeling of "my-ness" or ownership—and holds it as inherently existent. The absence of an inherently existent I or "mine" is the *selflessness of persons*.

Grasping the *inherent existence of phenomena* holds all other phenomena, especially the aggregates, to exist independently of other factors, including their causes and conditions, parts, and the mind that conceives and designates them. The absence of such a self is the *selflessness of phenomena*. Meditating on the emptiness of phenomena, specifically the aggregates, is essential because as long as we grasp the aggregates as inherently existent, we will also grasp the person as inherently existent, and liberation will elude us.

Meditators usually begin by negating the inherent existence of the I and thereafter the inherent existence of the aggregates. Identifying the object of negation—an inherently existent I—is the first, and most difficult, step. To do this, one corner of our mind unobtrusively observes how the sense of I manifests in our lives. It is easier to do this when grasping at I arises strongly, for example when we are unjustly blamed or when we strongly crave something.

Once we have identified how the false I appears, we need to investigate whether such an I can actually exist. Here reasoning and analysis are critical. We must investigate how the I exists until we are convinced that it cannot exist inherently. At that time, we rest the mind in the absence of an inherently existent self.

Seven-Point Refutation

Responding to Māra when he tries to interrupt her practice, Vajirā Bhikkhunī says (SN 5:10):

> Why now do you assume "a being"?
> Māra, is that your speculative view?
> This is a heap of sheer formations:
> here no being is found.
>
> Just as, with an assemblage of parts,
> the word "chariot" is used,
> so, when the aggregates exist,
> there is the convention "a being."[14]

The simile of the chariot to illustrate not-self (selflessness) is found in the Pāli suttas and was popularized in the first-century text *Milindapañha*. Here the Buddhist monk Nāgasena explains to King Milinda that while none of the parts are the chariot, the collection of the parts arranged in a certain manner is conventionally understood as a chariot. Similarly, the aggregates are not the person. The I is just a convenient designation for the aggregation of momentary material and immaterial processes that constitute the empirical person.

The Mādhyamika Candrakīrti also uses the simile of a chariot in his *Madhyamakāvatāra* to illustrate that a person is designated in dependence on the aggregates and does not exist inherently. If a person existed inherently, it should be findable in one of seven ways. The first five ways are those given by Dhammadinnā in the quotation above and by Nāgārjuna in his refutation of an inherently existent Tathāgata (MMK 22.1):

> The Tathāgata is neither the aggregates nor different from the aggregates;
> the aggregates are not in him, nor is he in the aggregates;
> he does not possess the aggregates.
> What Tathāgata is there, then?

If the I existed inherently, it would have to exist in one of these seven ways in relation to the aggregates:

1. The self would be inherently one with the aggregates: the person and the aggregates would be exactly the same, totally inseparable. In this case, five fallacies would arise: (a) The self and the aggregates would be synonymous, and therefore there would be no need to assert the existence of the self. (b) Since there is one person, there would be one aggregate. (c) Since there are many aggregates, there would be many persons. (d) Agent (person) and object (aggregates) would be one, and we could not say, "I have a body" or "The I appropriates the aggregates." (e) The aggregates and the person would arise and cease together. When the body ceased at death, the person would also cease with no continuity in future lives. Furthermore, one moment of the person would be totally unrelated to past and future moments of the person, and we could not speak of the I as a convention, saying, "In the past I was this, and in the future I will be that." This, in turn,

would bring three more unwanted consequences: (i) Recalling events from previous lives would be impossible because the past self and present self would be totally unrelated. (ii) Actions that we did would not bring results. If there were no continuity between one life and the next, we would not experience the results of actions we did in previous lives. (iii) We would experience the results of actions we did not do. If the person of each life were inherently different from preceding and subsequent ones, we could experience the results of actions done by other people because they would equally be inherently different. Even in this life, there would be no continuity of the person from one moment to the next, making it impossible to remember events or experience the results of actions done earlier in this life.

2. The person would be inherently different than the aggregates. On the conventional level, the self and the aggregates are different. They have different names and appear differently to the conceptual mind. However, if they were inherently different, they would be totally separate, and two faults would result: (1) We would be able to see the person and the aggregates separately. The person could exist in one place and the aggregates in another. (2) There would be no reason to label "I" in dependence on those aggregates because there would be no relationship between them and the person.

The remaining five possible relationships between the self and aggregates can be subsumed in the first two alternatives.

3. The self would inherently depend on its parts.
4. The parts would inherently depend on the self. If either of these were the case, the person and the aggregates would be inherently different.
5. The self would inherently possess the aggregates. In this case, either (a) the self would possess the aggregates like a person possesses a table, in which case they would be inherently different, or (b) the self would possess the aggregates like a person possesses her ear, in which case they would be inherently the same.
6. The self would be the collection of its aggregates. In this case, we couldn't differentiate the designated object—the person—and its basis of designation—the aggregates. They would be inherently one and the same. Furthermore, since each of the individual aggregates is not the self, the collection of aggregates could not be the self. For

example, an orange is not an apple, so a collection of oranges cannot be an apple.

7. The self would be the shape or arrangement of the aggregates. Since only the body has shape, the person would be the body and would not have mental aggregates.

Through analysis we see that the self does not exist in any of the seven ways. Therefore we can conclude that the self does not exist inherently, independently, or under its own power. However, the I does exist conventionally, by being merely designated, and its existence is established by an unimpaired conventional consciousness. The merely designated person creates karma, experiences its result, practices the path, and attains awakening. This middle-way view avoids eternalism by negating the inherent existence of the person and avoids annihilation by asserting the person's dependent existence.

Six Elements Are Not the Self

Both the Pāli tradition and Mādhyamikas analyze the relationship between the six elements and self. The Buddha says the person consists of six elements: earth, water, fire, wind, space, and consciousness (MN 140:8). The Pāli commentary on the Majjhima Nikāya explains:

> Here the Buddha expounds the reducibly existent by way of the irreducibly existent. The elements are irreducibly existent, but the person is not irreducibly existent. This is meant: "That which you conceive as a person consists of six elements. Ultimately there is no person here. 'Person' is a mere concept."[15]

Here "irreducibly existent" is contrasted with "conceived." According to the Pāli Abhidhamma commentaries, the six elements irreducibly exist in that they are fundamental properties of phenomena that exist apart from mental conceptualization, and in that sense they actually exist. They can be discovered on their own, in contrast to things that are conceptually constructed. This does not mean the elements exist independently; they are dependent, conditioned, and impermanent.

Conventional things, such as the person, exist due to conceptualization. The person is imputed or conceived dependent upon the six elements. Ulti-

Don Farber

CALLING MONASTICS FOR MORNING CHANTING, TAIWAN

mately there is no person. Only the six impersonal elements are present, and there is nothing about any of them that is a person or is personal. Earth, water, fire, and wind are metaphorical terms that represent the properties of solidity, cohesion, heat, and mobility. The internal space element is unoccupied space in the body. Proper wisdom sees these five physical elements as "This is not mine; this I am not; this is not my self." In this way insight into the material aspects of our existence is cultivated, and we become disenchanted with and dispassionate toward them.

The sixth element, consciousness, consists of the six primary consciousnesses as well as feelings, discriminations, and mental factors in the volitional factors aggregate. Nothing in the consciousness element is the person. There is a continuous flow of dependently arising mental states from one moment to the next without there being a substantial self holding them together to become an individual person.

The Buddha clearly states that consciousness is not the self. Bhikkhu Sati believed consciousness exists in and of itself, independent of conditions, and transmigrates from life to life, creating kamma and experiencing its results, without changing in the process. The Buddha reprimanded him, "Misguided man, have I not stated in many ways consciousness to be dependently arisen, since without a condition there is no origination of consciousness?" (MN 38:5).

The Buddha then explained the six consciousnesses, showing that consciousness is not unitary. Consciousness can be understood to be dependently arisen in three ways: (1) Each of the six consciousnesses depends on causes: its own cognitive faculty, object, and immediate condition. (2) Although conscious experience appears to be one unitary thing, it is composed of extremely brief moments of consciousness that can be vividly experienced in meditation with deep mindfulness. (3) Each moment of consciousness is also conditioned by its predecessor and in turn conditions the subsequent occasion. These different moments of consciousness form a continuity, not a jumble of disconnected events. The same conditioned process of successive moments of consciousness occurs at the time of death.

The Pāli Abhidhamma and commentaries posit the existence of a type of mental consciousness called the *bhavaṅga* that is seen as a prerequisite for the continuity of personal identity. The bhavaṅga is not a continuous consciousness but a succession of moments of mind occurring beneath the threshold of clear awareness; yet it maintains the continuity of consciousness when no distinct cognition is occurring, for example, during dreamless sleep. During waking hours, when an external object is perceived or a thought consciousness occurs, those clearly cognizing consciousnesses are at the forefront. But when they cease, if no other object is prominent, the bhavaṅga arises. The bhavaṅga is present at death and, in the very next moment, depending on the new physical organism, it arises as the rebirth consciousness. It is not a unitary or independent consciousness. Like all other states of consciousness, it is conditioned and consists of a series of mind moments arising and ceasing in every split second. The texts sometimes refer to it as the "stream of bhavaṅga."

Similarly, the third link of dependent arising, consciousness, is the mind that takes rebirth in the next life. It too does not exist independently but arises due to conditions such as ignorance and formative actions.

In summary, consciousness cannot be an independent self because consciousness consists of a series of mind moments, each of which arises and passes away very rapidly, and each moment of the various consciousnesses arises due to causes and conditions. Nowhere in the Pāli canon or commentaries is the mental consciousness or the collection of aggregates said to be the self. No phenomenon (*dhamma*) whatsoever is posited as the self. In the Pāli canon there is no notion of a foundation consciousness (S. *ālayavijñāna*) carrying kammic latencies. The "person" is a conceptual notion imputed on the basis of the five aggregates. It is designated dependent on the six elements, and the word "I" and its cognates are mere conventions that are mistakenly grasped as evidence of a true self.

The Sanskrit tradition also analyzes the relationship of the self and the six elements. Nāgārjuna explains in the *Ratnāvalī* (80–82):

> A person is not earth, not water,
> not fire, not wind, not space,
> not consciousness, and not all of them.
> What else could the person be?
>
> Just as a person is not real
> due to being a composite of six elements,
> so, too, is each of the elements
> not real due to being a composite.
>
> The aggregates are not the self, they are not in it;
> it is not in them, but without them, it is not;
> it is not mixed with the aggregates like fire and fuel.
> Therefore how could the self exist?

The six elements of a human being in the desire realm together constitute a person's existence and are the basis of designation of the person. The basis of designation cannot be the designated object (the person). The self is neither any of the elements individually nor their collection.

When refuting that the self is the consciousness, Nāgārjuna disagrees with those who identify the self as the mental consciousness or the continuity of consciousness. If we examine each successive state of ever-more subtle consciousness, we cannot isolate any of them, saying it alone is a self. Even the subtlest mind at the time of death is not the self because it is impermanent and composed of parts. Furthermore, we say, "My clear-light mind," conventionally indicating a person that possesses and the clear-light mind that is possessed. If the person and the clear-light mind were the same, this could not be.

If the person were the subtlest mind, then the self of this life would continue to the next life because the continuity of the subtlest mind is present in the next life. However, the person of this life dies and does not continue to the next life. If it did, then I would be Tenzin Gyatso in my next life. But that is not the case.

In the first verse, Nāgārjuna questions, "If the person is not any of the elements that are its basis of designation, what else could the person be?" This implies that the person cannot be found independently of the aggregates either. This negates the view of the non-Buddhists who assert a person independent from the aggregates. Nāgārjuna does not conclude that the person does not exist. Rather he says that the person depends on the collection of the six elements that are its basis of designation. Because the person is dependent, it is empty of inherent existence.

In the second verse, he speaks of the selflessness of phenomena, the elements' lack of inherent existence. They, too, are empty because they exist dependent on their causes and conditions, parts, and the mind conceiving and designating them.

The third verse returns to selflessness of the person, analyzing the person in relation to the aggregates. The aggregates are not the same as the person; the person is not separate from the aggregates, which it would have to be if either the aggregates were found in the person or the person were found in the aggregates. Nor does the person inherently possess the aggregates. Nevertheless, without the presence of the aggregates, a person cannot exist.

The person exists and depends on the aggregates although it cannot be found among them. How then does the person exist? By mere name, mere designation. "Mere" does not negate the basis of designation of the self—the aggregates—or the conventional self. It precludes the inherent existence of the self. While nothing can ultimately be identified as the person, the person exists on the nominal level. By weaving dependent arising in with the refutation of inherent existence, Nāgārjuna illustrates the compatibility of emptiness and dependent arising. This is the meaning of the middle way.

Refutation of Four Extremes of Arising

When composing the *Mūlamadhyamakakārikā*, Nāgārjuna relied on reasonings in the early sūtras, drawing out their implications in a way that no one had previously done. Based on the Prajñāpāramitā sūtras, the "self" that is negated is inherent existence, and "selfless" is an attribute of all phenomena, not just of persons.

The terms *inherent existence* (*svabhāva*), *selflessness of persons*, and *selflessness of phenomena* are not found in the Pāli suttas. They appear later on, first in Abhidhamma texts, where their meanings evolved and changed over time. Nāgārjuna refutes one meaning *svabhāva* had come to assume—self-existence or inherent existence. He says in the first verse of his treatise:

> Nothing ever at any time anywhere
> arises from itself, from another,
> from both [itself and another],
> or without a cause.

This fourfold refutation has antecedents in the Buddha's refutation of arising from self, other, both, and causelessly in the Pāli suttas. For example, the naked ascetic Kassapa asked the Buddha if suffering were created by self, another, both self and another, or fortuitously, to which the Buddha replied "no" to each. Then Kassapa asked if there were no dukkha or if the Buddha did not know or see dukkha. Again, the Buddha replied in the negative. Confused, Kassapa asked for clarification. The Buddha explained (SN 12:17):

> [If one thinks,] "The one who acts is the same as the one who experiences [the result]," [then one asserts] with reference to one existing from the beginning, "Dukkha is created by oneself." When one asserts thus, this amounts to eternalism.
>
> But, Kassapa, [if one thinks,] "The one who acts is one, the one who experiences [the result] is another," [then one asserts] with reference to one stricken by feeling: "Dukkha is created by another." When one asserts thus, this amounts to annihilation.
>
> Without veering toward either of these extremes, the Tathāgata teaches the Dhamma by the middle: "With ignorance as condition, formative actions [arise]; [the remainder of the twelve links are listed, with each conditioning the arising of the next.]...Such is the origin of this whole mass of dukkha. But with the remainderless fading away and cessation of ignorance comes cessation of formative actions...[the rest of the links]. Such is the cessation of this whole mass of dukkha."

How kamma is transmitted from one lifetime to the next and the relationship between the person creating the cause and the person experiencing the result have been topics of discussion for centuries. The first alternative—the person who creates the cause of dukkha is identical to the person who experiences the result—is eternalism, for it requires there be a permanent self continuing through many lifetimes who is both the agent of the action and the experiencer of the result. However, a permanent self cannot act as a cause for something else.

The second alternative—dukkha is created by another—is annihilation. Here someone who believes in rebirth thinks there is no continuity of the person: the creator of the cause ceases completely at death and someone new, who is totally unrelated, is born. Someone who does not accept rebirth thinks an external agent or omnipotent creator determines his suffering and happiness. However, if the agent and experiencer were totally unrelated, a relationship between a cause and its effect would not exist. Since everything would equally be unrelated to the result, anything could produce anything.

The third alternative—dukkha is caused by both self and other—would be thinking, for example, "A creator created me and the potential for my actions (arising from other), but I act and experience the results of my actions (arising from self)." This alternative has the faults of both these views.

The fourth alternative—there is no cause or condition for our experiences—is the view of annihilation. If results were random and causeless, farmers would not plant seeds to reap crops and students would not go to school to get an education. However, everything that functions arises dependent on its own causes.

People adhere to one or the other of these four alternatives based on conceiving a real self to exist. When all four are disproven, one must give up that wrong view.

The Buddha expounds the view of the middle way, free from eternalism and annihilation: causes produce their corresponding results. When an effect arises, its cause has ceased. Thus dukkha is not produced by a permanent cause or by someone completely distinct from the one experiencing the result. Dukkha is not predestined, nor does it happen haphazardly. The Buddha traces the evolution of dukkha and saṃsāra by teaching the twelve links of dependent arising. Similarly, he traces the cessation of dukkha to the eradication of each link in this causal chain.

The Buddha did not explicitly state in the suttas what kind of real self he was refuting: a permanent, unitary, independent self, a self-sufficient substantially existent person, or an inherently existent person. What the suttas mean to us will depend on what type of real self we aim to disprove.

The Buddha explains to the wanderer Timbaruka that pleasure and pain do not arise from self, other, both, or causelessly (SN 12:18):

> [If one thinks,] "The feeling and the one who feels it are the same," [then one asserts] with reference to one existing from the beginning: "Pleasure and pain are created by oneself." I do not speak thus. But, Timbaruka, [if one thinks,] "The feeling is one, the one who feels it is another," [then one asserts] with reference to one stricken by feeling: "Pleasure and pain are created by another." Neither do I speak thus. Without veering toward either of these extremes, the Tathāgata teaches the Dhamma by the middle: "With ignorance as condition, formative actions [arise]...[as above]. Such is the origin of this whole mass of dukkha. But with the remainderless fading away and cessation of ignorance comes cessation of formative actions...[the rest of the links]. Such is the cessation of this whole mass of dukkha."

Timbaruka is confused regarding not only cause and effect but also agent and object. The first position—that a feeling and the person feeling it are the same—is the extreme of eternalism because we think that feeling is created by feeling itself. In this case, the resultant feeling would exist in the past, before it arises.

The second position—that a feeling is one thing and the person feeling it is another—is annihilation. We think the feeling was created by another, unrelated person; that is, one person created the cause and another experiences the result. This would mean the continuity of the person who created the cause was annihilated at death and a totally different person who experiences the resultant feeling was born.

If pleasure and pain were created by both ourselves and another, the faults of both these positions would accrue, and if they arose randomly by neither oneself nor another, all causality would collapse. The Buddha does not negate the existence of pleasure and pain; he teaches that it arises dependently—feelings arise from impermanent causes that produce impermanent results concordant with those causes.

Assuming the existence of a real self, the monk Bhūmija asked Sāriputta how pleasure and pain arise from kamma (SN 12:25): Does it arise from itself, another, both, or causelessly? Sāriputta replies that the Buddha said pleasure and pain are dependently arisen. Specifically, they depend on contact. Here again, dependent arising is used to refute mistaken notions of self and causality.

This discussion is intimately related to our lives. Is the person who in the past created the causes for my life today the same person who experiences the results today? Is our suffering others' fault? Is suffering punishment from a supreme being? Do happiness and misery occur randomly? These questions are food for thought on our spiritual journey, and how we answer them will affect how we live our lives.

Buddhaghosa quotes the early commentators (Vism 19:20):

> There is no doer of a deed
> or one who reaps the deed's result;
> phenomena alone flow on—
> no other view than this is right.
>
> And so, while kamma and result
> thus causally maintain their round,
> as seed and tree succeed in turn,
> no first beginning can be shown....
>
> A monastic disciple of the Buddha
> with direct knowledge of this fact
> can penetrate this deep and subtle
> empty conditionality.

Mādhyamikas begin the refutation of the four extremes of arising by identifying the object of negation. Tsongkhapa says that grasping the object of negation is "to take both cause and effect not as merely nominally imputed, but as the objects that are the bases of nominal imputation, grasped as inherently existent produced and producer."[16] Here both the causes—such as seeds and karma—and the effects—sprouts and suffering or happiness—

are held to have their own inherent essence independent of all other factors, including nominal imputation.

If things existed inherently, they would have to arise either from self, other, both, or causelessly; there are no other alternatives. These four positions were held by various schools in ancient India. Let's examine each in turn.

Does a thing arise from itself? The Sāṃkhya school believes there is a primal or universal substance that is a cause from which things arise. They say things arise from self because they exist in an unmanifest form within their cause, as one nature with this primal substance, prior to their arising. If this were the case, a cause and its effect would exist simultaneously. That would mean an old man would exist in a newborn baby, and a sprout would exist in a seed. If cause and result existed at the same time yet the result still needed to arise and become manifest, four consequences would follow: (1) The sprout wouldn't need to arise because it already existed in the cause. Its arising would be senseless. (2) The seed would never cease because it could exist at the time of the sprout. Then it would keep producing sprouts endlessly. (3) We would be able to see the seed and its resultant sprout at the same time. (4) If the sprout existed as one nature with the seed, they would be inherently one and the same. In that case, we could not differentiate the seed from the sprout. Producer (seed) and product (sprout) would be exactly the same.

Some people nowadays hold a similar view, for example thinking the future is predetermined and already exists in an unmanifest form at present. Contemplating the faults of arising from self dispels these views.

Does a thing arise from other? Some Buddhists assert that things arise from causes that are inherently different from them. While on the nominal level, causes and effect are distinct, these Buddhists believe that the difference between the seed and the sprout is inherent and not merely posited by mind.

If the seed and sprout were inherently other, they would be totally unrelated. The sprout would then have the same kind of relationship with the seed that it has with any other thing. There would be no special relationship between a sprout and a seed because all things would be the same in being inherently other than the seed and thus totally unrelated. A sprout could then arise from a rock, and happiness could arise from nonvirtue.

Conventionally, a sprout grows from a seed. They are part of the same continuum. However, inherently different things cannot be part of the same continuum because they would be independent from and have no relationship with other things. Candrakīrti says in his *Prasannapadā*, "If things—volitional factors, sprouts, and so forth—have [inherent] nature, then what need have those existing things for causes and conditions?"

If the seed and sprout existed inherently, totally independently of each other, they could exist at the same time. However, while the seed exists, we speak of the sprout *that is about to arise* from it. After we plant carrot seeds, even before anything appears above the ground, we conventionally say, "The carrot is growing." In fact, the carrot is in the process of arising while the seed is in the process of ceasing. At that time the carrot does not yet exist, because if it did, cause and effect would exist simultaneously, which is impossible. The result arises only when the cause has ceased.

Three of the modes of arising—from self, both, and without a cause—do not exist even conventionally. Ultimate analysis is not needed to refute them. However, things arise from others that are *conventionally* different from them. Therefore, qualifying this thesis with "inherently" is important: "A sprout does not *inherently* arise from a seed." If we said simply that a sprout does not arise from a seed, we would be very ignorant!

Does a thing arise from both self and other? Jains believe a clay pot arises from clay, which is inherently the same as it, and a potter, who is inherently other than it. While it's true a clay pot arises due to both clay and the potter's efforts, neither of these is inherently the same as or inherently different from the pot. Arising from both self and other is susceptible to the faults of both positions individually.

Does a thing arise without a cause? Materialists (Cārvākas) do not refute obvious cause and effect as in a sprout arising from a seed. However, since they cannot explain the causes for the colorful design of a peacock's feathers or the roundness of peas, they say these arise without cause. Nowadays some people believe that miraculous experiences occur without causes. Other people believe that events occur randomly, without any cause. Buddhists explain that every functioning thing must have causes. While at present we may not know what those causes are, as our knowledge, wisdom, and meditative abilities develop, we may come to know these.

If things arose without causes, several faults would occur: (1) Nothing would arise, because there would be nothing to cause it to come into existence. (2) Things would arise chaotically and unpredictably. What arises at

TIBETAN MONKS IN PHILOSOPHICAL DEBATE, INDIA

one time and in one situation could arise anytime and anywhere, because the arising of a thing would not be constrained by requiring causes that have the ability to produce it. Flowers could grow in ice, and a pine cone could produce a rose. (3) All efforts to attain goals would be useless because things would happen randomly.

Initially we ascertain that if things existed inherently they would have to exist in one of the four ways. Then, with analysis, we examine and see the absurd consequences that follow if things arose in any of these ways and conclude they cannot arise in any of the four ways. We can then conclude that because things do not arise in any of the four ways, they are empty of inherent existence.

Language—including words such as "arising" and "ceasing"—is a means to understand things; it is approximation of reality. We cannot find the exact moment in which a sprout arises. The causal process of the seed producing a sprout makes sense only on this nominal level. It cannot be explained within a framework where things possess inherent nature.

When discussing the reasoning refuting the four extremes of arising, we often use the example of a sprout or another common object. However, when meditating, apply this reasoning to anger, dukkha, the path to liberation, and so forth, and contemplate how they arise.

Selfless and Deceptive

According to Mādhyamikas, dependently arising products are like reflections; they are false in that they appear to exist inherently although they do not. For example, although there is not a real face in the mirror, the appearance of a face exists. This appearance exists due to causes and conditions—the mirror, face, and light. Similarly, although persons and phenomena do not exist inherently, they appear and exist due to causes and conditions. They are falsities in that they appear inherently existent although they are not.

The notion of phenomena being deceptive appears in the Pāli suttas. The Buddha says, "All dhammas [phenomena] are not self" (*Dhammapada* 279). The *Suttanipāta* (1:1) speaks of phenomena as coreless and essenceless:

> He who does not find core or substance
> in any of the realms of being,
> like flowers which are vainly sought
> in fig trees that bear none—
> such a monastic gives up the here and the beyond [future lives],
> just as a serpent sheds its worn-out skin.[17]

And:

> This world completely lacks essence;
> it trembles in all directions.[18]

The Buddha says the aggregates are hollow (*tucchaka*), void (*rittaka, riktaka*), and insubstantial (*asāraka*). Regarding the form aggregate, he says (SN 22:95):

> Bhikkhus, suppose that this river Ganges was carrying along a great lump of foam. A person with good sight would inspect it, ponder it, and carefully investigate it, and it would appear to

> him to be void, hollow, insubstantial. For what substance could there be in a lump of foam? So too, bhikkhus, whatever kind of form there is, whether past, future, or present, internal or external, gross or subtle, inferior or superior, far or near: a bhikkhu inspects it, ponders it, and carefully investigates it, and it would appear to him to be void, hollow, insubstantial.

He then proceeds to use a similar verse for each of the other aggregates to show that they, too, are void, hollow, and insubstantial.

The Buddha did not say dhammas were ultimates (*paramattha*, *paramārtha*). Abhidhamma commentators said the four elements and so forth were ultimate in that they are the irreducible components of existence—that is, the final items of analysis of which all other things are composed. Pāli Abhidhammikas did not say they were partless particles, as did the Sarvāstivādins. Still, they saw the aggregates and so forth as more real than things that were designations (*paññatti*, *prajñapti*). Nāgasena in *Milindapañha* says the chariot does not possess ultimate reality but its components do.

The Sarvāstivāda school was popular in northern India, and its views later spread to Tibet as Vaibhāṣika tenets. Sarvāstivādins were substantialist, attributing to phenomena and persons an ontological existence that they in fact did not have. Specifically, they said that past and future phenomena were substantially existent. Nāgārjuna must have come into contact with these views, and seeing them as contrary to the Buddha's intent, he refuted *svabhāva* on phenomena as well as on persons. In doing so, he expanded the meaning of "self," saying all phenomena are selfless.

The Abhidhammikas' view is contrasted with suttas in which the Buddha clearly says that all dhammas are unreal, deceptive, and false (MN 140:26):

> That is false, bhikkhu, which has a deceptive nature, and that is true which has an undeceptive nature—nibbāna.

He also states that name and form—mentality and materiality—are deceptive, untrue, and unreal:

> What has been considered true by the world of humans, together with the gods, Māra, Brahmā, and among the renunciants, brahmans, gods, and humans, that has by the ariyas through their

> perfect knowledge been well seen to be really false.... What has been considered false by the world of humans, together with the gods, Māra, Brahmā, and among the renunciants, brahmans, gods, and humans, that has by the ariyas through their perfect knowledge been well seen to be really true.
>
> Behold this world together with the gods, imagining self in what is not self. Attached to name and form they imagine this is true or real. In whatever way they imagine it to be, in fact, it is other than that. For that is the falsity of it. For what is evanescent is of a deceptive nature. Nibbāna is of a nondeceptive nature; that the ariyas know as truth. They, by the penetration of truth, become free from craving and fully quenched.[19]

Emptiness

In the Pāli suttas, "selfless" (*anattā*) is found more frequently than "empty" (*suñña*), and both words are used more often as adjectives than in their noun forms. Also, "emptiness" does not necessarily indicate the ontological status of objects as it does in the Sanskrit tradition. Rather, "empty" has two main meanings: "empty of self or what pertains to self" and "empty of attachment, anger, and confusion." There are other meanings as well; for example, each meditative state in a series is empty of the features of the previous, lower state (MN 121).

The Buddha considers emptiness an important topic and encourages monastics to pay attention to it. He expresses concern about the long-term survival of the profound teachings and advises (SN 20:7):

> You should train yourselves thus: "When those discourses spoken by the Tathāgata that are deep, deep in meaning, supramundane, dealing with emptiness, are being recited, we will be eager to listen to them, will lend an ear to them, will apply our minds to understand them; and we will think those teachings should be studied and mastered."

The *Dhammapada* in verse 93 speaks of emptiness as meaning nibbāna, the object of an arahant's meditation. The *Paṭisambhidāmagga* says (2.179):

> What is the supreme emptiness (*agga suñña*)? This dhamma is supreme...the stilling of all formations, the relinquishing of all attachments, the destruction of craving, dispassion, cessation, nibbāna.

Nāgārjuna (MMK 15.7) indicates that emptiness of inherent existence is taught in the Pāli canon, even though the term *inherent existence* was not used there.

> The Transcendental Lord, through understanding
> "it exists" and "it does not exist,"
> refuted both existence and nonexistence
> in the *Katyāyana Sūtra* [*Kaccānagotta Sutta*].

In the *Kaccānagotta Sutta* (SN 12:15) the Buddha said:

> This world, Kaccāna, for the most part depends upon a duality—upon [the notion of] existence [eternalism] and [the notion of] nonexistence [nihilism]. But for one who sees the origin of the world as it really is with correct wisdom, there is no [notion of] nonexistence in regard to the world. And for one who sees the cessation of the world as it really is with correct wisdom, there is no [notion of] existence in regard to the world.

Here the Buddha refutes incorrect metaphysical assumptions in the minds of people who wonder if the world exists or not. Those with an eternalist view believe that if the world exists, it exists forever, permanently. Seeing some continuation of identity between a cause and its effect, they believe a permanent entity bridges the cause and its result. This view does not arise in a person who has right view, who knows that each moment in a continuum of cause and effect arises due to causes, ceases, and is followed by a new moment in the continuum.

A person with a nihilistic view sees something cease and concludes it has no continuation whatsoever; when a person dies, no being is reborn. Someone who thinks that the self and body are the same or that the mind is an emergent property of the brain concludes that when the body ceases at death, the person also totally ceases; there is no rebirth, no experience of kammic results, and no possibility of liberation. A person with right view knows that after death, someone new arises due to causes and conditions; the death of a person and the ending of the world serve as causes for what subsequently arises. This process of continuous, dependently arising change occurs without there being an enduring entity that goes from the previous time to a later time. To refute both eternalism and annihilation the Buddha speaks of dependent arising:

> "All exists": Kaccāna, this is one extreme. "All does not exist": this is the second extreme. Without veering toward either of these extremes, the Tathāgata teaches the Dhamma by the middle: "With ignorance as condition, formative actions [come to be]....Such is the origin of this whole mass of dukkha. But with the remainderless fading away and cessation of ignorance, comes cessation of formative actions....Such is the cessation of this whole mass of dukkha."

What Carries the Karma?

What carries the karmic seeds from one life to the next has been a topic of concern for Buddhists from early on. The Pāli tradition explains that a findable self is not required for rebirth to occur and for kamma to continue to the next life. Rebirth is based on the continuity of consciousness, with each moment of mind connected to the preceding and subsequent moments as members of the same causal continuity. It is through the continuity of the stream of mind that memories, habits, kammic energy, and so forth are preserved. At death the mindstream continues on, assuming the support of a new physical body. This impersonal process occurs without a findable self. A person is nominally identified because there is a causal continuity of the aggregates.

While the Pāli suttas and commentaries occasionally use the metaphor of seeds to illustrate kamma, they do not explain kamma as leaving seeds that have some kind of substantive nature. The prevailing view is that an action (*kamma*) establishes a potential to bring forth its fruits when suitable conditions come together. However, the action does not possess an enduring existence and does not exist somewhere. For example, the notes of a melody do not abide in a lute, ready to be brought forth when the lute is played. Rather, depending on the lute, the air, and the musician, the melody arises. Buddhaghosa says (Vism 17:170):

> When a result arises in a single continuity, it is neither another's nor from other [kamma] because absolute identity and absolute otherness are excluded there.

"Absolute identity" means a single, unchanging person that persists from the time of creating the kamma to the time of experiencing the result. "Absolute otherness" means that one person does the action and a totally different, unrelated person experiences the result. Instead, there is a continuity of experience—a continuity of an impermanent person—that is continuously changing and spans from one life to the next, enabling kamma to bring its results.

This explanation accords with the Madhyamaka explanation that the person who creates the action is neither inherently one with nor totally unrelated to the person who experiences the result. The person is designated in dependence on the aggregates, and therefore the I exists by mere name. *The Samādhirāja Sūtra* (LRCM 3:303) says:

> The states of saṃsāra are like a dream....
>
> There is no one who dies in this world
> and passes or migrates to another.
> Still, actions done are never lost,
> and virtuous and nonvirtuous effects ripen in the world.
>
> Neither permanent nor falling into annihilation,
> actions neither accumulate nor endure.
> Yet you cannot do actions without meeting their effects.
> Nor do you experience the effects of others' actions.

Mādhyamikas describe two repositories of karmic seeds, one temporary and the other constant. The continuity of the mental consciousness that functions during our lives is the temporary basis of karmic seeds. The "mere I"—the I designated in dependence on the aggregates—is the continuous basis. Existing even during an ārya's meditative equipoise on emptiness, deep sleep, and death, the mere I carries the karmic seeds. Nonetheless, the mere I exists only by designation; it is not findable under analysis.

This brief discussion of selflessness according to the Pāli and Sanskrit traditions demonstrates that there are many similarities. This is not surprising, since both traditions originate with the same Teacher, the Buddha.

8 | Dependent Arising

DEPENDENT ARISING is one of the most important teachings of the Buddha. Its essential principle is stated thus (MN 79:8):

> When this exists, that comes to be; with the arising of this, that arises. When this does not exist, that does not come to be; with the cessation of this, that ceases.

The Buddha employs this principle of conditionality in a variety of circumstances, especially when explaining the twelve links of dependent arising, the causal process for taking saṃsāric rebirth and attaining liberation from it. Dependent arising is also used to prove selflessness.

Twelve Links of Dependent Arising

As sentient beings, we exist in dependence on a body and mind, which themselves are dependent. Buddhaghosa explains (Vism 18:36):

> [The body and mind] cannot come to be by their own strength,
> nor can they maintain themselves by their own strength;
> relying for support on other states...
> they come to be with others as condition.
> They are produced by...something other than themselves.

The twelve links describe how our bodies and minds come into being by depending on their causal factors and how they give rise to further unsatisfactory results. Our lives arise due to causes we ourselves create. A supernatural power or external agent does not cause our experiences. Nor is there a substantially existent person who creates kamma and experiences their results. Rather one link arises from another in a natural process of conditionality.

In the suttas, Buddha presents the twelve links in a variety of ways, starting at different points in the chain to give a variety of perspectives on causation. Here we will follow the sequence (SN 12:2, MN 9) that begins with our present experience—aging and approaching death—and works backward in the sequence. This explains how we arrived at this point in our lives. It is also the sequence found in the Buddha's account of his own awakening, when he understood causation in its totality.

To fully understand each link, we need to understand its relation to its preceding and subsequent links, which are respectively its main cause and main effect. Contemplating these interlinking factors, we come to see our lives as a complex web of dependent causality. The following explanation from the Pāli tradition generally accords with that in the Sanskrit tradition.

Following the description of each link the question arises, "What is its origin, its cessation, and the path to its cessation?" The answer is that the previous link—the one that will be described next in this reverse ordering of the links—is the cause of this link. The cessation of the previous link brings the cessation of that link. The noble eightfold path is the path to its cessation. As you read below, you may want to pause after the description of each link to remember this.

12. *Aging* is the decline of life that begins immediately after birth; *death* is the dissolution of the body and mind of this life. Aging and death occur due to birth. Without being born, we would not age and die. To stop aging and death completely so that they are not experienced again, birth in saṃsāra must be stopped.

11. *Birth*, for human beings, is the time of conception, when the sperm, egg, and consciousness come together. This consciousness is the continuation of the mindstream of a being who left his former body and life. With it come all underlying tendencies of afflictions and kamma present in the previous life. These will condition many of the experiences of the new being. Birth is the "manifestation of the aggregates" of the new life. The five cognitive faculties of eye, ear, nose, tongue, and tactile are subtle material found deep inside each physical organ. They gradually develop so that contact with sense objects begins to occur.

Nalanda Buddhist Society Malaysia

TEACHING THE DHAMMA, MALAYSIA

In society, birth is seen as auspicious. This is because we do not see its inevitable result, death. When we train our minds to see the complete picture of life in saṃsāra, we will aspire for liberation.

There is discussion whether a period of time exists between death and the following rebirth. While no clear statement is found in the suttas, some passages suggest there may be a period of time between two lives. The Sanskrit tradition speaks of an intermediate state (*antarābhava*, or *bardo* in Tibetan) between one life and the next.

10. *Renewed existence* (or *becoming*) as a cause of birth refers to the kammic force that leads to rebirth in that particular state. The *Visuddhimagga* (17:250) distinguishes two aspects of renewed existence: (1) *Active kamma of renewed existence* is kamma that leads to a new rebirth: intentions and the mental factors of attachment and so forth conjoined with those intentions. It is the kammic cause propelling a rebirth. (2) *Resultant rebirth existence* is the resultant rebirth—the four or five aggregates propelled by kamma that experience the diverse results of our previous actions. Birth is the beginning of the resultant rebirth existence, aging is its continuation, and death is the end of that particular resultant rebirth existence. The Sanskrit tradition specifies renewed existence as the karma that is just about to ripen into the new rebirth.

During the time of this new life propelled by ignorance and kamma, many new kammas that will lead to future rebirths are created through our choices. Our choices are conditioned and limited by our previous actions and our current mental state, but they are not completely determined by them. We have the freedom to make responsible choices and nourish or counteract tendencies toward certain intentions.

9. *Clinging* makes us engage in activities that produce our next existence. It is of four types, clinging to (1) sensual pleasures, (2) wrong views other than the following two views, (3) a view of rules and practices—e.g., thinking self-mortification or killing nonbelievers is the path to good fortune—and (4) a view of self: an eternalist doctrine that holds there is a soul or self.

Clinging leads to renewed existence, birth, aging and death, and more dukkha. Therefore it is imperative to know the origin, cessation, and path to the cessation of clinging. It arises due to craving and ceases when craving ceases. The noble eightfold path is the way to cease clinging.

8. *Craving* is of three types: sensual craving, craving for renewed existence, and craving for nonexistence. These were explained in chapter 3.

Craving and clinging are closely related. An increase in craving stimulates clinging. The two bring dissatisfaction during our lives and great fear at the time of death, when we do not wish to separate from this life and cling to having another one.

7. *Feeling* is the nature of experience and has three types (pleasure, pain, and neutral), five types (physical pleasure, mental happiness, physical pain, mental pain, and neutral), or six types (feelings arising from contact through the six sources). So much of our lives is governed by our reactions to various feelings; we crave for pleasant feelings, crave to be separated from unpleasant ones, and crave for neutral feelings not to diminish. The latter applies especially to beings in the fourth jhāna and above, who have only neutral feelings and do not wish the peace of their state to cease.

One place where the forward motion of dependent arising can be broken is between feelings and craving. Feelings naturally arise as a result of previous kamma. By applying mindfulness and introspective awareness to our feelings, observing them as they are—impermanent, unsatisfactory, and selfless—we won't react to them with any of the three types of craving. Then feelings will arise and pass away without the arising of craving, clinging, and the remaining links. In this way ariyas and arahants experience feelings without craving.

6. *Contact* is the mental factor of contact arising with the meeting of the object with consciousness by means of the corresponding base. It occurs when, for example, a visible object such as color, the eye cognitive faculty, and the visual consciousness come together to create perception of that color. Contact is of six types corresponding to the six objects and six sources that produce it and the six types of feeling that it stimulates.

5. *Six sources* refers to the six internal bases—eye, ear, nose, tongue, tactile, and mental—that generate consciousness. They are called "sources" because they are the sources for the arising of the six consciousnesses. They are *internal* because they are part of the psychophysical organism. Of these, the first five are sense sources and the sixth is a mental source. The bhavaṅga is included in the latter. Each internal source is particular to its own object and consciousness. If it is injured or unable to function, the corresponding sensory function is also impaired. The six *external* sources—form up to mental objects—are the objects of consciousness. Together, these twelve include all conditioned phenomena.

4. *Name and form* is mentality and materiality. In the Pāli tradition, *name* (*nāma*) refers to five mental factors that are indispensable for making sense of and naming things in the world around us—feeling, discrimination, intention, contact, and attention. These help us to organize the data that flow in through our six sources and render them intelligible. The Sanskrit tradition says *name* consists of the non-form aggregates. *Form* (*rūpa*) is the form aggregate—our body constituted of the four elements and forms derived from them.

The way the six sources arise from name and form can be understood in two ways. (1) As the psychophysical organism conceived in the mother's womb develops, the six sources arise, and (2) the conditioning occurring in any cognition produces the six sources. For example, the eye source depends on the support of the body (material), which is alive due to the presence of consciousness and its accompanying mental factors (mentality).

3. *Consciousness* here refers to the mental consciousness that initiates the new life, connecting the mindstream from the previous life with the new

life. It simultaneously gives rise to the five mental factors that are called "name"—a shorthand term for the mental side of existence—and animates the new physical body, or "form." Without consciousness, the five mental factors of name cannot occur, and the body cannot function as a living being.

The six primary consciousnesses also condition name and form whenever we cognize an object. When consciousness is not present, the body dies and the six cognitive faculties cannot connect their corresponding objects and consciousnesses to produce cognition and contact.

Consciousness maintains the continuity of an individual's existence within any given life from birth until death and then beyond. It carries with it memories, kammic latencies, and habits, connecting different lives and making them into a series allowing later moments of consciousness to arise from former moments of consciousness and enabling future lives to relate to previous ones.

2. *Formative actions* are all the nonvirtuous and mundane virtuous intentions or kamma that bring rebirth in saṃsāra. While sense consciousnesses themselves do not create kamma, due to their contact with objects, virtuous and nonvirtuous mental factors arise in our mental consciousness and create kamma.

Not all kammas lead to rebirth. Weak intentions, neutral intentions, and physical and verbal actions that are incomplete lack the strength to produce saṃsāric rebirth. Supramundane virtuous intentions—those performed by ariyas—are not formative actions in relation to the twelve links because they do not perpetuate saṃsāra.

Formative actions may be meritorious, demeritorious, or unwavering, leading, respectively, to fortunate rebirths in the desire realm, unfortunate rebirths, and rebirth in the material or immaterial realms. (According to the Pāli tradition, rebirth in the material realm is the result of meritorious kamma.)

Formative actions generate rebirth into a new existence by serving as the condition for the consciousness that takes birth. This occurs in two ways. First, during our lives, we create kamma when we think, speak, and act. These intentions occur along with consciousness and also affect consciousness. Second, at the time of death, previous kamma is activated and propels the consciousness through the death process into a new existence. Formative actions determine whether this new consciousness is one of a human, animal, and so forth, corresponding with the body it has entered. Kamma accumulated in previous lives also determines which environment we are born into, the situations we experience, our habitual tendencies, and the feelings we experience.

While previous kamma influences consciousness, in general it is not an unalterable determining force. At any moment in our waking lives, we have the potential to change the course of our lives by changing our intentions.

1. *Ignorance* is the lack of understanding of the four truths. Oblivious to the three characteristics of conditioned phenomena, ignorance does not understand dependent arising and thus keeps us bound in saṃsāra. Mādhyamikas say ignorance apprehends the opposite of reality, grasping persons and phenomena as inherently existent when they are not.

As the first link, ignorance is the condition for the arising of both virtuous and nonvirtuous formative actions. Rooted in the underlying tendency (*anusaya*, *anuśaya*) of ignorance, attachment, anger, and other polluted mental factors motivate nonvirtuous actions. Ignorance also conditions virtuous mental states such as love and compassion in ordinary sentient beings. Only when ignorance is eradicated do all formative actions and saṃsāric rebirths cease.

Ignorance in one life is conditioned by ignorance in the previous life. There is no first moment of ignorance; thus saṃsāra is beginningless. However, ignorance can cease, and the path to that cessation is the noble eightfold path. When an ariya understands the pollutants, their origin, cessation, and the way to that cessation, she eradicates all underlying tendencies leading to saṃsāric rebirth and attains liberation.

Dependent arising applies not only to saṃsāra and what keeps it going (the first two truths of the ariyas) but also to liberation and the path that brings it about (the last two truths). Liberation has its nutriment—the seven awakening factors—and the links of conditioning factors leading to these are the four establishments of mindfulness, the three ways of good conduct, restraint of the senses, mindfulness and introspective awareness, appropriate attention, faith, listening to the true Dharma, and association with superior people (AN 10:61–62).

In explaining these forward and reverse series of causation for both saṃsāric existence and liberation, the Buddha does not imply that any one factor arises due to only the preceding factor. Rather he emphasizes that a momentum builds up as the various factors augment each other. In short, everything has multiple conditions, some more evident, others deeper. These conditions form a web of interrelated factors. It is like looking up a topic on the Internet. One page leads to five others, each of which takes us in a different but related direction.

Flow of the Links

Pāli commentaries explain the twelve links in terms of four groups, each with five links. This clarifies the relationships of the twelve links and the different lifetimes in which they occur. In the following table, lives A, B, and C occur in sequence, with life B being the present life.

Life	*Links*	*Twenty Modes (four groups of five)*
A	Ignorance (1) Formative actions (2)	Five past causes 1, 2, 8, 9, 10
B	Consciousness (3) Name and form (4) Six sources (5) Contact (6) Feeling (7)	Five present results 3, 4, 5, 6, 7
B	Craving (8) Clinging (9) Renewed existence (10)	Five present causes 8, 9, 10, 1, 2
C	Birth (11) Aging and death (12)	Five future results 3, 4, 5, 6, 7

The "links" column shows that our present life, B, is rooted in the ignorance and formative actions of a preceding life (A). Through the maturation of kamma (formative actions) conditioned by ignorance come the five resultant factors in this life (B): consciousness, name and form, six sources, contact, and feeling.

In this life (B), when feeling occurs, craving arises. That leads to clinging, which generates the active kamma of a renewed existence. These three are the force generating another rebirth (C) during which birth and aging and death are experienced.

In any given life all these factors intermesh. To understand how the twelve factors function in this life, we look to the last column with its twenty modes that fall into four groups of five each.

1. *Five past causes.* In the previous life, ignorance and formative actions as well as craving, clinging, and the active kamma of renewed existence were causes for the present life.
2. *Five present results.* Those five causes brought about the five present results: factors 3–7, which are an expanded way of speaking of birth and aging and death.
3. *Five present causes.* Five causes existing in this life—craving, clinging, renewed existence, ignorance, and formative actions—bring about a future birth. While these are the same as the five past causes leading to the present life, now they arise in the present life and condition the future life.
4. *Five future results.* Links 3–7—which include birth and aging and death—arise in the future life due to the five present causes.

The above explanation corresponds with the explicit teaching in the *Śālistamba Sūtra*, a Sanskrit sūtra, in which the items in the second column are respectively called *propelling causes*, *propelled results*, *actualizing causes*, and *actualized results*. Here link 3, consciousness, consists of the causal consciousness upon which the karmic seeds were placed and the resultant consciousness at the time the karmic seeds ripen. The former is a propelling cause, and the latter is a propelled result.

The twelve links can also be classified into three groups: (1) Afflictions—ignorance, craving, and clinging—underlie the entire process of rebirth by acting as the conditioning force for kamma. (2) Kamma—formative actions and the active kamma of renewed existence—actually propel rebirth. (3) Results—consciousness, name and form, six sources, contact, feeling, resultant rebirth existence, birth, and aging and death—are resultant dukkha.

The Sanskrit tradition speaks of the twelve links in terms of the *afflictive side*—how cyclic existence continues, and the *purified side*—how cyclic existence ceases. Each side has a forward and reverse order. These four combinations correspond to the four truths of the āryas. Emphasizing true origins of duḥkha, the *forward order of the afflicted side* begins with ignorance and shows how it eventually leads to aging and death. The *reverse order of the afflicted side* emphasizes true duḥkha. It begins with aging and death and traces back through birth and so forth to ignorance.

The purified side is the process of attaining liberation. The *forward order of the purified side* speaks of true paths by emphasizing that by ending ignorance, all the other links will cease. The *reverse order of the purified side* speaks of true cessations and liberation by emphasizing that beginning with aging and death, each link ceases with the cessation of its preceding link.

Sāriputta makes one of the most famous statements in the Pāli suttas (MN 28:28):

> Now this has been said by the Blessed One: "One who sees dependent arising sees the Dhamma; one who sees the Dhamma sees dependent arising."

Here "Dhamma" refers to truth, reality. It also refers to the Buddha's doctrine. Understanding dependent arising is the key to understanding both of these. It is also the key to countering saṃsāra. The Buddha says (DN 15:1):

> This dependent arising, Ānanda, is deep and appears deep. Because of not understanding and penetrating this Dhamma, Ānanda, this generation has become like a tangled skein...and does not pass beyond saṃsāra with its planes of misery, unfortunate births, and lower realms.[20]

In addition to the twelve links, the dependent evolution of saṃsāra can be explained by dissecting an instance of cognition (MN 28). In dependence on an intact cognitive faculty, an impinging object (these two are included in the form aggregate), and attention to that object, the eye consciousness arises. Together with it are factors of all five aggregates: visual form, eye faculty, feeling, discrimination, mental factors from the volitional factors aggregate, and the primary eye consciousness are all present. This is another way in which the five aggregates come into being dependent on causes and conditions, not under their own power. When the conditions are not present, the aggregates do not arise, and dukkha is ceased.

The noble eightfold path that eradicates the origins of dukkha is also conditioned. Thus it can be practiced and cultivated. Developing the path will eradicate the origins of dukkha, leading us to the unconditioned, nibbāna, true peace.

Who Circles in Saṃsāra?

In a Pāli sutta (SN 12:35) when a monk asks, "For whom is there this aging and death?" the Buddha responds that this is not a valid question because it presupposes a substantial self. If someone thinks the self and the body are the same and thus the self becomes totally nonexistent when the body dies, there would be no need to practice the path because saṃsāra would end naturally at the time of death. This is the extreme of annihilation.

If someone thinks the self is one thing and the body is another and that the self is released from the body at death and abides eternally, he falls to the extreme of eternalism. If the self were permanent and eternal, the path would be unable to put an end to saṃsāra because a permanent self could not change.

Not only did the Buddha refute a substantial self that is born, ages, and dies, he also denied that the body—and by extension the other aggregates—belong to such a person (SN 12:37). This body is not ours, because no independent person exists who possesses it. It does not belong to others, because there is no independent self of others.

Buddhaghosa answers the question, "Who experiences the result of kamma?" by quoting an ancient Pāli verse and then explaining it (Vism 17:171–72):

> "Experiencer" is a convention
> for mere arising of the fruit;
> they say "it fruits" as a convention
> when on a tree appears its fruit.

> Just as it is simply owing to the arising of tree fruits, which are one part of the phenomenon called a *tree*, that it is said "the tree fruits" or "the tree has fruited," so it is simply owing to the arising of the fruit consisting of the pleasure and pain called *experience*,

> which is one part of the aggregates called *devas* and *human beings*, that it is said, "A deva or a human being experiences or feels pleasure or pain." There is therefore no need at all here for a superfluous experiencer.

The words "experiencer" and "agent" are mere conventional labels. There is no need to assert a findable experiencer of kamma or a findable creator of kamma. Such a self is superfluous because we say "A person experiences pleasure or pain" simply because that feeling has arisen in that person's feeling aggregate. In speaking of the four truths, Buddhaghosa says (Vism 16:90):

> ...in the ultimate sense all the truths should be understood as void because of the absence of any experiencer, any doer, anyone who is extinguished, and any goer. Hence this is said:
>
> For there is suffering but no one who suffers;
> doing exists although there is no doer;
> extinction is but no extinguished person;
> and although there is a path, there is no goer.

Similarly, Mādhyamikas say that although we speak of a person who revolves in saṃsāra—one who creates karma and experiences its effects—this does not imply an inherently existent self. The resultant factors arise due to causal factors, which are themselves caused by other factors.

Similarly, there are no inherently existent āryas approaching nirvāṇa, and their going on the path—their activity of practicing—cannot bear analysis searching for their ultimate mode of existence. Still, āryas realize emptiness, purify their minds, attain awakening, and become qualified guides for others on the path. While all these agents and actions are not findable under ultimate analysis and have no inherent essence, they exist and function on the conventional level by being merely designated. Because they still mistakenly appear as inherently existent to āryas in post-meditation, they are said to be false, like dreams, illusions, mirages, and reflections.

We say "I studied hard as a child" from the perspective of our present I being a continuation of that child. The child self and the present self are different, yet because they exist as members of the same continuum, the adult experiences the result of the child's actions. The process is similar from one

MONASTICS FROM TWO DIFFERENT TRADITIONS
UNDER THE BODHI TREE, BODHGAYA, INDIA

life to the next: the self of one life isn't the same as the self of the next, yet the latter experiences the results of the karma done by the former because they are members of the same continuum.

Benefits of Meditating on the Twelve Links of Dependent Arising

Of the different levels of dependent arising, the Sanskrit tradition explains this process of dependent arising as *causal dependence*. Each link arises dependent on the preceding one; understanding this counteracts the extreme of eternalism, thinking that the links exist inherently or thinking that an external creator causes duḥkha. When each link is complete, it gives rise to the subsequent links; understanding this eliminates the view of annihilation, thinking that things totally cease.

Understanding causal dependence leads to insight into selflessness. We see there is no substantial person underlying the process of dependent arising and there are no inherently existent persons or phenomena that are bound to saṃsāra or liberated from it.

Reflection on causal dependence clears away wrong views, such as believing our duḥkha arises without causes or is due to an external creator or a permanent cause. Identifying that ignorance and formative actions cause future lives eliminates the wrong view that everything ceases at death. We also realize our actions have an ethical dimension and influence our experiences. Seeing the variety of realms we may be born into ceases the misconception that no other life forms exist. Furthermore, we understand that all the causes of suffering exist within us. Therefore relief from suffering must also be accomplished within ourselves.

Contemplating each link individually accentuates its unsatisfactory nature. Seeing the beginningless, unsatisfactory nature of saṃsāra stimulates strong renunciation and energizes us to make effort to terminate it. We ask ourselves, "What sense does it make to crave worldly pleasures when attachment to them brings endless rebirth?" Bodhisattvas meditate on the twelve links with respect to themselves and other sentient beings. This arouses their compassion, which spurs bodhicitta. They want to attain full awakening to be fully competent to lead others on the path out of saṃsāra. Bodhisattvas' compassion is so intense that if it were more beneficial for sentient beings for bodhisattvas to delay their own awakening, they would joyfully do this. However, seeing that they can be of greater benefit to others after they become buddhas, they exert effort to attain buddhahood as quickly as possible.

Sanskrit Tradition: Levels of Dependence

The following sections discuss the unique Prāsaṅgika Madhyamaka approach to dependent arising—because all phenomena are dependent, they are empty of inherent existence; because they arise dependent on other factors, they exist conventionally. Understanding this compatibility of dependent arising and emptiness—especially that karma and its results function although they lack inherent existence—enables us to practice the path to liberation and full awakening.

There are different ways of explaining and understanding dependent arising. According to one presentation, (1) *arising through meeting* refers to effects arising from causes. This is causal dependence and pertains only to impermanent things and is common to all Buddhist traditions. (2) *Existing in reliance* indicates that all phenomena depend on their parts. This applies to both permanent and impermanent phenomena. (3) *Dependent existence* refers to all phenomena existing by being merely designated in dependence on their basis of designation and the mind that conceives and designates them.

In another presentation of dependent arising, there are two levels: (1) *causal dependence* indicates that effects arise due to their own causes, and (2) *dependent designation* has two implications: (a) *mutual dependence* is phenomena's being posited in relation to each other, and (b) *mere dependent designation* refers to phenomena existing as mere name or mere designation. "Mere name" does not mean things are just words or sounds—that clearly is not the case. It means they exist by being merely designated.

In both presentations, the "arising" in *dependent arising* is not limited to arising due to causes and conditions but extends to other factors contributing to phenomena's existence. Also, in both presentations, the earlier levels of dependent arising are in general easier to understand than the latter and serve as a foundation to understand the latter ones. Focusing on the second presentation, let's look at these levels of dependent arising in more depth.

Causal Dependence

Dependence on causes and conditions is the meaning of dependent arising presented in both the Pāli and Sanskrit canons and practiced in the Śrāvaka, Pratyekabuddha, and Bodhisattva vehicles. This is the meaning explored above in the twelve links of dependent arising.

Because causal dependence is a fact, holding things to exist with an inherent nature is untenable. If things existed inherently or independently, they could not arise due to causes and conditions. Contemplating causal dependence leads us to understand that all functioning things do not exist by their own power. That they arise dependent on causes and conditions indicates that they exist. Thus they are both empty and existent.

Mutual Dependence

Based on causal dependence, mutual dependence and mere dependent designation are explained in the Prajñāpāramitā sūtras. Causal dependence is not too difficult to understand: we know that flowers grow from seeds, that knowledge comes from learning. Yet we don't usually think that causes depend on their effects.

On the basis of observing causal dependence, deeper reflection leads us to recognize the mutuality of the relationship. Not only does the effect depend upon the cause, but also the cause depends upon the effect. Although a cause does not arise from its effect, the identity of something as a cause depends upon there being an effect. A seed becomes a cause because it has the potential to produce its effect, a sprout. Without the possibility of a sprout arising, the seed cannot be a cause. This is not mere semantics; the meaning is deeper.

Things have no inherent identity as either a cause or an effect. When the term *cause* is imputed to a seed, nothing in the seed objectively makes it a referent for the term *cause*. The same holds true for an effect.

There are many obvious examples of things existing in mutual dependence on one another. East and west, suffering and happiness, goer and going, designated object and basis of designation, spiritual practitioner and path, whole and parts, ordinary being and ārya—all these are posited in relationship to each other.

Some pairs that are mutually dependent are also causally dependent, such as yesterday's mind and today's mind. However, many are not. Someone becomes an employer because he or she has employees and vice versa. None of our social roles are self-existent; they exist mutually dependent on each other.

Actions are called "constructive" or "destructive" not because they are inherently so. Constructive and destructive actions or karma are posited not only in relation to each other but also in dependence upon their results. When sentient beings experience happiness, the actions causing that are called "constructive," and when they experience suffering, those causative karmas are termed "destructive."

Agent, action, and object of action—giver, giving, recipient, and gift—are likewise mutually dependent upon each other. A generous action exists dependent on these three.

Whole and parts also depend on each other. A car (a whole) is dependent on an engine, wheels, and so forth (its parts), and a wheel is a "car part" because cars exist. Both permanent and impermanent phenomena depend on their parts. The mind depends on a continuity of moments of consciousness. Atoms are composed of even smaller particles. No smallest particle or moment of consciousness can be found because everything consists of parts. Emptiness, too, depends on parts. The generality *emptiness* is designated in dependence on the emptiness of the table, the emptiness of the chair, and so on. Emptiness also depends on phenomena—persons, aggregates, and so forth—that are empty. Thus emptiness is not an independently existent absolute.

Mere Dependent Designation

Delving deeper, we see that phenomena exist by being merely designated in dependence on their bases of designation. There is a designated object—a table—and its basis of designation—the collection of legs and top. The mind conceives the collection of these parts as a table and designates it "table." If we try to find an essence—the true referent of the word "table"—we can't find anything that *is* the table in the individual parts or in the collection of parts. Nothing in the parts can be objectifiably identified as the table. Dependence on other factors means that phenomena are empty of inherent existence.

When "snake" is imputed to a coiled, speckled rope in a dimly lit area, nothing on the side of the rope is a snake. Similarly, when we impute "snake" in dependence on a long coiled being, nothing on the side of that being—its body, mind, or the collection of the two—is a snake. We may think, "But there has to be something that is a snake from the side of the coiled being. Otherwise there is no reason for it, and not the coiled rope, to be a snake." However, when we search for something that makes the coiled being a snake, we can't pinpoint anything.

Similarly, when I is designated in dependence on the aggregates, there is nothing from the side of the aggregates that is I or me. The person is not one aggregate, the collection of aggregates, or the continuum of the aggregates.

What makes designating "snake" in dependence on a long, coiled being or designating "I" in dependence on the aggregates valid, while designating "snake" on a rope and "I" on the face in the mirror erroneous? The coiled being can perform the function of a snake, and the I can function as a person. The coiled rope and the reflection of a face cannot perform those functions.

The fact that things exist dependent on being merely designated does not mean that whatever our mind thinks up is real or that whenever we designate something with a term, it becomes that object. Thinking there are real people in the television doesn't mean there are, and calling a telephone "grapefruit" doesn't make it one.

Three criteria establish something as existent: (1) It is well known to a conventional consciousness—some people can identify the object. (2) It is not discredited by another conventional reliable cognizer—the perception of someone with unimpaired senses does not negate that. (3) It is not discredited by ultimate analysis—a mind realizing emptiness cannot refute its existence. In short, while all conventionally existent phenomena exist by being merely designated by mind, everything that is designated does not necessarily exist conventionally.

Emptiness and Dependent Arising Are Compatible

The levels of dependence are related to each other. We know through direct experience that things depend on causes and conditions: certain medicines cure particular diseases, and pollution adversely affects our health. By reflecting deeply on the observable fact of causal dependence, we will see that the ability for effects to arise from causes is due to their being interdependent by nature. Their possessing an interdependent nature enables causal influences to produce effects when suitable conditions come together.

But what makes phenomena have this dependent nature? Through examination, we see that only because everything lacks inherent existence and nothing is a self-enclosed, independent entity can things have a dependent nature that enables them to have conditioned interactions with other things. Thus, on the basis of the observed fact of causal dependence, we go through this chain of reasoning culminating in the realization of the emptiness of inherent existence, which, in turn, enables us to understand that all phenomena exist by mere designation, mere name.

Although phenomena are empty of inherent existence, they exist. We see that each thing has its own effects. How do they exist? There are only two possibilities: either inherently in their own right or by mere designation. Probing deeper, we see that inherent existence—phenomena existing from their own side, unrelated to anything else—is untenable. If they possessed such reality, the more we searched for their identity, the clearer it should become. In fact, when we subject phenomena to critical analysis, they are unfindable, indicating that they lack inherent, independent, or objective existence. When we understand that things exist but not inherently, the only conclusion we can reach is that they exist depending on mere designation by term and concept, i.e., by thought and language. Since they do exist, their existence can only be established on the level of dependent designation. In this way, understanding emptiness in terms of causal dependence eventually leads us to understand dependent arising in terms of emptiness.

Emptiness and dependent arising are seen as fully integrated and noncontradictory after arising from meditative equipoise on emptiness. The world does not cease to exist with the realization of emptiness; rather, our understanding of how it exists becomes more accurate. The I, aggregates, karma and its effects, and other phenomena are falsities in that they do not inherently exist although they appear to do so to our ordinary senses. Knowing they exist dependently, not inherently, enables us to relate to people and our environment in a more spacious way. Nāgārjuna says (MMK 24.18–19):

> That which arises dependently
> we explain as emptiness.
> This [emptiness] is dependent designation.
> Just this is the middle way.
>
> Because there is no phenomenon
> that is not dependently arisen,
> there is no phenomenon
> that is not empty.

Arising dependent on other factors—such as causes and conditions, parts, and term and concept—is the meaning of emptiness of inherent existence. Because actions depend on other factors, they produce results. This would be impossible if they existed inherently or independent of other factors. This understanding, which unites dependent arising and emptiness, negates both inherent existence and total nonexistence. Dependent arising and emptiness are inseparable qualities of all existents. It is the true middle way.

Although emptiness and dependent arising are compatible and come to the same point, they are not the same. If they were, then just by perceiving an instance of dependent arising, such as a book, or the principle of dependent arising, we would perceive emptiness. Empty and arising dependently are two ways of looking at phenomena. The fact that they are empty does not prevent conventional distinctions among objects. Pens and tables still have their own unique functions. Someone who realizes emptiness discerns these when she emerges from meditative equipoise on emptiness.

If dependent arising referred only to causal dependence, it would refute the inherent existence of only causally conditioned phenomena. Because here "dependent arising" means dependent designation, it establishes the emptiness of all phenomena. To understand this subtlest level of dependence, understanding mutual dependence is necessary, and to understand that, understanding causal dependence is vital. These three levels of dependence are progressively subtler although they are not mutually exclusive.

Dependent arising is called "the king of reasonings" because it not only negates independent existence but also establishes dependent existence. The term *dependent arising* itself shows the middle way view that phenomena are empty and yet exist. "Dependent" shows they are empty of independent existence, eliminating eternalism. "Arising" indicates they exist, eliminating annihilation. All phenomena that exist lack any inherent nature; nevertheless, they exist dependent on other factors and are established by reliable conventional consciousnesses.

Pāli Tradition: Terms, Concepts, and Conventions

The Buddha explains the danger of not correctly understanding terms and concepts (SN 1:20):

> Those who go by names, who go by concepts,
> making their abode in names and concepts,
> failing to discern the naming process,
> these are subject to the reign of death.[21]

The commentary says what "goes by names and concepts" is the aggregates. When ordinary people perceive the aggregates, their minds misconceive them to be permanent, pleasurable, and having or being a self. Due to distorted conceptions, people then "make their abode in names and concepts," generating all sorts of afflictions in relation to the aggregates. People familiar with the Madhyamaka view may understand these same verses from that perspective.

The *Itivuttaka* commentary explains the same verse saying that beings "who make their abode in names and concepts" apprehend the aggregates as I or mine, or when the aggregates are not their own, they apprehend them as another person. Those who do this are subject to death and rebirth in cyclic existence. The sutta continues:

> He who has discerned the naming process
> does not suppose that one who names exists.
> No such case exists for him in truth,
> whereby one could say: "He is this or that."

Someone who understands the naming process understands the aggregates and knows them as impermanent, unsatisfactory, and selfless and abandons craving for them by actualizing the supreme path. This arahant does not grasp what is labeled as I, mine, or "my self" in dependence on the aggregates to be a real person. After leaving behind the aggregates and attaining nibbāna without remainder, the arahant cannot be said to be "this or that."

In several suttas, the Buddha explains that seeing not-self (selflessness) with wisdom does not destroy conventional discourse and the ability to communicate with others through the use of language. Conventional discourse, he says, does not necessitate grasping a self. Words, names, expressions, and concepts can be used by arahants who have eliminated all self-grasping.

The Buddha clarifies that an arahant uses words and concepts in accord with how things are done in the world, without grasping them as self. An arahant with his last saṃsāric body still uses conventional language that corresponds to how ordinary beings speak (SN 1:25). The commentary says "they do not violate conventional discourse by saying, 'The aggregates eat... the aggregates robe.'" If they didn't speak in a way that others could understand, how could they teach the Dhamma?

While arahants use words such as "I," "mine," and "my self," this does not indicate they are subject to the conceit "I am." They are beyond conceiving due to craving, views, and conceit.

The Buddha elucidates (DN 9:53), "There are merely names, expressions, turns of speech, designations in common use in the world, which the Tathāgata uses without grasping them." Names and concepts can be used in two ways: someone who has ignorance and the view of a personal identity uses words and concepts believing there is a true object to which they refer, a self in these phenomena. Those free from ignorance and the view of a personal identity do not grasp at true referents of words and concepts. They use them merely as conventions to convey a meaning, without grasping at a self in the objects to which they refer.

9 | Uniting Serenity and Insight

Pāli Tradition

The Buddha practiced the jhānas and recommended this meditation to his disciples to overcome hindrances by drawing the mind away from sensual pleasure to more refined states of happiness and then to awakening. However, if we are not vigilant about maintaining a Dharma motivation, there is danger of becoming attached to the bliss and peace of the jhānas and thus being distracted from eliminating defilements. To remedy this, the Buddha advised meditators, after emerging from a jhāna, to examine the jhāna in terms of the three characteristics. Seeing that it is impermanent, unsatisfactory, and not-self, they will not become attached to it and will cultivate liberating insight.

The ultimate purpose of developing deep concentration is to unite it with insight wisdom and use the union of the two to eradicate defilements completely. The fourth jhāna is the door to the three higher knowledges: knowledge of past lives, knowledge of the passing away and rebirth of beings according to their kamma, and knowledge of the destruction of all pollutants. The Buddha used the concentrated mind of the fourth jhāna to gain these three knowledges, whereby he uttered (MN 4:32), "I directly knew, 'Birth is destroyed, the holy life has been lived, what had to be done has been done, there is no more coming to any state of being.'"

How we balance the cultivation of serenity and insight to attain liberation depends on our faculties and the guidance of our spiritual mentor. Ānanda speaks of four ways through which practitioners may attain arahantship (AN 4:170): (1) We first practice serenity and, based on that tranquil, undistracted mind, cultivate insight by contemplating the three characteristics so the supramundane path will arise. (2) We cultivate insight by contemplating the three characteristics, thus weakening the five hindrances. We then develop serenity, unite it with insight, and attain the supramundane path. (3) We cultivate serenity and insight together, alternating between the two. We attain the first jhāna and, after emerging from it, examine its constituents with insight, seeing them as impermanent, unsatisfactory, and not-self. We then do this with the second jhāna and so forth. (4) The mind is seized by restlessness regarding the Dhamma. According to the *Visuddhimagga*, this mental agitation is due to the ten imperfections of insight (*vipassanā upakkilesa*)—exceptional experiences that practitioners overestimate as indications of attainments instead of seeing their impermanence (Vism 20:105). When this agitation is stilled and the mind settles down, becoming unified and concentrated, the supramundane path arises. Another interpretation is that this agitation is mental restlessness produced by exceptional eagerness to realize the Dhamma. In some cases this can precipitate realization of the truth, as seems to have been the case for the ascetic Bāhiya Dārucīriya (Ud 1:10).

Each of the above four ways leads initially to stream-entry and ultimately to the elimination of all fetters, underlying tendencies, and pollutants. Everyone who has attained liberation has done so in one of these four ways. The first three ways are taught by Theravāda meditation masters at present.

Both serenity and insight are necessary to actualize stream-entry, even though an individual may emphasize one or the other at the beginning. When our practice is mature, serenity and insight are brought into harmony so that both are present supporting each other. When they are unified, the mind remains steady and tranquil on the meditation object while insight sees deeply into the nature of phenomena. In the supramundane path, serenity and insight arise simultaneously in a balanced way, the former being right concentration, the latter being right view.

The suttas are not clear about the degree of samādhi needed to become an arahant. Some suggest that at least the first jhāna is necessary, while some commentaries say access concentration (*upacāra samādhi*) is sufficient. In the latter case, the person is called a "dry wisdom arahant" because wisdom without the moistening effect of jhāna is "dry," even though it can still eradicate the defilements. In general, because the five hindrances are not well suppressed in access concentration and may rebound, it is more secure to develop at least the first jhāna as a basis for insight.

While the jhānas are states of full absorption on one object, *momentary concentration* (*khaṇika samādhi*)—a concept introduced in the Pāli

Yann Pinczon du Sel

BOROBODUR, INDONESIA

commentaries—does not restrict the range of awareness to one object. To develop momentary concentration, we direct mindfulness to the changing states of mind and body and maintain continuous awareness of whatever object enters the field of perception. Not clinging to any object, we note the variety of sensory objects, feelings, mental states, and so forth that arise and pass away. Concentration thereby gains in strength until it becomes established one-pointedly on the changing stream of events. While constant change in meditation objects usually inhibits concentration, with momentary concentration single-pointed unification of the mind remains. In time, mindfulness on the changing phenomena in the field of awareness becomes strong enough to suppress the five hindrances. The four establishments of mindfulness develop this flexible-yet-steady concentration, enabling us to progress along the path of insight leading to the supramundane path that realizes nibbāna.

In jhāna, the mind is focused single-pointedly and unwaveringly on an unchanging object, whereas insight requires observation, analysis, and mindfulness of a changing object—mental functions not usually operative within jhāna. Thus, according to the *Visuddhimagga* and the Abhidhamma system, insight is practiced in a non-jhānic state of concentration. Such a state, which some call *vipassanā samādhi*, arises when we have just emerged from jhāna and thus are still infused with the power of the jhāna. While not as concentrated as jhāna, the mind is sufficiently focused to analyze an object without distraction.

Sanskrit Tradition

Finding the correct view of selflessness and proper insight requires learning, reflection, and meditation. Wrong views concerning emptiness and insight abound. By incorrectly identifying the object of negation, some people negate all existence. Other people remain single-pointedly in a nonconceptual state, incorrectly thinking that since all thoughts grasp inherent existence, abandoning thoughts altogether brings liberation. In this way they abandon compassion, generosity, ethical conduct, and other important practices, saying they involve conceptions of true existence.

However, not all thoughts are conceptions of inherent existence. When we first hear teachings on emptiness and reflect on them, we use thought. Such conceptual reflection is useful, even though our ultimate goal is to go beyond it. Furthermore, not all analytical meditation is conceptual; yogis on the paths of seeing and meditation employ nonconceptual analysis to meditate on emptiness. When some scriptures state that emptiness is inconceivable and beyond awareness, it does not mean we can dispense with analysis aimed at discovering the ultimate nature. These statements indicate only that emptiness cannot be experienced fully through the intellect.

When we have strong concentration, we may have many wonderful experiences. The coarse appearance of subject and object may vanish; our mind may be very clear; objects may appear insubstantial like rainbows or may even disappear. However, these experiences do not necessarily indicate insight into selflessness or meditation on illusion-like appearances.

To avoid going astray, we must correctly identify self-grasping ignorance and its object, inherent existence. Then we analyze whether phenomena exist in the way they appear to the mind obscured by ignorance. Only by irrefutably proving to ourselves the nonexistence of inherent existence—the object apprehended by ignorance—can we generate the wisdom realizing the emptiness of inherent existence. Since the object of this wisdom—emptiness—directly contradicts the object held by ignorance, such wisdom counteracts ignorance.

Emptiness is not an object ordinary beings can know directly through our senses. We must use reasoning to understand it, and the initial realization of emptiness is inferential and conceptual. While excellent, this understanding lacks sufficient power to undermine innate ignorance and destroy afflictions. Direct perception of the emptiness of all phenomena is necessary, and this requires uniting serenity and insight.

Serenity is a concentration arisen depending on the nine stages of sustained attention and held by pliancy in which the mind is able to remain on its object as long as wanted. *Insight* is a wisdom discriminating its object with discernment and is held by the bliss of pliancy induced by analyzing its object within serenity. Experiencing mental and physical pliancy induced by stabilizing meditation is the mark of success in attaining serenity. Experiencing this same pliancy induced by analytical meditation is the measure of success in attaining insight. Until that time, stabilizing and analytical meditations still subtly interfere with each other. The determining factor for actual insight on emptiness is being able to refute the object of negation and remain single-pointedly on that emptiness of inherent existence without laxity or excitement, with pliancy being induced by the power of analytical meditation.

To unite serenity and insight, after attaining serenity and gaining the correct view in meditation sessions, first do analytical meditation to discern emptiness, then do stabilizing meditation on emptiness. Analysis ensures that the ascertainment of emptiness remains correct and vibrant, and stabilizing meditation ensures that the mind remains clear and stable on emptiness. Thus, within one meditation session, practice analytical and stabilizing meditations alternately. If stability decreases due to too much analytical meditation, do more stabilizing meditation. If your discernment of emptiness declines, do more analytical meditation.

Then, while doing analytical meditation, go through the nine stages of sustained attention and develop the four mental engagements. At the conclusion of the ninth stage, when spontaneous engagement arises, if analysis itself induces nondiscursiveness and a special serenity focused on emptiness, the union of serenity and insight is attained. This mind is very powerful. Whereas previously serenity and insight were different entities, they now occur simultaneously. In one consciousness, the stability aspect is serenity and the analytical aspect is insight.

Before arising at the end of a meditation session on emptiness, think, "All phenomena do not exist inherently but depend on other factors. Thus sentient beings' actions bring their corresponding results. Not seeing this, ordinary sentient beings become confused, attached, and angry, thus creating the causes for duḥkha. Having a precious human life, I must fulfill the collections of merit and exalted wisdom to become a buddha and lead them to awakening."

Between meditation sessions, bow, make offerings, and practice generosity, ethical conduct, and fortitude with bodhicitta. While doing so, reflect that the agent, object, and action depend on each other and do not exist inherently; they are like illusions. In this way, all your meritorious practices will be complemented by wisdom.

Chinese Buddhism

Zhiyi emphasized that successful Dharma practice depends on balancing the quiescence of serenity and the analytical wisdom of insight. Cultivating serenity without the wisdom realizing emptiness does not bring liberation. However, if beginners are taught Nāgārjuna's view of emptiness, they may not understand it well and may even generate wrong views. Therefore we must first be well grounded in the method aspect of the path—generosity, ethical conduct, and other practices—as explained by Maitreya and Asaṅga. Since the first five perfections without wisdom are like a barren house, incorporating the wisdom of reality into them is essential. Through repeated practice, practitioners conjoin great compassion and bodhicitta with all meditation practices and reflect on the emptiness of the agent, object, and action of all the practices they do.

By learning, reflecting, and meditating on Nāgārjuna's texts, practitioners gain the Madhyamaka view. Since the understanding gained from learning and reflecting is conceptual, they seek the union of serenity and insight in order to generate unpolluted wisdom directly realizing the eight negations in Nāgārjuna's homage in his *Mūlamadhyamakakārikā*: no ceasing and arising, no annihilation and permanence, no coming and going, and no singularity and plurality.

In ninth-century China, there was much discussion on the role of serenity and insight. Some Chan practitioners stated that Chan was beyond words and concepts and was thus beyond Buddhist scriptures. Zongmi, the Huayan school's fifth patriarch and a respected Chan master, accepted that final awakening was beyond words and conceptions. However, he said that Chan should not disengage from the philosophical traditions of Buddhism that employ words and concepts to lead sentient beings toward the truth. He encouraged practitioners to study the scriptures, and he cautioned that meditation was not about emptying the mind of all thought but about cultivating the wisdom of reality. Highly valuing the method aspect of the path, Zongmi saw the gradual accumulation of merit as essential for developing wisdom.

Zongmi described two types of *sudden teachings*: one for beings of sharp faculties, the other as a method of exposition. The Buddha gave the sudden teachings for those of sharp faculties when he spontaneously and directly revealed the true Dharma to unawakened beings who immediately attained awakening. Here "awakening" refers to the first direct perception of reality. For Zongmi, this means for the first time seeing that one's own true nature is, and always has been, the same as the nature of all the buddhas. At this time, although a practitioner has an experience of awakening, she is not yet fully awakened; she must still remove all afflictions and karmic latencies obscuring the mind. This is done through gradual practice after the initial, sudden experience of awakening.

Sudden teachings are not the same as the *highest teachings*, which also include teachings given for gradual practice. In other words, the highest teachings could be approached in two ways, either gradually through consistent development or suddenly through a direct experience of reality. Sharp-faculty disciples are suited for the sudden teachings, while middle- and low-faculty practitioners fare better with the gradual approach. The Buddha leads the latter group progressively until they are capable of understanding the teachings on the ultimate meaning. This is the approach shown in the *Saddharmapuṇḍarīka Sūtra* and *Nirvāṇa Sūtra*, where the highest teaching is expounded in a gradual manner, beginning with how to create the causes for fortunate rebirths by abandoning nonvirtue and creating virtue.

I once discussed gradual and sudden awakening in a public forum in New York City with Master Sheng Yen (1930–2009), the founder of the Dharma Drum Mountain organization and a wise, respected Chan master from Taiwan. He affirmed that in Chan, *awakening* refers to having the initial, direct perception of emptiness. While Tibetan Buddhists occasionally use "awakening" in that way, more often we use it to refer to the endpoint of a path—the arhatship of a śrāvaka, for instance, or the full awakening of a buddha.

Understanding the path in light of the differing use of the word *awakening*, there does not seem to be a big gap between our traditions. To paraphrase what Master Sheng Yen told me: "At the time of the Buddha many people attained awakening suddenly after the Buddha spoke only a few words to them. Chan stories of people realizing emptiness after being hit or scolded by their teacher apply only to highly accomplished, exceptional students. Not everyone is capable of sudden awakening, and those who are not must begin with the basics of Dharma practice. While those with sharp faculties and good karma may attain awakening quickly or suddenly, they still have to practice method and wisdom after their first experience of awakening because they are not yet free from all afflictions. Only with buddhahood is one free from all obscurations. Everyone else practices a gradual path to amass the necessary virtue and wisdom before their awakening. While sudden awakening is possible, it is not easy; it is not like getting something for nothing. People must still keep pure precepts and cultivate bodhicitta, concentration, and wisdom."

A few Tibetan texts mention a sudden or instantaneous approach that isn't limited to the structure of gradual practice. I read a Kagyu text that explicitly explained *mahāmudrā* as a sudden path. In Sakya writings we find mention of the "simultaneity of realization and liberation," and the Nyingma *dzogchen* practice also speaks of this. Tsongkhapa accepts the notions of simultaneity and instantaneous liberation. However, he points out that what appears to be sudden realization is actually the culmination of many causes accumulated over time coming together. This is the case with the Buddha's first five disciples, who realized emptiness immediately after listening to one teaching on the four truths, and with Milarepa, who had engaged in serious practice for many lifetimes before attaining full awakening in that life. So whether we speak of gradual or sudden awakening, accumulating causes and conditions over time is needed for true spiritual development.

10 | Progressing on the Path

BOTH THE Pāli and Sanskrit traditions contain explanations of progressive steps taken along the path to arhatship and buddhahood. Knowing these enables us to practice in a systematic way and to accurately assess our progress.

Pāli Tradition: Purification and Knowledge

By cultivating the four establishments of mindfulness, the seven awakening factors, and the noble eightfold path, we cultivate wisdom, the direct antidote freeing us from cyclic existence. The suttas (MN 24) and the *Visuddhimagga* set out the structure of the path in terms of seven purifications (*satta visuddhi*).

Buddhaghosa gives the analogy of a tree growing. The *soil* in which wisdom grows is wisdom's field of examination: the five aggregates, twelve sources, eighteen elements, twenty-two faculties, four truths, and dependent arising. Just as *roots* of the tree make it stable, the first two purifications—the purification of ethical conduct and the purification of mind—form the foundation for wisdom. Just as branches, leaves, flowers, and fruit grow from the *trunk* of a tree, the excellent qualities of the ariyas grow from wisdom, and so the five subsequent purifications are included in the higher training of wisdom (Vism 18–22).

The seven purifications are practiced in order, each one depending on the preceding ones. The first six are mundane, the last is supramundane.

1. **Purification of ethical conduct** (*sīla visuddhi*) is the higher training of ethical conduct. There are four ways to accomplish it. (1) The *ethical conduct of restraint* is taking and living in precepts, which prevents physical and verbal nonvirtues. (2) The *ethical conduct of restraining the senses* involves

practicing mindfulness and introspective awareness to avoid attachment to attractive objects and aversion toward unattractive ones. (3) The *ethical conduct of pure livelihood* is to receive the four requisites in an honest and nonharmful way. (4) The *ethical conduct of proper use of requisites* is to use the requisites after reflecting on their purpose, shedding attachment, and dedicating for the donors' welfare.

2. Purification of mind (*citta visuddhi*) is the higher training of concentration, accomplished by subduing the five hindrances by means of access and full-absorption concentration.

Practitioners may cultivate insight in two ways. Following the vehicle of serenity, some attain access concentration or a higher state of absorption and use it as the basis for generating insight. Here the meditator emerges from the absorption, analyzes the factors of that absorption in terms of the five aggregates, understands their conditions, examines their nature, and sees they are marked by the three characteristics. The purification of mind for this person is whatever degree of concentration he or she develops from access on up.

Others, following the vehicle of pure insight, cultivate *momentary concentration* (see chapter 9) on the ever-changing physical and mental events. This is comparable to access concentration and is the purification of mind for these practitioners.

3. Purification of view (*diṭṭhi visuddhi*), also known as the analytical knowledge of mind and matter, begins the process of cultivating wisdom by discerning the characteristics, functions, manifestations, and immediately preceding causes of the five aggregates. Through this, meditators discern that what is called the person is a collection of interdependent mental and physical factors. This purifies the wrong view of a unitary, permanent self.

4. Purification by overcoming doubt (*kaṅkhāvitaraṇa visuddhi*) discerns the conditions of the mind and matter in the past, present, and future, thus eliminating doubts concerning them. By meditating on dependent arising, meditators view the present collection of aggregates as dependently arisen, conditioned phenomena, thus understanding their body-mind complex does not arise due to a transcendent creator, is not a manifestation of a primal or permanent cosmic substance, and did not appear causelessly.

DEVOTEE PROSTRATING AT BOUDHANATH STUPA, NEPAL

5. Purification by knowledge and vision of what is and is not the path (*maggāmagga ñāṇadassana visuddhi*) and the following purification involve cultivating *ten insight knowledges*. Having discerned the mind and matter of the three realms and their conditions, meditators prepare to cultivate the first knowledge by contemplating the three realms in terms of the five aggregates. That is, all matter whatsoever is included in the form aggregate, all feelings are consolidated in the feeling aggregate, and so on.

To cultivate the *knowledge of comprehension* (1), meditators apply the three characteristics to the five aggregates. Beginning with a longer time—"The body of this lifetime is impermanent"—they meditate on increasingly shorter periods of time—"The feelings of this year are unsatisfactory"—until they see that in each split second, the aggregates are impermanent, unsatisfactory, and not a self.

The *initial phase of the knowledge of arising and passing away* (2a) is developed by contemplating that the arising and ceasing of conditioned things is due to the presence or absence of their respective conditions. This contemplation is not done conceptually but by observing the very moment in which arising and passing away occur. In each nanosecond everything arises and passes away, giving way to the next moment that is equally transient.

As meditation deepens, *ten imperfections of insight* arise: (a) meditators see an aura of light radiating from their bodies; (b–d) they experience rapture, pliancy, and bliss in a way they never have before; (e) their resolution becomes stronger; (f) they exert themselves in practice; (g) their knowledge matures; (h) their mindful awareness becomes stable; (i) their equanimity becomes immovable; and (j) there is subtle enjoyment, clinging, and attachment to these experiences. This last factor is why they are called "imperfections": the mind relates to the first nine in an incorrect way. While these intriguing experiences that are natural byproducts of insight may give meditators the impression that their meditation is going well and they are developing special qualities—even the supramundane path and fruit—this is not the case. Not seeing the error in their discernment, they may stop insight meditation.

Purification by knowledge and vision of what is and is not the path is the ability to discern that these ten imperfections, no matter how fascinating they may be, are not the path to liberation and that insight into the three characteristics is the correct path to liberation. This purification is instrumental in keeping meditators on the right track so they will actualize their spiritual goal.

6. Purification by knowledge and vision of the way (*paṭipadā ñāṇadassana visuddhi*) involves generating the remaining nine insight knowledges with regard to the three characteristics. These become clearer and more stable due to the absence of the ten imperfections of insight during the *mature phase of the knowledge of arising and passing away* (2b).

To cultivate *knowledge of dissolution* (3), meditators focus only on things' ceasing. This reveals impermanence more deeply because they see that the conditioned things of saṃsāra are in a process of constant disintegration. There is nothing stable or trustworthy in them; they are wholly unsatisfactory; because they are only ceasing, how can a self exist in them?

With *knowledge of fearfulness* (4), they see these constantly disintegrating things of saṃsāra as fearful in that being attached to them binds one to dukkha. With *knowledge of danger* (5), they know with certainty that the fearful things of saṃsāra have the nature of dukkha and lack any core of a real self, and that safety exists only in the unconditioned, which is free from the unpredictability of impermanent things. With *knowledge of disenchantment* (6), meditators become disenchanted and disillusioned with saṃsāric phenomena. They clearly see the disadvantages of clinging to existence in the three realms.

With *knowledge of desire for liberation* (7), the momentum of turning away from saṃsāra and turning toward nibbāna increases, and meditators' motivation to be free from the world of conditioned existence grows stronger. With *knowledge of reflective contemplation* (8), they repeatedly review and examine conditioned things in light of the three characteristics in an expansive way. With *knowledge of equanimity toward formations* (9), they leave aside both attraction and aversion toward conditioned things and abide in equanimity. This mental state is a great relief that comes from the cultivation of proper wisdom regarding the five aggregates.

Knowledge of conformity (10) arises in the desire-realm consciousness that precedes the consciousness of the change of lineage (*gotrabhū*) that leads to the supramundane path. This knowledge conforms to the truth of the previous insight knowledges and of the supramundane path to follow.

7. Purification by knowledge and vision (*ñāṇadassana visuddhi*), according to Buddhaghosa, is knowledge of the four supramundane paths and thus is the only supramundane purification. Some moments of transition from purification by knowledge and vision of the way precede the breakthrough to the supramundane path as the mind "changes lineage" from being a mundane mind perceiving conditioned phenomena to a supramundane mind knowing nibbāna. The culmination of insight that occurs just before the first moment of the supramundane path focuses on the three characteristics. It is called *insight leading to emergence* because it leads to the supramundane path that emerges from conditioned phenomena by taking nibbāna, the unconditioned, as its object, and that emerges from mundane consciousness by eliminating some of the defilements.

This last moment of insight, called *change of lineage* consciousness, marks the transition from an ordinary being to an ariya. While it resembles the path by focusing on nibbāna, it is unlike the path because it cannot dispel the defilements that obscure seeing the four truths. The path consciousness that arises subsequent to the change of lineage consciousness performs four functions of: fully understanding dukkha; abandoning the origin of dukkha; realizing nibbāna; and cultivating the noble eightfold path.

Each path consciousness of stream-enterer and so forth performs these four functions, and when the corresponding level of defilements has been reduced or eradicated, that path consciousness is followed by the fruition consciousness.[22] After the fruition consciousness, a reviewing knowledge (*paccavekkhaṇañāṇa*) arises. It looks back and reflects on the path, fruit, and nibbāna, and often on the defilements that have been abandoned and those that remain. There is a tremendous sense of satisfaction, relief, and joy at this time, and meditators continue to practice until they reach the fruit of arahantship. In this way the knowledge of the four supramundane paths is accomplished, and the final goal, nibbāna, is attained.

Sanskrit Tradition: Five Paths and Ten Bodhisattva Grounds

Sentient beings' minds are obscured by two levels of obscurations, which are gradually eradicated as we progress along the path. *Afflictive obscurations* mainly hinder the attainment of liberation. They include the afflictions, their seeds—potentials producing another moment of the affliction—and polluted karma causing rebirth in saṃsāra. Afflictive obscurations have been eliminated by arhats, by bodhisattvas on the eighth ground and above, and by buddhas.

Cognitive obscurations are more subtle and difficult to remove. Mainly impeding omniscience, they prevent beings from directly perceiving both conventionalities and their emptiness simultaneously. They consist firstly of latencies (*vāsanā*) of the afflictions that remain on the mindstream even after the afflictions and their seeds have been eliminated, and secondly of the aspect of the mind that continues to mistakenly see inherent existence. Only buddhas have completely eradicated these. The Pāli tradition also refers to cognitive obscurations (*ñeyyāvaraṇa*) impeding full knowledge, which a buddha has abandoned.

Other cognitive obscurations are *dysfunctional tendencies* (*duṭṭhulla, dauṣṭulya*), latencies on the mindstreams of arhats that manifest in peculiar physical, verbal, and mental behavior. The Pāli commentary to the *Udāna* speaks of latencies (*vāsanā*) built up by defilements that produce similar dysfunctional actions in the future. These exist in the mindstreams of ordinary beings and arahants.

A consciousness that is a spiritual realization is called a *path* (*magga, marga*) because it leads out of saṃsāra and to awakening. A consciousness that is a spiritual realization is called a *ground* (*bhūmi*) because it is the foundation for the growth of good qualities and release from obscurations. The explanations of the paths of the Śrāvaka, Pratyekabuddha, and Bodhisattva vehicles are described here according to the Madhyamaka system.

Each of the three vehicles has five paths. The common features of the five paths in all three vehicles are described below; differences will be explained afterward.

1. The **path of accumulation** (*sambhāramārga*) is a clear realization of the doctrine—the words of the scriptures. It is called "accumulation" because at this stage practitioners accumulate great learning of the doctrine and begin accumulating the merit and wisdom leading to the goal of their chosen vehicle. Śrāvakas and pratyekabuddhas enter the path of accumulation of their vehicles when they have, day and night, the determination to be free from saṃsāra. Bodhisattvas enter their path of accumulation when they have genuine bodhicitta in addition to the determination to be free from saṃsāra.

2. The **path of preparation** (*prayogamārga*) is a clear realization of the meaning of the truth—emptiness, the ultimate nature. This path is a union of serenity and insight on emptiness. This realization is inferential: emptiness is known conceptually via a conceptual appearance. On this path practitioners prepare for direct perception of emptiness.

3. The **path of seeing** (*darśanamārga*) is a clear realization of the truth itself—emptiness. As āryas, these practitioners realize emptiness directly and nonconceptually, without any sense of subject and object. The mind and emptiness are fused like water poured into water. The path of seeing has three phases. (1) The *exalted wisdom of meditative equipoise* (*samāhitajñāna*) directly realizes emptiness and has no dualistic appearance whatsoever. It has three types: (a) The *uninterrupted path* (*ānantaryamārga*) abandons the acquired afflictions. (b) The *liberated path* (*vimuktimārga*) directly follows the uninterrupted path and is a wisdom that has definitely abandoned the acquired afflictions forever. (c) The *exalted wisdoms of meditative equipoise that are neither* occur when practitioners meditate on emptiness at other times. (2) The *exalted wisdoms of subsequent attainment* (*pṛṣṭhalabdhajñāna*) occur when practitioners arise from meditative equipoise, practice illusion-like meditation, and accumulate merit in order to attain higher paths. (3) The *exalted wisdoms that are neither meditative equipoise nor subsequent attainment* are nonmanifest exalted wisdoms.

4. The **path of meditation** (*bhāvanāmārga*) begins when practitioners have accumulated enough merit and their wisdom is powerful enough to begin eradicating the innate afflictions. The word for "meditation" has the same verbal root as that for "familiarize," and this path is so called because practitioners mainly familiarize themselves with the emptiness directly realized by the path of seeing.

The path of meditation has exalted wisdoms of meditative equipoise, exalted wisdoms of subsequent attainment, and exalted wisdoms that are neither of those. Here the uninterrupted paths counteract progressively subtle levels of obscurations, and liberated paths have definitely abandoned them.

5. The **path of no-more-learning** (*aśaikṣamārga*) of each vehicle is the highest goal of that vehicle. For śrāvakas and pratyekabuddhas, this wisdom has eradicated all afflictive obscurations and the person has attained arhatship; for bodhisattvas it has also eradicated cognitive obscurations and actualized buddhahood.

Spread over the bodhisattva paths of seeing and meditation are *ten bodhisattva grounds*. These ten are ultimate bodhicitta—unpolluted wisdom directly realizing the emptiness of inherent existence. This wisdom is conceptually divided into its earlier and later moments, forming these ten grounds. However, not every instance of a ground is ultimate bodhicitta; ārya bodhisattvas also meditate on conventional bodhicitta and engage in practices to create merit.

The ten grounds are differentiated by four features: (1) Each successive ground has a greater number of twelve sets of good qualities. These twelve qualities include seeing buddhas, receiving their inspiration, going to pure lands, having long lives, ripening sentient beings, and emanating bodies. (2) Each successive ground has greater power to eradicate obscurations and advance to a higher path. (3) Each ground has its own surpassing perfection that refines bodhisattvas' body, speech, and mind. (4) On each successive ground, bodhisattvas are able to take higher rebirths in which they have more power to benefit sentient beings.

Bodhisattvas finish eliminating afflictive obscurations at the beginning of the eighth ground. They finish eliminating cognitive obscurations at the end of the tenth ground and become buddhas in the very next moment.

Differences among the Three Vehicles

Śrāvakas meditate principally on the four truths and attain their awakening in three lifetimes according to the Sanskrit tradition and within seven lifetimes according to the Pāli tradition. Pratyekabuddhas meditate principally on dependent arising and accumulate merit for at least a hundred eons to attain their awakening. Bodhisattvas practicing Sūtrayāna accumulate merit for three countless great eons to attain buddhahood.

Stream-enterers are on the path of seeing; once-returners, nonreturners, and approachers to arhat are on the path of meditation. Arhats are on the path of no-more-learning. As liberated beings, they are no more bound in cyclic existence and will no longer take rebirth under the control of afflictions and polluted karma.

While the Pāli tradition does not use the schema of the five paths, it does use the names of four of the five paths to refer to similar stages of practitioners' development. In the late commentaries, *collections* (*sambhāra*) refers to requisites a practitioner must assemble to attain liberation. In the Abhidhamma, *seeing* (*dassana*) indicates the path of a stream-enterer, and *meditation* (*bhāvanā*) refers to the paths of once-returner, nonreturner, and arahant that gain familiarity with the view attained at stream-entry. *No training* (*asekha*) refers to arahantship or buddhahood and is the last ground. Buddhahood is called a ground and not a path because it marks the end of cultivation.

According to Mādhyamikas, āryas of all three vehicles directly and nonconceptually realize the same selflessness of persons and phenomena: their emptiness of inherent existence. Bodhisattvas attain a buddha's awakening due to special factors they cultivated on the path: the bodhicitta motivation, the vast collection of merit created over many eons, their training in the six perfections, their use of many reasonings to realize emptiness in order to teach them to others, and their abandoning of both the afflictive and cognitive obscurations.

Sanskrit Tradition: Nirvāṇa

In general, *nirvāṇa* or *liberation* (*vimokkha, vimokṣa*) is a state or quality of mind. It is not an external place or something reserved for a select few. Nirvāṇa is attainable by each and every sentient being.

The emptiness of mind—its natural purity or naturally abiding buddha nature—is the basis. On this basis, we undergo a process of purification by applying antidotes to eradicate the adventitious obscurations until the mind is totally free from afflictive obscurations. The purified state of the emptiness of the mind that is free from afflictive obscurations is true nirvāṇa. By realizing the ultimate nature of mind that itself is free from all afflictive obscurations, we attain nirvāṇa. Thus the understanding of emptiness eliminates the obscurations, and emptiness is also the resultant state present when all defilements have been cleansed from the mind.

In general, there are four types of nirvāṇa, although not all of them are actual nirvāṇa:

(1) *Natural nirvāṇa* is the ultimate nature of a mind that is primordially pure and empty of inherent existence. It is the basis allowing for the attainment of actual nirvāṇa. As the nature of the mind, it is a quality of the mind, so attaining actual nirvāṇa does not involve gaining a quality from outside. Rather it involves recognizing a quality of the mind that is already present.

In a more general sense, natural nirvāṇa is emptiness. Everything around us—as well as the four truths, the paths, and the resultant attainments—is empty of inherent existence, and in this way we can say it possesses natural nirvāṇa. However, only sentient beings can attain the nirvāṇa free from obscurations because that nirvāṇa is the emptiness of the mind.

In the terms (2) *nirvāṇa with remainder* and (3) *nirvāṇa without remainder*, "remainder" refers to the ordinary aggregates, which are true duḥkha because they arise due to ignorance and polluted karma. When śrāvakas and pratyekabuddhas eradicate all afflictive obscurations, they attain nirvāṇa with remainder and become arhats. When they later shed their body at death, there is nirvāṇa without remainder because the polluted aggregates have ceased.

Some Buddhists say at the time of nirvāṇa without remainder, the continuum of consciousness of the person ceases although the nirvāṇa without remainder exists. However, other Buddhists assert that all sentient beings will eventually attain buddhahood and the continuum of consciousness exists even after arhats pass away. At that time, arhats have a mental body and reside in a pure land, where they remain in meditative equipoise on emptiness. At the appropriate time, the Buddha arouses them from their meditative equipoise and causes them to enter the bodhisattva path and attain a buddha's awakening.

ANGKOR WAT, CAMBODIA

Mādhyamikas assert a second meaning of nirvāṇa with and without remainder. Here "remainder" refers to the appearance of inherent existence and the dualistic appearance of subject and object. *Nirvāṇa without remainder* is a true cessation occurring during āryas' meditative equipoise on emptiness when the mind is free from these two mistaken appearances. Upon arising from meditative equipoise on emptiness, āryas again experience the false appearance of inherent existence, even though they see things as like illusions in that they appear inherently existent although they are not. This is called *nirvāṇa with remainder* because dualistic appearances are present.

In the first presentation, nirvāṇa with remainder occurs first, followed by nirvāṇa without remainder. In the second presentation, the order is reversed.

Nāgārjuna says that what the Pāli tradition calls *extinction* or cessation, the Sanskrit tradition calls *nirvāṇa* (RA 386):

> The non-arisal taught in the Mahāyāna
> and the extinction [taught] for other [Buddhists]
> are [both] emptiness. Therefore, one should admit
> that extinction and non-arisal are ultimately the same.

Extinction in the Pāli tradition refers to nibbāna without remainder, the nibbāna of an arahant who has abandoned the polluted aggregates at death. Nāgārjuna extends the meaning of extinction to include the nonappearance (non-arisal) of inherently existent phenomena because in the Sanskrit tradition "remainder" also refers to the appearance of inherent existence.

(4) *Nonabiding nirvāṇa* is the nirvāṇa of a buddha who does not abide in either saṃsāra or the personal nirvāṇa of a śrāvaka arhat. All Buddhists see saṃsāra as undesirable. Wishing to actualize a buddha's awakening to benefit sentient beings most effectively, bodhisattvas see the personal nirvāṇa of an arhat as limited. They seek a buddha's nirvāṇa, the purified aspect of the ultimate nature of a mind that is forever free of both afflictive and cognitive obscurations.

Pāli Tradition: Nibbāna

Nibbāna refers to the elimination of clinging to the five appropriated aggregates (*sakkāya*). It is the state of cessation in which both dukkha and its origins have been eradicated. Nibbāna is also spoken of as the object of meditation, the reality that is directly seen by ariyas' supramundane wisdom.

When speaking of "nibbāna as the cessation of dukkha and its origins," the Buddha described his awakening (MN 26:19):

> I considered: "This Dhamma that I have attained is profound, hard to see and hard to understand, peaceful and sublime, unattainable by mere reasoning, subtle, to be experienced by the wise.... It is hard for such a population to see this truth, namely, specific conditionality, dependent arising. And it is hard to see this truth, namely, the stilling of all formations, the relinquishing of all attachments, the destruction of craving, dispassion, cessation, nibbāna."

The Pāli commentary says "this Dhamma" refers to the four truths. "Specific conditionality, dependent arising" refers to true origins, and "stilling of all formations, the relinquishing of all attachments, the destruction of craving, dispassion, cessation, nibbāna" refers to true cessation. The reference to true origin implies true dukkha, and the reference to true cessation implies true path. Thus in nibbāna all four truths have been realized. Here *nibbāna* is the extinguishment of all attachment and craving (true origins) and leads to the extinguishment of the aggregates (true dukkha) at death. Similarly, Sāriputta said nibbāna is "the destruction of sensual desire, the destruction of hatred, the destruction of confusion" (SN 38:1). This meaning of nibbāna focuses on the cessation of true origins.

Many suttas present nibbāna as the "object of a supramundane path." The Buddha said there are three unconditioned marks of nibbāna: no arising, vanishing, or changing is discerned (AN 3:47). Unlike conditioned phenomena that arise and pass away, nibbāna—the unconditioned—is free from such fluctuation. It does not arise or vanish due to causes and conditions, nor does it change into something else. Nibbāna is true, in contrast to the world, which is deceptive. Nibbāna is a distinct phenomenon that has nothing to do with matter or the deepest samādhis of saṃsāra. Nibbāna is illustrated via negation—no coming, no going, not made, and so forth—without anything being posited in their stead (Ud 8:1). The *Abhidhammattha Saṅgaha* explains nibbāna as the object of only a supramundane path—the supreme, ultimate mind cognizing the supreme, ultimate object (CMA p. 258).

The suttas and Abhidhamma say nibbāna has three aspects: Nibbāna is emptiness (*suññatā, śūnyatā*) because it is empty of ignorance, anger, and attachment and empty of the conditioned. It is signless (*animitta*) because it is free from the signs of ignorance, anger, and attachment and the signs of conditioned things. Nibbāna is wishless (*appaṇihita, apraṇihita*) because it is free of hankering for ignorance, anger, and attachment and is not wished for by craving (CMA p. 260).

The Sanskrit tradition speaks of these three attributes as three perspectives of selflessness. Emptiness refers to the lack of inherent existence of the *entity* of an object, signlessness to the lack of inherent existence of its *cause*, and wishlessness to the lack of inherent existence of its *result*.

Buddhaghosa refutes a number of misconceptions about nibbāna. Nibbāna is not nonexistent. It exists because it is apprehended by the supramundane path. The fact that ordinary beings' limited minds cannot perceive it does not render it nonexistent. If nibbāna were nonexistent, practicing the path would be futile.

Nibbāna is not simply the absence of defilements and the ceasing of existence. It is called the "destruction of craving" because realizing it brings about the destruction of craving. If nibbāna were the destruction of craving, it would not be the unconditioned because the destruction of craving is a conditioned event. While the destruction of craving is produced by causes, nibbāna is uncaused and has no beginning or end (Vism 16:71).

While nibbāna is realized by cultivating wisdom over time, it does not come into being through the act of being realized. Nibbāna always exists as the unconditioned element; it is the unborn, unoriginated, unchanging, deathless. Because nibbāna exists, the eradication of defilements is possible (Ud 8:3). The ariya path realizes the unconditioned, and this realization cuts off the defilements.

Pāli commentators show the compatibility of the two senses of nibbāna in the suttas: (1) as the goal, it is a blissful state free from dukkha and its origins that can be experienced in this life and, (2) as the object of meditation, it is the unconditioned, the unborn that always exists and is seen by the supramundane path and fruit. It is called the "destruction of attachment, anger, and confusion" because the realization of the unconditioned element has the effect of cutting away and finally eliminating these three.

Nibbāna is the unconditioned, in contrast to saṃsāra, which is conditioned. Nibbāna is completely separate from the saṃsāric world governed by dependent arising. Nibbāna, which is reality, is also distinct from selflessness, which is a characteristic of saṃsāric phenomena.

For Mādhyamikas, all phenomena of both saṃsāra and nirvāṇa lack inherent existence and thus are selfless and empty. While *nirvāṇa* is often used to refer to the cessation of true duḥkha and true origins, its real meaning is the emptiness of the purified mind.

11 The Four Immeasurables

THE FOUR IMMEASURABLES or "boundless states"—love, compassion, joy, and equanimity—are widely taught and practiced in both the Pāli and Sanskrit traditions. They are called "immeasurable" because they are directed toward immeasurable sentient beings with a mind free from partiality and because they are states of jhāna that are not limited by the five hindrances of the desire-realm mind. They are also called the *brahmavihāras* after the brahmā worlds of the first jhāna, where beings' minds are gentle. *Brahma* also implies "pure," for these four are free from attachment, anger, and apathy. They are called *vihāras*, or "abodes," because they are peaceful resting places for our mind.

Pāli Tradition

The four immeasurables (*appamañña*, *apramāṇa*) are spoken of in many Pāli suttas, and the *Visuddhimagga* devotes a full chapter to this practice. The *Mettā Sutta* (Sn 1:8) speaks of immeasurable love and is one of the most popular and oft-recited suttas. While meditation on the four immeasurables can lead to rebirth in a material realm, the further aim of this meditation is to attain a pliable, concentrated mind—a liberation of mind—that can be used as a basis for insight into the three characteristics.

One way to practice the four immeasurables enriches our relationships with others. *Love* has the aspect of friendliness toward sentient beings and wishes them to be well and happy. This should be our basic attitude toward living beings. When seeing sentient beings' suffering, we respond with *compassion*, thus abandoning fear and disgust, and do what we can to be of assistance. When we witness their happiness, success, virtue, and good qualities, our response is *joy*—the opposite of jealousy. When our aim for others' welfare is not accomplished or others are not receptive to our help, we remain balanced and *equanimous*.

Love "has the aspect of friendliness.... Its proximate cause is seeing others as loveable. When it succeeds, it eliminates malice. When it fails, it degenerates into selfish affectionate desire" (Vism 9:93). The latter is the affliction of clinging attachment, which is often called "love" in society. Genuine love spreads to both those who treat us well and those who don't. It is firm and does not waver according to our mood or how others treat us. It is ready to help but does not coerce others to fulfill our wishes.

Combining love with the understanding of not-self demolishes any sense of possession. This love knows that ultimately there is no possessor or person to possess, no substantially existent person to give or receive love. The highest love wishes beings to have the highest happiness, nibbāna.

Compassion "has the aspect of allaying suffering.... Its proximate cause is seeing helplessness in those overwhelmed by suffering. When it succeeds, it reduces cruelty. When it fails, it produces personal distress" (Vism 9:94). Compassion enables us to look at suffering in all its tortuous varieties without succumbing to despair. It motivates us to reach out to others directly or indirectly in order to alleviate their suffering. Compassion does not favor some and exclude others: it isn't limited to those who are obviously experiencing suffering. It does not blame others for their suffering but realizes that suffering ultimately stems from ignorance.

Joy delights at the happiness and good fortune of others and opposes jealousy. Meditating on joy enables us to see the goodness in the world. Joy "is characterized by bringing joy.... Its proximate cause is seeing beings' success. When it succeeds, it reduces jealousy and boredom. When it fails, it produces overexcitement" (Vism 9:95).

Equanimity is a balanced mind that remains tranquil and steady no matter what we encounter. It is not apathetic indifference that builds walls to protect us from pain. Equanimity allows our spiritual practice to stay on track, without being buffeted around by excitement or intense emotions. Clinging to nothing, equanimity gives space to appreciate everything. Equanimity "is characterized by promoting the aspect of balance toward beings. Its proximate cause is seeing the ownership of kamma thus: 'Beings are owners of their kamma....' When it succeeds, it makes anger and attachment subside. When it fails, it produces an unknowing equanimity" (Vism

9:96). Understanding kamma engenders equanimity. People meet with results caused by their own actions. Understanding that there is no I or mine releases craving and other afflictions, allowing equanimity to arise.

Joyous effort is crucial when beginning to practice the four immeasurables. Taming the hindrances by applying their antidotes is important in the middle, as practice continues. Meditative absorption is essential at the end.

Love

Since hostility is the opposite of love and prevents its development, we begin by reflecting on the disadvantages of hostility and the benefits of fortitude. Hostility crushes trust and tears apart valued relationships; it destroys our merit and compels us to act in ways we later regret. Fortitude, or patience, is like a soothing balm. It attracts others to us and protects our virtue.

At the beginning, it is important to cultivate love toward specific people in a definite order. Do not begin the cultivation of any of the four immeasurables toward someone to whom you are or could be sexually attracted. The people should be alive because we don't know what form the deceased are in now.

When cultivating love, begin by using yourself as an example. Contemplate repeatedly, "May I be happy and free from suffering. May I be free from hostility, affliction, and anxiety and live happily." Generating love toward ourselves isn't selfish because the goal is to generate love toward *all* beings, which includes ourselves. We, too, are worthy of love and kindness. This meditation counteracts self-hatred, freeing us to develop our potential.

Then contemplate, "Just as I want to be happy, so too do other beings." Cultivate love for someone you respect and hold in high regard, such as your spiritual mentor or another teacher. If we begin by cultivating love for a dear one, attachment may easily arise under the guise of love; however, this will not happen toward someone you respect. Recalling the help you have received from this person, contemplate, "May he be happy and free from suffering. May he be free from hostility, affliction, and anxiety and live happily."

Then extend your love more broadly, first to a dear friend, thinking in the same way as above. When the mind is malleable, generate love for a neutral person, seeing her as a very dear friend. When you can do this, cultivate love for an enemy, seeing her as neutral. "Enemy" means someone you are hostile or critical toward. The person does not have to be one who reciprocates those disturbing emotions.

This step can be difficult because anger or the wish for revenge may arise toward those who have harmed you. If you cannot get past these disturbing emotions, return to meditating on love toward one of the previous persons, and when the mind is drenched in that feeling, again generate love for the enemy.

If hostility persists, apply an antidote, such as the ones offered below. If one doesn't release the anger, try another. Begin by remembering the disadvantages of hostility. The Buddha details seven disadvantages of anger (AN 7:64): While an enemy may wish us to be ugly, experience pain, lack prosperity, wealth, a good reputation, harmonious relationships, and have an unfortunate rebirth, we bring all these upon ourselves through our own anger. Letting our mind dwell in animosity destroys our virtue and inhibits our spiritual progress.

Hearing others' disturbing speech often triggers anger in the mind. Here the Buddha counsels us (MN 21:11):

> ...you should train thus: "Our minds will remain unaffected, and we shall utter no evil words; we shall abide compassionate for their welfare, with a mind of love, without inner hate. We shall abide pervading that person with a mind imbued with love, and starting with him, we shall abide pervading the all-encompassing world with a mind imbued with love, abundant, exalted, immeasurable, without hostility and without malice."

This is love in the state of jhāna (Vism 9:44). Such love will carry over when we leave the jhāna state and return to an everyday state of mind. Even if we have not attained jhāna, training our mind to approach all beings with a loving attitude will overwhelm our discomfort, suspicion, and malice and imbue us with ease and affection for all.

Reflecting on the person's good qualities when he is in a congenial situation enables us to dispel our critical attitude. We can then recall this when he creates trouble. If it is difficult to see any good qualities in the person, generate compassion for him, thinking of the destructive kamma he is creating and the suffering he will experience as a result. There is no use wishing harm to someone who is bringing harm upon himself. It is better to generate compassion for him.

Thinking of the Buddha's responses to aggression in his previous lives as a bodhisatta can inspire us to forgive others for their faults. The *Jātaka* collection tells many stories of the bodhisatta's previous lives in which he responded to aggressors with compassion.

Reflecting that all sentient beings have been our mother, father, siblings, and children, we see that they have all benefited us in the past and that it is therefore unfitting to harbor enmity for them. Our affection and gratitude for others then overpowers any resentment.

We can also ask ourselves, "Who am I angry at? Among the five aggregates in dependence on which this person is called so-and-so, what aggregate am I angry with?" Searching for the real person who is the source of our anger becomes like painting in space.

Another suggestion is to give the person a gift. Others' hostility toward us and ours toward them subsides when a gift is given and received earnestly.

Once the anger and resentment have dissipated, cultivate love toward the enemy just as you did toward the others.

Reciting the formula "May you be happy and free from suffering! May you be free from hostility, affliction, and anxiety and live happily!" is a tool to help us generate the mental state those words indicate. If the recitation becomes mechanical, express the meaning in your own words. Alternatively, think in more detail about the types of happiness you wish someone to have and imagine her having them. Make the meditation more personal. Slowly your love will arise and gain momentum. After a while the meditation will carry on by itself without need to use the formula.

The next step is to "break down the barriers" by seeing the five individuals—yourself, the respected person, the friend, the neutral person, and the enemy—as equal and generate love for them equally. When the barriers between the five people have been broken down and you are able to extend love equally to all five, simultaneously the counterpart sign appears and access concentration is attained. Repeatedly practicing the counterpart sign, you will attain the full concentration of the first jhāna. With this, the five hindrances have been suppressed, the five absorption factors are present, and the liberation of mind by love (*mettācetovimutti*) is attained. It is so called because in that absorption the mind is liberated from anger and hostility. This is also called "love as a divine abode."

Only upon gaining the first jhāna, a meditator (MN 43:31):

> ...abides pervading one quarter with a mind imbued with loving-kindness, likewise the second, likewise the third, likewise the fourth; so above, below, around, and everywhere, and to all as to himself, he abides pervading the entire world with a mind imbued with loving-kindness, abundant, exalted, immeasurable, without hostility and without malice.

To gain this further development of love, extend love to one direction—the east—so that it pervades all sentient beings there. When doing this, begin small, thinking of one dwelling and extending love to everyone there. Then expand love to two dwellings and, gradually, to the town, state, and so forth in one direction. When that meditation is firm, gradually add the beings in the other three cardinal directions, the four intermediate directions, and up and down—radiating love in each place, one by one.

Then extend love everywhere without specifying a particular direction, realm of existence, social status, race, ethnicity, religion, gender, and so on. Unmarred by negative feelings, grief, or suffering, this immeasurable love is pure, impartial, and unconditional.

Together with extending the range of your love, intensify it by remembering that in our beginningless rebirths we have all been each other's mothers. This helps to break down feelings of separateness and open our hearts to love all beings as if they were our children. The *Mettā Sutta* says, "As a mother would, with all her life, protect her only child, so one should develop a boundless heart toward all beings."

Practicing love as a divine abode entails practicing it at all times when you are awake and in all postures—sitting, standing, lying down, and walking. As meditation continues, the second and third jhānas in the fourfold schema will be gained.

In the early stages of cultivating love, thought and imagination are necessary. But once love is aroused and becomes strong and stable, these are unnecessary. The mind becomes absorbed in the experience of love, and radiating love takes on a momentum of its own.

The liberation of mind by love is practiced with *universal pervasion* by extending it to all beings, then all breathing things, all creatures, all persons, and all those with a personality. While these five terms are synonymous, meditating on them individually gives us different perspectives on the object of our love. The liberation of mind by love is practiced with *specific pervasion* by extending love to groups of women, men, ariyas, ordinary beings, devas, human beings, and those born in unfortunate realms.

The liberation of mind by love is cultivated to pervade the ten directions in ten ways, by thinking as above toward all beings in the ten directions and then thinking of the twelve types of beings—the five unspecific and the seven specific—in each of the directions. In addition, each of the phrases in the formula—"be free from hostility," "be free from affliction," "be free from anxiety," and "live happily"—is one meditative absorption, so when combined there are quite a number.

The Buddha said that practitioners of the liberation of mind through love will experience eleven benefits (AN 11:15):

> You sleep well; you awaken happily; you do not have bad dreams; you are pleasing to human beings; you are pleasing to spirits; deities protect you; fire, poison, and weapons do not injure you; your mind quickly becomes concentrated; your facial complexion is serene; you die unconfused; and if you do not penetrate further, you fare on to the brahmā world.

Using the liberation of mind by love as the basis for developing insight, you can attain arahantship. This is done by meditating in a jhāna, then leaving that state and analyzing its components. Through doing this, you see that even this blissful state of concentration is impermanent, unsatisfactory, and selfless. Such insight into the three characteristics will lead to the realization of nibbāna and the eradication of all fetters.

Compassion

Similar to meditation on love, the cultivation of compassion begins with contemplating the disadvantages of lacking compassion and the benefits of having it. The first person you cultivate compassion for should be someone in great suffering. You may or may not know him personally, although compassion will arise more strongly by directly seeing the person. If you do not encounter an appropriate person, you can cultivate compassion for someone creating horrendous destructive kamma, even if he appears happy

CALLING THE ASSEMBLY AT A VIETNAMESE TEMPLE

at the moment. Do this by comparing him to someone given delicious food just before being executed.

After generating compassion for a suffering person, do so for a dear person, followed by a neutral person, and finally an enemy. Should you feel anger toward an enemy, counteract it through the methods described above. If any of these people are not experiencing gross suffering at the moment, cultivate compassion by recalling that they are still under the control of afflictions and kamma and therefore are not free from the suffering of pervasive conditioning.

Then break down the barriers between the four kinds of people—ourselves, dear ones, neutral people, and enemies—until the counterpart sign appears and access concentration is attained. By repeatedly meditating on that sign, you attain the first three jhānas. Such concentration enables your mind to be pliant and versatile so that you can meditate on compassion for all sentient beings in all the directions as described in the meditation on love. The eleven advantages as detailed above also accrue.

When viewing others' suffering and cultivating compassion, if you become overwhelmed by feelings of despair or helplessness, you have missed the mark. Distress about others' suffering, anger at societal forces that cause suffering, or frustration with others for getting themselves into predicaments may be natural emotions for ordinary beings, but they are far from the Buddhist meaning of compassion. Compassion is the wish for others to be free from suffering, and to cultivate it we must remain focused on responding with tender concern and the wish to help.

Joy

Empathetic joy rejoices at success, good qualities, and happiness. Cultivate joy first for a dear person who is good-natured and happy and whose happiness and success merits rejoicing. If the person had success in the past or you expect she will in the future, rejoice about that too. Having generated joy for this dear person, cultivate joy for a neutral person and then an enemy. The means of subduing anger for the enemy, breaking down the barriers, cultivating and repeatedly practicing the sign, increasing the absorption up to the third jhāna, cultivating versatility, and reaping the benefits are as explained above.

Equanimity

Having become familiar with the third jhāna on love, compassion, and joy, emerge from it and contemplate the "risks" of the previous three immeasurables and the benefits of equanimity. The preceding three immeasurables are "risky" because attachment and anger are not far away. For example, while developing love, attachment could arise instead. Also, the previous three immeasurables are associated with happiness, which decreases the depth of concentration. Thus seek equanimity, a constancy or steadiness of mind. With equanimity, we are free from longing and aversion for others. We accept happiness and suffering by understanding that they arise due to kamma created by that person. This equanimity is not indifference, for meditators have already gained jhāna on love, compassion, and joy. While equanimity remains peaceful and receptive, the three previous immeasurables imbue it with calm affection for sentient beings and balanced involvement with them.

Having contemplated love, compassion, and joy, focus on a neutral person and cultivate equanimity. When this is stable, meditate on equanimity toward a dear one followed by equanimity toward an enemy.

Breaking down the barriers and cultivating and repeatedly practicing the sign are as above. Through this you will enter the fourth jhāna. Only after attaining the first, second, and third jhānas on love, compassion, and joy can you attain the fourth jhāna on equanimity.

Your practice will expand by being versatile in the levels of jhāna you enter and in the range of positive emotions you experience. This affects your ability to reach out and benefit others in your daily life.

Even after attaining awakening, the Buddha continued to meditate on all four immeasurables. He was a loving, compassionate, and joyful individual whose evenness of mind enabled him to be effective in diverse situations with a variety of people.

Buddhaghosa compares the sequential cultivation of the four immeasurables with the changing attitude parents have toward their children. When the baby is in the womb, the parents think with a loving mind, "When will we see our child healthy?" After he is born, when the adorable baby lies on his back and cries because he had a bad dream, the parents feel compassion. When the child grows up and the parents see him playing and learning, they feel joy at their child's happiness. When the child is grown and becomes a responsible adult in his own right, the parents have equanimity knowing he can take care of himself. This analogy shows the usefulness of each attitude in specific situations.

Four Immeasurables and Insight

A "liberation of mind" is a state of concentration resulting from serenity. It is liberated in that it is free from the five hindrances. Alone it cannot bring liberation from saṃsāra, but when it is used to meditate on the three characteristics and nibbāna, the resulting insight leads to liberation.

For example, meditators who develop the first jhāna based on love enter into that jhāna through love. After stabilizing the jhāna on love, they emerge from that state, look back at it, and examine it. The experience of jhāna is so blissful that if they did not examine it, they would easily become attached to it, forgoing liberation in favor of the bliss of samādhi.

But when they analyze the jhāna, they see it is simply a mental state. There is a pleasant or equanimous feeling, some discrimination, various other volitional factors such as love, attention, contact, intention, and concentration. The mental primary mind, the three other mental aggregates, and the physical body are also present. By dissecting the jhāna of love into its parts, they see it is a composite phenomenon consisting of the five aggregates. With insight, these meditators see the jhāna is impermanent because it arises and ceases due to conditions. Because it arises and perishes in every moment, it cannot bring lasting happiness and is unsatisfactory in nature. Being impermanent and unsatisfactory, it is not worth clinging to; it is not I, mine, or myself. There is no substantially real person findable within or different from the ever-changing collection of body and mind.

Continuing to investigate their experience of the jhāna more deeply by seeing it in light of the three characteristics, their wisdom increases until there is a breakthrough and they perceive the unconditioned, nibbāna. They become stream-enterers and begin the process of abandoning the fetters, eventually becoming arahants.

Some ariyas cultivate the four immeasurables and are reborn in the brahmā worlds after death. They continue to practice insight there and become arahants. This is very different from a worldling who cultivates the four immeasurables for the purpose of being born in the brahmā worlds. This person lacks insight and wisdom as well as interest in developing them; he will be born in an unfortunate realm after the kamma for rebirth in the brahmā worlds has been exhausted.

Near and Far Enemies

Each of the four immeasurables has a "near enemy" and a "far enemy," the former being an affliction that is similar in some way to the unafflicted immeasurable, and the latter being an affliction that is the opposite of that immeasurable. We must ensure that we are free from both.

Near enemies are hard to detect. The near enemy of love is attachment because both emotions see the good qualities in the other person. However, attachment clings to others with unrealistic expectations, and the affection we feel is polluted with possessiveness and neediness. Compassion's near enemy is personal distress. This grief is based on worldly life and is the sadness felt when our dear ones are unhappy. It is similar to compassion in that both have an element of sorrow due to others' misery. The near enemy of joy is happiness based on worldly life—delight at receiving sense pleasures or status in the past or present. Giddy with excitement, we become too involved and attached to someone else's happiness. Equanimity's near enemy is indifference and apathy based on worldly life. They are similar to equanimity in that they don't notice the faults or good qualities of others.

The far enemy of love is anger and malice; the far enemy of compassion is cruelty; the far enemy of joy is jealousy and boredom; the far enemy of equanimity is attachment, anger, prejudice, and partiality.

Sanskrit Tradition

The four immeasurables are extensively explained in the *Bodhisattvapiṭaka Sūtra* and are essential in the Bodhisattva Vehicle. In general, they are contemplated at the beginning of a meditation session to stabilize and increase bodhicitta. One version of the four immeasurables is:

> May all sentient beings have happiness and its causes.
> May all sentient beings be free of suffering and its causes.
> May all sentient beings not be separated from sorrowless bliss.
> May all sentient beings abide in equanimity, free of bias,
> attachment, and anger.

Another version is:

> How wonderful it would be if all sentient beings were to abide in equanimity, free of bias, attachment, and anger. May they abide in this way. I shall cause them to abide in this way. Buddha, please inspire me to be able to do so.
>
> How wonderful it would be if all sentient beings had happiness and its causes. May they have these. I shall cause them to have these. Buddha, please inspire me to be able to do so.
>
> How wonderful it would be if all sentient beings were free from suffering and its causes. May they be free. I shall cause them to be free. Buddha, please inspire me to be able to do so.
>
> How wonderful it would be if all sentient beings were never parted from upper rebirth and liberation's excellent bliss. May they never be parted. I shall cause them never to be parted. Buddha, please inspire me to be able to do so.

In the first version, equanimity comes at the end. This emphasizes our wish that others enjoy the peace of being free from attachment to friends, anger toward enemies, and apathy for strangers.

In the second version equanimity comes at the beginning, providing the basis to generate impartial love, compassion, and joy. Here the sequence of the four immeasurables is a synopsis of the sevenfold cause-and-effect instruction to generate bodhicitta, which is explained in more detail in the next chapter. First we release attachment, anger, and apathy toward sentient beings—this is the equanimity meditation that is preliminary to the seven instructions. Second we meditate on love, which comprises the first four instructions—seeing all sentient beings as our mother, recognizing their kindness, wishing to repay it, and love. Third we cultivate compassion, which is the fifth instruction. This leads to the great resolve and bodhicitta, the sixth and seventh instructions. With bodhicitta, we work for sentient beings' temporal and definitive welfare—their upper rebirth and liberation respectively. This is the expanded meaning of joy wishing sentient beings are never separated from whatever happiness they have obtained.

In the second version of the four immeasurables, each verse has four parts, which gradually intensify the emotion: (1) a wish ("How wonderful it would be..."), (2) an aspiration ("May they..."), (3) a resolution ("I shall cause them..."), and (4) a request to the Buddha for inspiration ("Buddha, please inspire me to be able to do so").

Using love as an example, first we have the wish that sentient beings have happiness and its causes. Focusing on this wish, our feeling intensifies and we aspire that they have these. Then we get involved and make a resolution, taking responsibility to actualize our wish. Because energy and determination are needed to fulfill this resolution, we seek inspiration and support from the Buddha and our spiritual mentor. Our feeling of love becomes strong and stable, as does our confidence to engage in whatever is necessary so that sentient beings will have happiness and its causes.

The phrase "and its causes" is explicitly added when generating love and compassion, indicating a wish that sentient beings understand the law of karma and its effects and the path to awakening so that they will create causes for happiness and cease creating causes for suffering.

Joy is expressed as wishing all beings to attain liberation—undeclining peace that is free from sorrow. It also rejoices in others' temporal happiness and does not want them to be separated from the happiness they already have. We also rejoice that sentient beings already have buddha nature, the pure nature of mind that makes awakening possible.

Equanimity refers to both equanimity toward others in the meditator's mind and equanimity in the minds of all sentient beings. We wish all sentient beings to experience equanimity so that their minds will be free from gross attachment and anger and they receive equal benefit.

In his *Abhisamayālaṃkāra* Maitreya says equanimity, love, compassion, and joy are not immeasurable unless they are accompanied by an actual dhyāna. Thus meditation on these four qualities may be done to increase our bodhicitta and/or to develop dhyāna.

Combining the four immeasurables with wisdom is done by viewing agents, objects, and actions as empty of inherent existence. Taking love as an example, that means contemplating that the meditator generating love for sentient beings, the sentient beings who are the object of that love, and the action of wishing them to have happiness and its causes are dependent events and thus empty of inherent nature. This wisdom conjoined with the four immeasurables and bodhicitta leads to full awakening, whereas without this wisdom, meditation on the four immeasurables will at best lead to rebirth in the brahmā worlds.

12 | Bodhicitta

BODHICITTA—the aspiration to attain full awakening for the benefit of all sentient beings—is the magnificent motivation that enabled Siddhārtha Gautama to become a bodhisattva and then a buddha and to turn the Dharma wheel. Both the Pāli and Sanskrit traditions speak of bodhicitta, bodhisattvas, and bodhisattva practices.

Tibetan Buddhism

Deep and continuous meditation on the defects of saṃsāra gives rise to *renunciation*—the aspiration for liberation. This aspiration is self-compassion wanting ourselves to be free from suffering and its causes. Knowing all sentient beings also experience the defects of saṃsāra and wanting them to be free is compassion that is the basis for bodhicitta.

The benefits of bodhicitta are many. Bodhicitta makes the mind very joyful due to having great love and compassion for all beings. It is the distinguishing cause of a buddha's full awakening. Bodhisattvas manage problems and difficulties with ease and act in ways that bring peace in the larger society. At the beginning of our Dharma practice, bodhicitta inspires us to practice diligently, in the middle it motivates us to eliminate all defilements, and at the end it enables us to do limitless work to benefit sentient beings and lead them to liberation and full awakening.

Bodhisattvas must engage in all practices of the Śrāvaka Vehicle, including the prātimokṣa ethics of restraining from harmful physical and verbal actions. In addition, they train in the bodhisattva ethical code to counter self-centeredness. Bodhisattvas seek to attain the dharmakāya—a buddha's omniscient mind—to fulfill *their own purpose* of having a totally purified mind, and they want to attain a buddha's form body (*rūpakāya*) to fulfill *the purpose of others* by manifesting in different forms to lead them on the path.

Bodhisattvas' compassion is so strong that if it were more beneficial for sentient beings for bodhisattvas to stay in saṃsāra, they would do that. However, since they can benefit sentient beings more after eliminating their defilements, they practice diligently. Upon eliminating all afflictive obscurations, bodhisattvas do not abide in nirvāṇa but have a mental body and emanate various forms that benefit saṃsāric beings and accumulate merit. They continue practicing until they eradicate all obscurations and attain full awakening.

Śāntarakṣita in his *Madhyamakālaṃkāra* explains the sequence of meditation for two types of bodhisattva aspirants. Those with *modest faculties* initially generate renunciation, followed by compassion for all sentient beings. They admire bodhicitta due to having strong confidence in those who teach bodhicitta, and their aspiration to attain awakening derives from their ardent faith in the Three Jewels. They generate bodhicitta, practice the perfections, and then cultivate insight into emptiness.

Bodhisattva aspirants with *sharp faculties* are not content to believe that awakening is possible because the Three Jewels and their spiritual mentors say so. They investigate to determine if ignorance can be eliminated. Seeing that the wisdom realizing emptiness can overcome it, they strive to gain at least a correct inference of emptiness, thus generating certainty that awakening is possible. On this basis, they generate bodhicitta. With bodhicitta informed by the wisdom realizing emptiness, they then practice the perfections.

Cultivating compassion and wisdom in tandem is very beneficial. As our understanding of emptiness increases, so will our compassion for sentient beings, who are under the influence of ignorance. Meanwhile compassion temporarily counteracts many of the coarser afflictions, facilitating meditation on emptiness.

Two methods exist to train the mind in bodhicitta: (1) the sevenfold cause-and-effect instruction and (2) equalizing and exchanging self and others. In both of these, the principal cause of bodhicitta is great compassion. This in turn depends on seeing others as pleasing and loveable and feeling the depth of their duḥkha.

Equanimity

To have unbiased love and compassion for all beings, we must first free our minds from coarse attachment to friends and relatives, apathy toward strangers, and hostility toward enemies. As mentioned above, cultivating equanimity is the way to do this.

To develop equanimity we reflect that our categorization of people as friends, enemies, and strangers is unstable and highly subjective. If someone is nice to us today, we consider her a friend and become attached. But if tomorrow she criticizes us, our fondness evaporates, and she becomes an enemy. When we lose touch with a friend or an enemy, that person becomes a stranger. Meanwhile today's strangers may become friends or enemies in the future, and if we meet an enemy in a different situation, he becomes a friend. There is nothing fixed in any of these relationships. We have been each other's friends, enemies, and strangers countless times in beginningless saṃsāra. Given this, there is no reason to be partial for or against any sentient being.

Having equal, openhearted care for others does not mean we treat or trust everyone equally. Conventional roles and relationships still exist. We trust old friends more than strangers, even though we want both equally to be happy and free from suffering. While maintaining equanimity internally, we can still prevent someone from harming us.

Sevenfold Cause-and-Effect Instruction

Founded on the practice of equanimity, the first three causes help us to cultivate love and compassion. These are (1) *recognizing that all sentient beings have been our parents* in previous lives, (2) *contemplating their kindness* when they were our parents, and (3) *wishing to repay their kindness*. These three bring forth (4) deep affection and *heart-warming love* for all beings, which leads to (5) *compassion*.

Compassion has two principal aspects: a sense of closeness to others and concern for their suffering. Seeing sentient beings as loveable through remembering their kindness creates a sense of intimacy, affection, and dearness in our hearts. Meditating on the fact that sentient beings undergo the three kinds of duḥkha—especially duḥkha of pervasive conditioning—stimulates heartfelt concern for their suffering. Bringing these two together arouses genuine compassion for all beings.

The torment others undergo due to the two obscurations becomes unbearable to us, and the compassion arising from that produces (6) *great resolve*, assuming the responsibility to work for the welfare of sentient beings. This primarily means liberating them from saṃsāra, although benefiting them temporarily in saṃsāra is also included. The great resolve is the wholehearted commitment to act to bring about others' happiness and protect them from duḥkha.

These six causes lead to (7) the effect, *bodhicitta*. To transform great resolve into bodhicitta, we reflect that for sentient beings to be happy and free from suffering, they must create the appropriate causes for these. To teach them how to do this and guide them on the path, we must know through our own experience all the practices and paths to full awakening. We must also discern others' spiritual dispositions and tendencies and know the practices suitable for them. To fully develop these abilities necessitates attaining buddhahood, the state in which all obscurations have been abandoned and all excellent qualities developed limitlessly. Bodhicitta is the motivation to do this. It is a primary mental consciousness informed by two aspirations: to benefit all sentient beings and to attain full awakening in order to do that.

While the method for developing bodhicitta is not difficult to understand, it requires patience and consistent effort to actualize. After generating bodhicitta, we need to make it firm through repeated meditation and then live this magnificent motivation through practicing the perfections. No matter how long it takes and no matter what hardships we experience along the way, becoming a buddha so that we may benefit sentient beings most effectively is worthwhile.

Equalizing and Exchanging Self and Others

The second method to cultivate bodhicitta has several steps: equalizing self and others, contemplating the disadvantages of self-centeredness and the benefits of cherishing others, exchanging self and others, and taking and giving.

To *equalize ourselves and others*, we investigate our innate feeling of self-importance and realize there is no reason to justify it: others and ourselves are equal in wanting happiness and freedom from suffering. Both we and others deserve happiness and the cessation of suffering because we equally are sentient beings who have buddha nature. We are only one single individual, while other sentient beings are countless. It makes no sense to ignore their welfare, while counteracting others' misery and bringing them happiness is beneficial.

The Luminary International Buddhist Society

SHAVING THE HEAD BEFORE ORDINATION, INDIA

The *disadvantages of self-centeredness* are many. Our self-centered attitude has brought all manner of undesirable consequences from beginningless saṃsāra up to the present. Although we want to be happy, our self-preoccupation has led us to engage in unimaginable destructive karma as well as create havoc in the lives of those around us. We have spent countless eons looking out for our own benefit at the expense of others but haven't accomplished our own or others' aims. Self-preoccupation fuels guilt, anxiety, and fear. Had we cherished others instead, we would certainly have become buddhas long ago.

When contemplating the faults of self-centeredness, it is important to remember that self-centeredness is not an inherent part of us and that we are not "bad" because we are plagued by selfishness. Furthermore, being happy does not mean we are self-centered or that, for our compassion to be genuine, we must suffer. Practicing the path involves joyful effort and leads to the supreme bliss of full awakening.

All good comes from *cherishing others*. The best way to achieve our own happiness is to benefit others. We live in a world where we depend on others simply to stay alive. If we consider only our own good and ignore others' plight, we will soon find ourselves surrounded by unhappy people. Their unhappiness will surely affect us; they will complain, resent our success, and try to steal our possessions. However, if we work for the benefit of others, those around us will be content and kind, and this will certainly make our own life more pleasant!

Cherishing others brings happiness in this and future lives. With a mind that genuinely cares about all others, we create constructive karma. As a result, we will die without fear or regret and secure a good rebirth. Realizations of the path will come easily because our mind has been made fertile with merit created by cherishing others. We will generate bodhicitta, progress through the bodhisattva's paths and grounds, and attain full awakening.

Seeing that self-preoccupation leads to misery and cherishing others brings joy, we now *exchange self and others*. This entails changing the focal point of the wish to avoid suffering and have happiness from ourselves to others. Initially we may think this is impossible because living beings are biologically programmed to look out for themselves first. We don't feel the pain and pleasure in another person's body, so of course we don't care about it as much as we do our own bodies. However, considering this mass of organic matter "*my* body" is a matter of ignorant habit. Nothing about this body is ours: the sperm, egg, and genes belong to our parents. The rest is the result of the food we have eaten, which came from the earth and was given to us by others. It is simply by habit that we consider this body "mine." Examining the body, feelings, mind, and mental factors with mindfulness, we see there is no I or mine in them. There are simply material elements and moments of mind and mental factors. Thinking there is a real person who either is the aggregates or who owns them is a fabrication.

Two main obstacles block our exchanging self and others. First, we think ourselves and others are inherently separate. In fact, self and others are posited in mutual dependence on each other, similar to one side of the valley being called "this side" in dependence on the other side being "that side." Being "this side" and "that side" depends on where we stand. To others, what we call "I" they regard as "you." Exchanging self and others means imputing "I" on other people so that "my happiness is most important" refers to other sentient beings' happiness.

The second obstacle to exchanging self and others is thinking that dispelling others' suffering is unnecessary because their suffering doesn't harm us. This, too, is based on seeing self and others as entirely separate when in fact we depend on each other. It is similar to thinking, "There's no need to save money for my old age because that old person is a different person and his suffering doesn't harm me." It is also similar to our hand refusing to pull a thorn out of our foot because the foot's pain doesn't hurt the hand.

Our actions affect the well-being of others, be that another individual or the old person we will become. Just as we create conditions for that old person's happiness, we should create the conditions for others' happiness. Just as the hand helps the foot without any expectation of appreciation because they are parts of the same body, we should help other living beings because we are all parts of the body of life. Śāntideva asks (BCA 8:115):

> Through acquaintance has the thought of I arisen
> toward this impersonal body;
> So in a similar way, why should it not arise
> toward other living beings?

Whereas previously we held ourselves as most important, now we hold others as supreme. The benefits of doing this are enormous. Śāntideva says (BCA 8:129–30):

> Whatever joy there is in this world
> all comes from desiring others to be happy,
> and whatever suffering there is in this world
> all comes from desiring myself to be happy.
>
> What need is there to say much more?
> The childish work for their own benefit,
> while buddhas work for the benefit of others.
> Just look at the difference between them!

Bodhisattvas' joy in exchanging self and others is much greater than any happiness we self-centered beings could even dream of.

The meditation on *taking and giving* deepens our love, compassion, and ability to exchange self and others. *Taking* comes from the compassionate wish, "I will take all problems, sufferings, and defilements of other sentient beings on myself so that they may be free of them." *Giving* is motivated by love: "I will give my body, possessions, and merit to others, so that all their wishes may be fulfilled." Nāgārjuna aspires (RA 484):

> May I bear the results of their negativity,
> and may they have the results of all my virtue.

We imagine taking all others' suffering upon ourselves, and we use this thought to destroy our self-centered attitude. Then we transform our body, wealth, and virtue into whatever others need and give these to others. Through this they receive all they need, and we are freed from our self-preoccupation.

Self-Interest, Self-Confidence, Self-Centered Attitude, and Self-Grasping Ignorance

Hearing about bodhisattvas' ability to cherish others more than themselves, we may doubt, "If I abandon all self-interest and only cherish others, I will neglect myself and my suffering will increase." Cherishing others does not mean ignoring our own needs and caring only for others. If we did that, we would fall into a deplorable state in which benefiting others and practicing the Dharma would be nearly impossible. In that case, instead of our helping others, they would need to take care of us!

While one form of self-interest is selfish, stingy, and irritable, another is wise self-interest that understands that benefiting ourselves and helping others need not be contradictory. As mentioned above, bodhisattvas' self-interest leads them to fulfill their own purpose by attaining a buddha's dharmakāya, which in turn enables them to benefit others through gaining a buddha's form body.

Similarly, while one sense of self—self-grasping ignorance—is a troublemaker, stable and realistic self-confidence is necessary to accomplish the path. Bodhisattvas must have exceptionally strong self-confidence to be able to complete all the perfections. Free from arrogance, such self-confidence aspires for what is positive without clinging to it.

Self-confidence is essential to begin, continue, and complete the path to awakening, and our buddha nature is a valid basis on which to generate it. Reflecting on emptiness helps us to recognize our buddha nature, for we see that the defilements are adventitious and can be removed. Compassion for others also builds self-confidence, as does remembering our precious human life, its meaning, purpose, and rarity.

The *self-centered attitude* considers ourselves the most important, whereas *self-grasping ignorance* misapprehends how the self exists. Aside from the self-centered attitude's grosser manifestations, which are obviously detrimental, its subtler aspect seeks liberation for ourselves alone. In general, this is not an object of abandonment; it is an unmistaken mind that motivates śrāvakas and pratyekabuddhas to fulfill their spiritual aspirations, generate virtuous qualities, and attain liberation—all admirable activities. However, self-centeredness is an object of abandonment for those following the bodhisattva path to buddhahood.

The self-centered attitude is neither an afflictive nor a cognitive obscuration; it is not a pollutant and is not the root of saṃsāra. Self-grasping, on the other hand, is the root of saṃsāra and an afflictive obscuration that must be eradicated to attain both liberation and full awakening.

The self-centered attitude and self-grasping have neither a causal relationship—one does not cause the other—or a same-nature relationship—if one exists in a person's mindstream, the other doesn't necessarily exist. Arhats have eliminated self-grasping but have self-centeredness. Bodhisattvas who freshly enter the bodhisattva path (that is, they are not arhats who later become bodhisattvas) and are below the eighth ground have self-grasping but do not necessarily have self-centeredness. The self-centered attitude and self-grasping ignorance also have different counterforces. Bodhicitta is the counterforce to the former and the wisdom realizing emptiness to the latter.

Integrating the View with Bodhicitta

When we consider emulating the deeds of the great bodhisattvas, our minds may be overcome with anxiety. "What will happen to *me* if I altruistically help others?" Integrating either the Madhyamaka or Yogācāra view of emptiness helps us overcome this unnecessary and limiting fear. It aids our cultivation of bodhicitta by loosening the unrealistic grasping to self and others, to suffering and happiness, and to friend, enemy, and stranger. It also deepens our compassion for sentient beings, who are under the control of afflictions and karma.

According to the Yogācāra view, the seemingly external objects that appear to our sense consciousnesses have arisen due to karmic latencies on the consciousness. While these objects do not exist as entities separate from our mind, they appear that way due to ignorance. In fact, they are like things in a dream, for they do not exist as they appear.

Seeing both good and bad experiences as karmic appearances arising due to latencies on the mindstream loosens the solidity with which we view sentient beings and the environment. From this perspective, friends, enemies, and strangers are simply karmic appearances, and having attachment, anger, and apathy toward them is misguided. Similarly, attractive and unattractive objects, praise and blame, reputation and notoriety, and wealth and poverty simply appear to the mind due to the activation of latencies. They lack any external existence separate from the mind to which they appear. Therefore, there is no sense in clinging to some things and having aversion for others.

According to the Madhyamaka view, nothing exists from its own side; everything exists by being merely designated by mind. "Self" and "others" exist dependent on labels; there is no inherently existent I or others and no inherently existent suffering or happiness. Contemplating that all these exist in mutual dependence and thus are empty of their own inherent nature lessens our fear of suffering and our clinging to our own happiness. In this way, our minds become more courageous and joyful in practicing the bodhisattva deeds.

Chinese Buddhism

Nāgārjuna's *Daśabhūmikavibhāṣā* speaks of seven factors that may cause people to generate bodhicitta, depending on their dispositions and tendencies: (1) being instructed by a buddha who understands their faculties, (2) observing that the Dharma is on the verge of destruction in our world and wanting to guard and protect it, (3) feeling compassion for suffering sentient beings, (4) receiving instructions from a bodhisattva who influences them to generate bodhicitta, (5) observing the conduct of a bodhisattva and wanting to emulate it, (6) having performed an action of generosity that makes them recall the virtues of bodhisattvas, (7) feeling delight upon seeing or hearing about the thirty-two signs and eighty marks of a buddha.

People may generate bodhicitta due to any of these seven causes and conditions. However, only those who have generated bodhicitta in the first three ways will certainly attain full awakening. This is because the roots of virtue created by generating bodhicitta in these three ways are very deep, while the roots of virtue created in the other four ways are not necessarily firmly established. However, by practicing well and stabilizing their roots of virtue, the latter group will also attain buddhahood.

Shixian (1685–1733), a meditation master and Pure Land patriarch, in his *Quan fa pu ti xin wen* (*Exhortation to Resolve on Buddhahood*), gives ten points for reflection to spur the generation of bodhicitta. But first, to ensure we cultivate bodhicitta purely and properly, he discusses four pairs of distinctions in practitioners' bodhicitta.

Practitioners who do not examine their minds but instead seek wealth, fame, and sense pleasures practice *perversely*. Those unattached to personal profit, reputation, and pleasure either in this life or the next practice *correctly*.

Constantly directing the mind to the Buddha's path, trying to benefit sentient beings with every thought, and being undeterred by having to practice bodhicitta for eons is *genuine* resolve. Neglecting to purify destructive karma, undertaking projects with enthusiasm but not completing them, and having virtuous thoughts mixed with attachment to wealth and reputation constitute *false* resolve.

Resolving to attain full awakening and keep the bodhicitta motivation and bodhisattva precepts until all sentient beings have become awakened is *great* resolve. Aspiring only for personal liberation without caring for others indicates *small* resolve.

Thinking that the Buddha's path is outside our mind and remaining attached to our own merit, knowledge, and views is *one-sided*. Generating bodhicitta, taking the bodhisattva precepts, and practicing the perfections with a mind supported by wisdom realizing emptiness is *perfect*.

Understanding these eight distinctions, we must continuously examine our mind to ensure our bodhicitta is correct, genuine, great, and perfect. Done in this way, our practice will certainly be successful.

The first five of the ten points for reflection to inspire us to generate bodhicitta are mindfulness of the great kindness we have received from the Buddha and from our parents, teachers, benefactors, and all sentient beings. Recognizing this inspires us to repay their kindness by generating bodhicitta and practicing the bodhisattva path. The remaining five points support and direct our bodhicitta. We should (1) be mindful of the suffering of repeated birth and death in saṃsāra, (2) respect our buddha nature, (3) think of the disadvantages of nonvirtuous karma, repent, and purify; (4) aspire to be born in the pure land, and (5) pray that the Buddha's pure teachings remain in our world forever. After we generate bodhicitta, Shixian then counsels us:

> Do not, fearing difficulty, shrink back in timidity. Do not, regarding this matter as easy, take it but lightly. Do not, seeking a swift conclusion, fail to make a long-enduring commitment.... Do not claim that a single thought is insignificant.[23]

Bodhicitta is tremendously important for our own and others' well-being, and we must never give it up. If we reflect on bodhicitta at times of suffering, our mental distress will decrease, and by generating compassion, our physical suffering will be transformed and become meaningful on the path to awakening.

Chinese Buddhism contains several meditations to cultivate love and compassion. One is meditation on the four immeasurables. Another is the "seven-round compassion meditation," which has its source in Vasubandhu's *Abhidharmakośabhāṣya*. This meditation consists of seven rounds, each round having seven steps in which we contemplate our relationship with seven groups of people.

(1) Recall the kindness of your *elders* in this life, remembering each person who has taken care of you, taught you, guided you, protected you, and served as a good role model. Think, "My elders have done so much for me. Since they have selflessly helped me, it would seem natural that I try to repay their kindness. However, instead of doing that, I argue with them and cause them worry. I don't listen to their suggestions and don't appreciate all they have done for me. I confess and regret this." Feel this in your heart. Now dedicate all your merit to your elders for the cessation of their suffering and attainment of buddhahood. Then think about your elders in past lives and do the same.

(2) Recall your *peers*—siblings, friends, and colleagues—and consider that they have kept you company, befriended you, and assisted you when you needed help. Recall that instead of caring about them in return, you have criticized and blamed them, called them names, been inconsiderate or jealous of their successes. Confess this, purify, and dedicate your merit to them. Contemplate your peers in previous lives and think in the same way.

(3) Meditate in the same way regarding your *juniors* (children, students, employees), (4) *enemies of your elders* (people who have hurt, betrayed,

or taken advantage of your elders), (5) your own *enemies*, (6) *enemies of your juniors*, and (7) *neutral people* who have neither helped nor harmed you. Contemplate their kindness. Then recall that instead of repaying their kindness, you sometimes had malice and harmed them. Confess and purify, and dedicate your merit to them so that they may be happy and free from duḥkha, take refuge in the Three Jewels, and become awakened. Do the same for all those with whom you have had that relationship in previous lives.

Contemplating the seven steps in this way constitutes one round. The second round is thinking in the same way toward these various groups, beginning with neutral people and going in the reverse order, ending with your elders. The third round is going through the seven steps again in forward order. The meditation is performed, back and forth, in this way for seven rounds.

At the conclusion, empty your mind of all thoughts, ideas, graspings, and keep pure awareness. Contemplate emptiness.

Those who practice this compassion contemplation for some months will definitely see a change in their lives and relationships with sentient beings.

Four Great Vows

Chan (Zen) practitioners generate bodhicitta by reflecting on the four great vows:

> Sentient beings are countless; I vow to free them.
> Defilements are endless; I vow to eradicate them.
> Dharma doors are limitless; I vow to cultivate them.
> The Buddha's way (bodhi) is supreme; I vow to attain it.

The last of the four is the generation of bodhicitta. To actualize this vow, we need the support of the first three. Therefore the first great vow is to liberate each and every one of the countless sentient beings because we feel their suffering in saṃsāra as our own. This great compassion leads to the second great vow, to eradicate our own and all others' numberless defilements by cultivating the wisdom that realizes the ultimate nature. This leads to the third great vow, to cultivate countless approaches, realizations, and skillful means.

Bodhisattvas maintain these four vows in their minds thought after thought, so there is no time in which they are not present. Bodhisattvas are not intimidated by the vastness of these four vows. Their minds are focused on the full awakening of all sentient beings, and they are willing to do everything necessary to bring it about.

Gāthas—short verses extracted from sūtras or written by great masters—guide us to train our minds, imbue ordinary actions with a bodhicitta motivation, and transform neutral actions into virtue. These are also found in the "mind training" practice in Tibetan Buddhism. Some gāthas from chapter 11 of the *Avataṃsaka Sūtra* are:

> When giving something:
> May all sentient beings be able to relinquish everything with hearts free from clinging.
>
> In danger and difficulty:
> May all sentient beings be free and unhindered wherever they go.
>
> When sitting up straight:
> May all sentient beings sit on the seat of awakening, their minds without attachment.
>
> When traveling on a road:
> May all sentient beings tread the pure realm of reality, their minds without obstruction.
>
> When using the toilet:
> May all sentient beings discard their attachment, anger, and confusion and eliminate destructive conduct.

According to Chinese Buddhist scriptures, bodhicitta is cultivated and expanded in five stages: (1) making the vow to become a buddha and liberate all the countless sentient beings, (2) engaging in many practices to counteract afflictions and progress toward awakening, (3) directly realizing the ultimate nature, which is the actual awakening of bodhicitta, (4) continuing to cultivate the bodhisattva practice to become fully and perfectly awakened, and (5) attaining supreme, ultimate bodhicitta—buddhahood.

THERAVĀDA MONKS CUTTING KAṬHINA CLOTH, MALAYSIA

These five stages are similar to the five paths of a bodhisattva as explained in the Tibetan tradition.

In Chan the third stage is considered one form of awakening. Here one realizes the pure mind, the buddha nature that is empty and is the actual bodhicitta. As in Theravāda Buddhism, Chinese Buddhism uses "awakening" to apply to any direct, nonconceptual realization of reality.[24] Neither tradition considers this first experience to be final awakening; both say it needs to be cultivated over time to eradicate all obscurations forever and attain the final goal.

Aspiring and Engaging Bodhicitta

According to its nature, bodhicitta may be of two kinds: *Aspiring bodhicitta* is the wish to attain full awakening for the benefit of all sentient beings. *Engaging bodhicitta* is the maturation of that wish so that it is accompanied by the bodhisattva ethical restraints and the commitment to practice the perfections and the four ways of gathering disciples, which are discussed in the next chapter.

Initially our bodhicitta is contrived. Continuing to reflect on the two methods to generate bodhicitta, we develop it so that it becomes uncontrived. Participating in the ceremony of generating aspiring bodhicitta in the presence of our spiritual mentor helps us to do this. This is "receiving aspiring bodhicitta in a ceremony," and it helps stabilize our determination to cultivate bodhicitta.

Later, when we feel capable of training in the causes for keeping our bodhicitta from deteriorating, we can again generate bodhicitta in the presence of our teacher with the thought never to give it up. This is "receiving aspiring bodhicitta with commitment in a ceremony." At this time we assume the precepts of aspiring bodhicitta to prevent our bodhicitta from deteriorating in this and future lives.

After training the mind in aspiring bodhicitta with commitment, we can assume the bodhisattva ethical restraints. Doing this is engaging bodhicitta. Most bodhisattva aspirants take the bodhisattva precepts before they are full-fledged bodhisattvas with uncontrived bodhicitta. The bodhisattva precepts at this point are a similitude, not actual bodhisattva precepts, but they help us develop bodhicitta and practice the bodhisattva conduct.

In the Tibetan tradition, the bodhisattva ethical restraints consist of eighteen root and forty-six auxiliary precepts. These were taught by the Buddha at different times and initially were scattered throughout the Sanskrit sūtras. Asaṅga, Śāntideva, and Candragomin collated them, and the present set was formed by combining their lists.

Two renditions of the bodhisattva ethical code exist in Chinese Buddhism. The *Brahmajāla Sūtra* contains ten root and forty-eight auxiliary precepts, and the *Yogācārabhūmi Śāstra* has four root and forty-one auxiliary precepts. There is much overlap between the lists in these two scriptures, as well as with the bodhisattva precepts of Tibetan Buddhism.

In the Chinese and Tibetan traditions, both monastics and lay followers take the bodhisattva ethical restraints with the intention to keep them until full awakening. All transgressions, no matter how serious, can be purified through confession and repentance.

In the Chinese tradition, a voluntary ceremony in which people "offer their body to the Buddha" precedes the taking of the bodhisattva precepts.

For monastics, this is done by making three small burn marks on the top of the head; for lay followers these are made on the arm. This symbolizes offering one's body to the buddhas and bodhisattvas and being willing to endure suffering when working for the benefit of sentient beings and striving for full awakening. Additionally, in ancient China, monastics were exempt from punishment by civil law because they were governed by the vinaya precepts. To avoid arrest by the police and to gain offerings, some criminals would don monastic robes. To discriminate genuine monastics from imposters, the custom arose to burn three or more cones of incense on monastics' heads.

In general, Japanese priests and committed lay followers take sixteen bodhisattva precepts. The first five correspond to the five lay precepts, and the last three are taking refuge in the Three Jewels. The others are to abandon speaking of the misdeeds of others, praising oneself and disparaging others, withholding spiritual or material aid, indulging in anger, and reviling the Three Jewels. The remaining three are to abandon evil, do good, and liberate all sentient beings.

In short, while differences exist in the delineation of the bodhisattva precepts in various traditions, their essence and purpose remain the same.

Pāli Tradition: Bodhicitta and Bodhisattas

For followers of the Pāli tradition, which vehicle to follow is an individual choice, and seeking the full awakening of a buddha is one option.[25] Although most practitioners seek arhatship, the bodhisatta path is set forth for exceptional individuals. The *Buddhavaṃsa*, *Cariyāpiṭaka*, *Jātakas*, *Mahāpadāna Sutta* (DN 14), and *Apadāna* are canonical scriptures that speak about previous buddhas fulfilling the bodhisatta practices. The twelfth-century Pāli treatise *Upāsakajanālaṅkāra* by Thera Ānanda from the Mahāvihāra tradition speaks of the awakening of sāvakas, paccekabuddhas, and bodhisattas in detail.

Some Pāli suttas emphasize compassion as the motivating force for the Buddha's attainment of awakening. He was the "one individual who arose and came to be for the welfare of the multitude, for happiness of the multitude, out of compassion for the world, for the benefit, welfare, and happiness of gods and humans" (AN 1:170). The Buddha told his disciples to cultivate the Dhamma with that same compassionate motivation so the holy life will last for a long time (DN 16:3.50). He sent the monastics to spread the Dhamma for that same reason (SN 4:5).

Monastics are to engage in the path to liberation not only for their own benefit but also to preserve the Dhamma for future generations and to become exemplars inspiring others to practice the path and attain liberation. Out of concern and compassion for others, the Buddha instructs his followers to abide harmoniously. He praises Mahākassapa for teaching the Dhamma with compassion, and Mahākassapa himself says that he became a monastic and cultivated contentment with simple food, clothing, and shelter to benefit others. His hope was that others would see value in this lifestyle, adopt it for themselves, and attain liberation.

Monastics show compassion by being receptive, accepting offerings, and counseling those from all socioeconomic, racial, ethnic, and educational classes. Their duty is to receive their livelihood in a nonharmful manner, show people how to live ethically, encourage them to practice mindfulness, teach them the Dhamma, and be grateful recipients of their gifts so that the laity will accumulate merit from making offerings.

The oldest Pāli scriptures speak of bodhisattas who, in their last lives as sentient beings, become fully awakened buddhas without the aid of a teacher. They begin a dispensation (*sāsana, śāsana*), turning the Dhamma wheel so the enlightening teachings will exist in the world. This is the awakening attained by buddhas, and it is extolled as superior to the awakenings of sāvakas and paccekabuddhas. While some ancient Pāli sages said that the bodhisatta path is only for those who are destined to become wheel-turning buddhas, the South Indian commentator Dhammapāla did not concur and instead described a bodhisatta path open to others who aspire to follow it.

In a post-canonical Pāli composition, *Dasabodhisattupattikathā*, the Buddha says, "There have been...and will be limitless and countless ariyas who...with courage and determination having successively fulfilled the pāramīs, will attain buddhahood and pass away having completed a buddha's duty."[26] It then tells the stories of ten bodhisattas who will do this in the future.

The bodhisatta ideal is not foreign to Theravāda countries. Historically there was interest in the bodhisatta path in Sri Lanka, and statues of the bodhisatta Avalokiteśvara have been unearthed in Sri Lanka, Thailand, and other Theravāda countries. In the past and present, kings and the populace in Theravāda areas found the bodhisatta ideal exemplary. Beginning around the eighth century, some kings in Sri Lanka, Burma, and Thailand either were referred to as bodhisattas by others or declared themselves to be bodhisattas or practitioners of the bodhisatta path.[27] Some Theravāda scholars and textual scribes, in the colophon of their writings, declared their bodhicitta motivation, saying "*Buddho bhaveyyam*" or "May I become a buddha." Buddhaghosa was regarded as the incarnation of Metteyya Buddha (Maitreya) by the monks of Mahāvihāra Monastery.

Some Theravāda practitioners find the bodhisatta path appealing and practice it.[28] Nowadays there are both monastic and lay Buddhists in Theravādin countries who make the resolve to become buddhas for the benefit of all sentient beings.[29] In Thailand two Thai masters are regarded as incarnations of the bodhisatta Metteyya.

The pure intention of a bodhisatta is illustrated in the story of the Buddha's previous life as King Sivi, who desired to give his eyes to someone in need. To test him, Sakka (Śakra), lord of the devas, appeared as a decrepit, blind old man who asked the king for his eyes. With great joy King Sivi immediately had the doctor remove his eyes to give to the old man. After doing this, he said:

> While I was desiring to give, while I was giving, and after the gift had been given by me, there was no contradictory state of mind; it was for the sake of awakening itself.... Omniscience was dear to me; therefore I gave the eyes.[30]

The *Buddhavaṃsa* relates the inspiring story when Gotama Buddha generated bodhicitta in his previous life. Born into a wealthy family, the brahman Sumedha lived a life of luxury. When his parents died, however, he realized the impermanence of mundane happiness, resolved to seek liberation, and became a matted-hair ascetic. One day he learned that Buddha Dīpaṃkara and his disciples were to visit the city near his hermitage. Descending from his hermitage, he began to clear the path for them but was unable to finish before they arrived. As the Buddha Dīpaṃkara approached, Sumedha, elated to see him, prostrated and lay down in the mud. Sumedha relates this moving event (Bv 52–54):

> Loosening my hair, spreading my bark-garments and piece of hide there in the mire, I lay down prone. "Let the Buddha tread on me with his disciples. Do not let him tread in the mire—it will be for my welfare."

When he initially invited the Buddha and his disciples to use him as a bridge across the mud, Sumedha was focused on his own welfare. He knew that if he wished, he could eradicate defilements and become an arahant that very day by listening to a discourse by Buddha Dīpaṃkara. Questioning his self-centered intention, he made an unshakable resolve to become a buddha and lead all other beings out of saṃsāra (Bv 55–58):

> What is the use while I remain ignorant of realizing Dhamma here? Having reached omniscience, I will become a buddha in this world with its devas. What is the use of my crossing over alone, being a person aware of my strength? Having reached omniscience, I will cause the world together with its devas to cross over.
>
> By my merit toward the supreme among humans, I will reach omniscience; I will cause many beings to cross over. Cutting through the stream of saṃsāra, shattering the three renewed existences, embarking in the ship of Dhamma, I will cause the world with its devas to cross over.

Dīpaṃkara Buddha then predicted Sumedha's full awakening: he would actualize his vow to attain full awakening, becoming a buddha with the name Gotama after four countless ages and a hundred thousand eons. Going into seclusion, Sumedha contemplated how to fulfill his aim of full awakening and saw that the main virtuous qualities to develop were the ten pāramīs. Here a full-fledged bodhisatta path is set out in Pāli scriptures.

All twenty-four buddhas, whose life stories are found in the *Buddhavaṃsa*, went through a similar process. First, they make an unshakable resolve (*paṇidhāna*, *praṇidhāna*) to become a bodhisatta and then a buddha by practicing the path with great diligence for a long time. This mental determination is made once. Then, in the presence of a series of buddhas, they make an aspiration (*abhinīhāra*) to attain full awakening for the benefit of all sentient beings. Bodhisattas then perform an act of merit (*adhikāra*) to demonstrate to each buddha their sincerity and dedication to fulfill that aspiration, and that buddha predicts (*vyākaraṇa*) their success in doing this.

For the bodhicitta aspiration to be fulfilled in buddhahood, it must be supported by eight conditions: the person is a human being, is male,[31] has the necessary supportive conditions (firm Dhamma practice), has generated the bodhicitta aspiration in the presence of a buddha, is a renunciant, has achieved noble qualities such as the superknowledges and the higher states of meditative absorption, has such deep dedication and devotion for the Buddha that he is willing to give up his life to perform great acts of merit for the Three Jewels, and has strong virtuous desire and determination to cultivate the qualities leading to buddhahood (Bv 59). A bodhisatta's desire for full awakening should be so intense that "if he were to hear 'Buddhahood can only be attained after experiencing torture in hell for four countless ages and a hundred thousand eons,' he would not deem that difficult to do but would be filled with desire for the task and would not shrink away" (TP sec. 6). The bodhisattva then investigates the pāramīs, trains in them, and fulfills them.

In addition to generating the aspiration for full awakening, great compassion and skillful means are needed to practice the pāramīs. Skillful means (*upāyakosalla, upāyakauśalya*) is the wisdom that transforms the pāramīs into the collections necessary to attain full awakening. Uniting the practices of wisdom and compassion, he fulfills the ten pāramīs, practices zeal, competence, stability, and beneficent conduct, and cultivates six inclinations—renunciation, solitude, nonattachment, nonhatred, nonconfusion, and release (from saṃsāra).

13 | Bodhisattva Training in the Perfections

THE PERFECTIONS (*pāramī, pāramitā*) are the method to attain awakening ourselves, and the four ways of gathering disciples (*saṅgahavatthu, saṃgrahavastu*) are the method to lead others on the path to awakening.

The Sanskrit tradition enumerates ten perfections: generosity (*dāna*), ethical conduct, fortitude, joyous effort, meditative stability, wisdom (*paññā, prajñā*), skillful means, unshakable resolve, power (*bāla*), and exalted wisdom (*ñāna, jñāna*). The last four are refined aspects of wisdom, making six perfections. In the Pāli tradition the ten are generosity, ethical conduct, renunciation (*nekkhamma, naiṣkramya*), wisdom, joyous effort, fortitude, truthfulness (*sacca, satya*), determination (*adhiṭṭhāna, adhiṣṭhāna*), love and compassion, and equanimity.

Pāramī and *pāramitā* mean "going beyond the end" or "reaching perfection." When done with the bodhicitta motivation, these practices take us beyond saṃsāra to buddhahood, where all obscurations have been eliminated and all good qualities have been developed limitlessly. The perfections become supramundane when conjoined with the wisdom realizing emptiness: the bodhisattva knows the agent, object, and action of each perfection arise dependently and are therefore empty of inherent existence.

SANSKRIT TRADITION

Having generated bodhicitta, we need to accumulate all the appropriate causes and conditions for full awakening. These are subsumed in the two collections of merit and wisdom. The *collection of merit* ripens the mind, makes it more receptive, and is the principal cause for a buddha's form body. The *collection of wisdom* eradicates defilements and is the principal cause of a buddha's dharmakāya. The two collections encompass the perfections.

The *basis*—the person who engages in the perfections—is those who have awakened their bodhisattva disposition by generating bodhicitta. They rely on a qualified spiritual mentor and receive extensive teachings on texts about the perfections. Not satisfied with intellectual knowledge, they reflect and meditate on these teachings and practice the perfections at every opportunity they have.

Regarding the *nature* of each perfection: (1) Generosity includes physical, verbal, and mental actions based on a kind intention and the willingness to give. (2) Ethical conduct is restraint from nonvirtue. (3) Fortitude is the ability to remain calm and undisturbed in the face of harm from others, physical or mental suffering, and difficulties in learning the Dharma. (4) Joyous effort is delight in virtue and in creating the causes to attain the dharmakāya and form bodies of a buddha. (5) Meditative stability is the ability to remain fixed on a virtuous object without distraction. (6) Wisdom is the ability to distinguish and deeply understand conventional and ultimate truths and to discern what to practice and what to abandon on the path.

Each perfection accomplishes the welfare of other sentient beings in a specific way. Generosity alleviates poverty and provides others with the basic necessities of life and other things they can enjoy. Ethical conduct eases others' fear and pain. Fortitude bears others' inconsiderate or harmful behavior without retaliating and causing them pain. Joyous effort helps others without laziness, resentment, or empathic distress. Meditative stability leads to the superknowledges. Wisdom teaches others so that they can generate wisdom, thus eliminating their doubts and leading them to awakening.

Since fulfilling the collections of merit and wisdom takes a long time, we need to ensure that we have precious human lives in our future rebirths so we will be able to continue practicing the path. Generosity ensures we have the material resources needed to practice. Ethical conduct is the principal cause of attaining good rebirth. Fortitude results in being attractive and having good companions who encourage our Dharma practice. Joyous effort enables us to complete virtuous projects in future lives. Meditative stability leads to a stable, peaceful mind that can meditate without distraction. The wisdom correctly understanding karma and its effects enables us to know what to practice and what to abandon on the path and thus to discern teachers imparting the correct path from charlatans. Engaging in each perfection and experiencing its results in future lives is important. Lacking

Brian Harris, Tibetan Nuns Project

TIBETAN NUNS DOING PUJA, INDIA

even one will limit our opportunity to progress on the bodhisattva path in future lives.

The six perfections can be included in the three higher trainings. Generosity, ethical conduct, and fortitude are included in the higher training of ethical conduct; dhyāna is in the higher training of concentration; and wisdom is in the higher training of wisdom. Joyous effort is needed for all of them.

All six perfections can be included in the practice of each one. For example, a small act of generosity such as giving someone a cup of tea can be done with bodhicitta. Not harming others physically or verbally when giving the tea is ethical conduct. If the recipient harms us or doesn't appreciate the gift, fortitude keeps the mind calm. Giving the tea is done with joyous effort, taking delight in being generous. Stability of mind is necessary so the mind maintains a bodhicitta motivation and is not polluted by afflictions while giving. Prior to giving, wisdom is needed to know what, when, and how to give. While giving, contemplating the emptiness of the giver, gift, recipient, and act of giving cultivates wisdom.

Fulfilling the perfections requires time, practice, and patience. Instead of expecting to be experts, we can accept our present abilities and at the same time work to increase them in the future. The Buddha did not start off fully awakened, and there was a time when he found the perfections challenging.

However, because causes bring their corresponding results, by steady practice we can begin, develop, and complete all the bodhisattva practices.

Pāli Tradition: Ten Pāramīs

The *Treatise on the Pāramīs*—written by the great Pāli commentator Dhammapāla and found in his commentary on the *Cariyāpiṭaka* and subcommentary to the *Brahmajāla Sutta*—explains the ten pāramīs as bodhisatta practices. Dhammapāla's audience and purpose were "clansmen following the suttas (*suttantikas*) who are zealously engaged in the practice of the vehicle to great awakening (*mahābodhiyāna*), in order to improve their skillfulness in accumulating the collections (requisites) for awakening." Praising the Buddha for having completed the bodhisatta path and becoming a fully awakened buddha, Buddhaghosa comments (Vism 1:33), "The virtue of the perfections done for the liberation of all beings is superior."

The perfections are good qualities to cultivate no matter which of the three vehicles we follow, and many people seeking arahantship practice them. Bodhisattas must practice them more intensely and for a longer time to attain their spiritual goal. Disciples in Theravāda countries frequently praise their teachers for their great accumulation of pāramīs.

Buddhaghosa explains the progression from one perfection to the next (Vism 9:124). Having generated the four immeasurables, bodhisattas

> ...*give gifts*, which are a source of pleasure, without discriminating thus: "It must be given to this one; it must not be given to this one." To avoid doing harm to beings they undertake the precepts of *ethical conduct*. They practice *renunciation* for the purpose of perfecting their ethical conduct. They cleanse their *wisdom* for the purpose of nonconfusion about what is good and bad for beings. They constantly arouse *effort*, having beings' welfare and happiness at heart. When they have acquired heroic *fortitude* through supreme effort, they become patient with beings' many kinds of faults. They *do not deceive* when promising, "We shall give you this; we shall do this for you." They have unshakable *determination* for beings' welfare and happiness. Through unshakable *love*, they place them first. Through *equanimity*, they expect no reward. Having thus fulfilled the pāramīs, they per-

> fect all the good states classed as the ten powers, four kinds of fearlessness, six kinds of knowledge not shared [by sāvakas], and eighteen unique qualities of a buddha.

The ten perfections share many characteristics: they function to benefit others, are motivated by the aspiration to attain awakening, and are done with a mind unpolluted by craving, conceit, and wrong views. Great compassion and skillful means—the wisdom transforming them into the requisites of awakening—are their proximate causes and accompany each of them.

When contemplating the perfections, we should reflect: What afflictions do I need to be particularly on guard against when practicing each pāramī? What are the antidotes to that affliction? How can I energize mindfulness and introspective awareness to recognize the afflictions and apply their antidotes?

To develop inner strength to complete the path, bodhisattas offer themselves to the buddhas. Then, if they encounter difficulties in practicing the pāramīs—for example, they lack requisites for living, are insulted, experience illness or injury, or become exhausted—they reflect, "I have given myself to the buddhas for the sake of the awakening of all beings. Whatever comes, comes." In this way they trust the Three Jewels and have confidence in the law of kamma and its effects. Not succumbing to fear or worry, they remain firm and determined to continue on the bodhisatta path.

Destroying self-centeredness and cultivating love are the means to accomplish the pāramīs. Bodhisattas treat all beings as equal to themselves in importance and remain emotionally stable in all circumstances. By contemplating sentient beings as their precious children or relatives, bodhisattas' love, compassion, and affection increase. Having subdued their own ignorance, attachment, and anger, they mature others' minds with the four ways of gathering disciples, causing sentient beings to enter and then complete any of the three vehicles.

The time necessary to accomplish the perfections depends on the inclination of each bodhisatta—whether wisdom, faith, or energy is predominant. All bodhisattas receive predictions of their awakening directly from a buddha and then proceed to fulfill the perfections in the time corresponding to their inclination. Since full awakening is attained by the power of wisdom, bodhisattas inclined toward wisdom proceed more rapidly.

Bodhisattas are a supreme field of merit, held dear by humans and nonhumans, protected by deities, and unharmed by wild animals. Free from malice, jealousy, competitiveness, hypocrisy, miserliness, stubbornness, and arrogance, bodhisattas' presence in a place prevents danger and disasters. Due to practicing the pāramīs, bodhisattas have long life, enabling them to accumulate excellent qualities, deepen their meditation, and complete a multitude of virtuous actions to benefit sentient beings. They have an attractive form drawing others to them, are born in excellent families, are influential, and have many helpers for their virtuous activities that benefit others. They are trustworthy and reliable, so sentient beings value their advice and give them authority. Because their minds have been transformed into the Dhamma, bodhisattas cannot be subjugated by others but instead subdue others through their noble qualities. Through these accomplishments, bodhisattas are capable and have many opportunities to guide others in the Dhamma of the three vehicles.

Nevertheless, we should not expect every bodhisatta to display all these benefits. Bodhisattas manifest in whatever ways benefit sentient beings according to sentient beings' kamma. Thus they may be from a lower social class, physically unattractive, or have a short life.

The result of bodhicitta and the bodhisattas' pāramīs is buddhahood, with the attainment of the magnificent form body with the thirty-two signs and eighty marks of a great person (*mahāpurisa*, *mahāpuruṣa*), and the dhammakāya, glorious with wondrous qualities such as the ten powers.

Five of the ten perfections in the Pāli and Sanskrit traditions have the same names—generosity, ethical conduct, fortitude, joyous effort, and wisdom. Unshakable resolve (Sanskrit tradition) and determination (Pāli tradition) have different names but similar meaning, as do meditative stability (Sanskrit tradition) and renunciation (Pāli tradition). While truthfulness, love, and equanimity are listed as perfections only in the Pāli tradition, and skillful means, power, and exalted wisdom only in the Sanskrit tradition, the meaning of each of these is found in the teachings of both traditions. Dhammapāla says that when seen according to their nature, the ten perfections become six, which are the six perfections found in the Sanskrit tradition. Thus the great majority of the material is shared in common.

The perfections taught in both traditions will be explained together. This will be followed by the perfections found in one tradition but not another.

Material from Dhammapāla's treatise has Pāli spelling, and material from the Sanskrit tradition has Sanskrit spelling.

Perfection of Generosity

Based on nonattachment and the relinquishing of miserliness, generosity is the mind of giving. Generosity is of four types:

1) *Giving material resources* is giving possessions or money. Bodhisattas give whatever is needed to whoever needs it. They give even if not asked, and they give a suitable amount, not just a little so that the other person will leave them alone. They give without expecting to receive a gift, praise, or fame in return, and when there is not enough to go around, they distribute it equitably among all those in need. They do not give things that may cause harm or stimulate afflictions to arise in others' minds, such as weapons, intoxicants, pornography, and dangerous chemicals. They give only what is appropriate for the recipient and conducive for the other's well-being.

Should bodhisattas notice they are becoming attached to a particular object, they immediately give it away. When asked for things, they contemplate the disadvantages of clinging and see the person asking as a close friend helping to free him from bondage to these items and giving him the opportunity to be generous.

Bodhisattas also give their own body by serving others or giving parts of their body, but they do this only when it is suitable. If they hesitate to give their body, they should think that if people in need of the various parts of a medicinal tree were to come and take them, the tree would not complain. Similarly, since this body has the nature of dukkha and since they have entrusted it to the service of others, there is no sense clinging to it thinking, "This is mine, this am I, this is my self."

Ārya bodhisattvas are able to give their body without hesitation or fear. Practitioners below this level are allowed to give only parts of their body if doing so does not jeopardize their lives. It is wiser for ordinary bodhisattvas to maintain their precious human lives and use them to practice the Dharma. Meanwhile, they can aspire to give their bodies in the future, after they become āryas.

Ārya bodhisattvas who give their bodies do not experience physical suffering due to their great merit and do not experience mental suffering due to their wisdom. Ordinary bodhisattvas feel physical suffering when giving parts of their body. However, the pain they experience serves only to intensify their compassion for other sentient beings, who experience far greater pain in unfortunate rebirths.

We should practice giving possessions as much as we can, making offerings to the Three Jewels each day, offering our food before eating, and giving to those in need. Doing practices in which we imagine giving our body, possessions, and virtues of the past, present, and future are also beneficial, especially if we reflect that the giver, recipient, and gift exist dependently and are empty of inherent existence.

2) *Giving fearlessness* is offering protection to those who are frightened, lost, or in danger. It calms sentient beings' minds and shields them from physical suffering.

3) *Giving love* includes volunteering in social welfare projects, consoling the grieving, and encouraging others' good qualities.

4) *Giving the Dhamma* is giving correct Dhamma teachings that lead to well-being and peace in this and future lives and to liberation and full awakening. Bodhisattas introduce the Dhamma to sentient beings who have not met it and mature the minds of those who are already practicing. They give discourses on the three vehicles according to the disposition of the audience. When sharing the Dhamma, they do not expect special treatment, respect, or offerings but simply give advice or instructions to others as one close friend to another.

Generosity has many benefits. It is the cause to receive resources. Making offerings to the Three Jewels creates a karmic connection that will enable us to meet holy beings who will guide us on the path. Bodhisattvas give whatever is required and beneficial with a joyful heart, knowing that through this, they will attain full awakening.

If we think of the benefits of giving and the disadvantages of stinginess but still cannot bring ourselves to give to a person who has asked for something, the Buddha tells us to humbly explain to him:

> At this point my strength is meager and my roots of virtue are immature.... I still have the perspective of grasping and am stuck in grasping things as I and mine. And so, good person, I beg you to forgive me and not to be upset. [In the future] I will act,

> accomplish, and exert myself in order to fulfill your desires and those of all beings.[32]

Being generous does not mean abolishing all the poverty in the world. If we have the wish to give but lack resources, there is no fault. Each situation in which we are requested to help needs to be examined individually, in light of our motivation, capability, and the repercussions of our action.

Perfection of Ethical Conduct

Ethical conduct is the attitude of abandoning all thoughts of harming others through relinquishing the self-centered attitude. There are three types of ethical conduct:

1) *Restraining from destructive actions* entails abandoning the ten nonvirtues and abiding in whatever precepts and commitments we have taken. It is the best protection from being harmed and is more effective than thousands of warheads and the best bodyguards. Ethical conduct gives us sovereignty over our body, speech, and mind. Those with pure ethical conduct exude the "fragrance of virtue," making them more attractive to others and thus more effective in benefitting them.

If afflictions arise in the mind threatening their virtue, bodhisattas reflect, "Didn't I resolve to attain awakening for the benefit of all beings? To do this, I must teach the Dhamma, and to be a trustworthy guide, I must have a pure character and possess attainments such as the jhānas and wisdom. All these are founded upon pure ethical conduct. Therefore I should protect my ethical conduct." Thus bodhisattas strengthen their ethical resolve, personal integrity, and consideration for others; take lay or monastic precepts; avoid transgressing their precepts by exercising mindfulness and introspective awareness; and purify all transgressions.

Bodhisattvas guard the four gates through which ethical errors occur: (1) ignorance regarding what to practice and abandon, (2) lack of respect for the precepts—not thinking that ethical conduct is important, (3) carelessness, and (4) strong afflictions that overpower the mind. They practice the antidotes to these four by (1) studying the ten virtues and the precepts, (2) developing faith and respect for the precepts by understanding the disadvantages of unethical behavior and the benefits of ethical conduct, (3) being careful and conscientious in their actions by maintaining mindfulness and introspective awareness, and (4) applying antidotes to the afflictions.

2) *Collecting positive qualities* is taking every opportunity to enhance the collections of merit and wisdom in order to progress on the path. Bodhisattas respect their spiritual mentors and those worthy of respect, offer service to them, and care for them during illness. They appreciate advice and instructions given by the wise and rejoice in the merit of others. With gratitude for those who have helped them, they benefit and honor others in return.

3) *Benefiting sentient beings in need* involves caring for the ill and injured, comforting the grieving, giving wise advice to those about to act recklessly, helping others in danger, and facilitating reconciliation and forgiveness. It also entails aiding the blind, deaf, and those who are physically or mentally challenged, helping those without faith to cultivate it, teaching the lazy how to be energetic, and instructing those plagued by the five hindrances in their antidotes. Bodhisattas rehabilitate those with faulty ethical conduct, addictions, and criminal records. In short, in whatever way their companionship, knowledge, or abilities can benefit others, they employ these without hesitation.

Being judicious, bodhisattas are accessible to others but only at the right time, in a suitable place, and in a proper situation. They neither push their help and advice on others nor refuse them when needed. In guiding others, bodhisattas behave only in ways that increase others' good qualities and virtuous actions and avoid abusing or humiliating others. As much as possible, bodhisattvas act in accordance with others' wishes and needs as long as these do not harm themselves or others and do not distract from Dharma practice.

The three types of ethical conduct occur in a fixed sequence. Restraint from harm establishes the foundation for engaging in virtuous actions, which in turn enables us to work for the welfare of sentient beings.

When hearing of the wondrous deeds and spiritual accomplishments of previous bodhisattas, bodhisattas do not become discouraged or overwhelmed but reflect, "Those great beings were once human beings too. They trained in the pāramīs and fulfilled the collections, thus attaining their great abilities. I too will train as they did and attain the same realizations and abilities to benefit others." In this way, bodhisattas generate faith and inspire themselves.

Bodhisattas do not become arrogant due to the purity of their ethical conduct but always remain humble, concealing their virtues and revealing their faults. They are content, do not complain, and are not conceited or manipulative. They are honest and direct yet tactful.

Cultivating the unpolluted wisdom that does not grasp the inherent existence of the sphere of three—the person abandoning the destructive action, the destructive action, and the being who was to be the recipient of harm—makes a bodhisattva's practice of ethical conduct supramundane.

Bodhisattas dedicate their merit for full awakening, not for a fortunate rebirth, release from saṃsāra, or attainment of the superknowledges. Dhammapāla (TP sec. 10) says they dedicate it:

> ...only for the purpose of becoming an omniscient buddha in order to enable all beings to acquire the incomparable adornment of ethical conduct.

Perfection of Fortitude

Fortitude or patience is the ability to remain resolute and calm in the face of hardship or suffering. Remembering the disadvantages of anger as explained earlier inspires us to practice fortitude. Since we cannot identify who is a bodhisattva and who is not, it is better to restrain our anger toward all beings.

Cultivating fortitude brings many benefits. Others find us attractive, we are close to holy beings, our discriminating wisdom is keen, our future rebirths will be fortunate, and our nonvirtues decrease. Fortitude is the basis for a good reputation, enabling us to benefit others. The perfection of fortitude is of three kinds:

1) *The fortitude undisturbed by harm from others* involves not retaliating when others harm us, those dear to us, or our possessions. Here are some themes for reflection to avoid anger, resentment, and spite when others harm us:

- Anger is the real enemy because it destroys all that is good, perpetrates harm, and spreads negativity.
- Enemies are the result of angry thoughts and preconceptions. To free myself from enemies, I must relinquish anger.

- Anger destroys my virtue and merit. Without these I cannot fulfill my bodhisatta aspiration. Until I do that, all sentient beings will be immersed in dukkha.
- No good comes from anger. Due to it, my good qualities and reputation decline. I cannot sleep or eat well.
- This suffering will consume that karma, no longer enabling it to obscure my mind.
- Although this suffering arises from the harmful deeds of others, this body of mine is the field for that suffering, and the karma that made me take this body was created by me alone. There is no reason to blame others for my misery.
- The person harming me is my teacher, enabling me to cultivate fortitude.
- Although this person is harming me now, in the past he has been my friend and someone who has helped.
- All beings are like my children. How can I become angry at their misdeeds done through unknowing?
- This harm is showing me the suffering nature of saṃsāra. I must work to end the dukkha of myself and others.
- It is the nature of the cognitive faculties to encounter pleasant and unpleasant objects.
- The harmer, harmful action, and recipient of harm have ceased at this very moment. They are past. With whom shall I be angry, and who is becoming angry? Since all phenomena are selfless, who can harm whom?
- The Buddha looks at all these beings as dear ones. How can I hate someone the Buddha holds dear?
- Mere phenomena alone exist, devoid of being I or mine. Arising and disintegrating due to causes and conditions, they do not come from anywhere, they do not go anywhere, they are not established anywhere. There is no self-sufficient agency in anything whatsoever.
- The person and the action are different. While an action may be harmful or wrong, the person who does it is not evil. He has the potential to become a buddha. The real troublemaker is his afflictions that make him act in detrimental ways.

Mike Nowak

CAVE OF THE GREAT TIBETAN MEDITATOR MILAREPA,
TSUM VALLEY, NEPAL

The Pāli tradition explains that bodhisattas dissect the experiences of harm and anger into their parts and see that each factor arises dependent on other ones and is transient, arising and passing away in the briefest moment. What is there to cling to? Being impermanent, these factors are unsatisfactory, and being both impermanent and unsatisfactory, they are not suitable to be considered mine, I, or my self. There is no person being criticized and no person feeling hurt due to it.

The Sanskrit tradition explains that after meditating on emptiness, bodhisattvas view all elements of the harm—the harmer, the harmed, and the act of harming—as deceptive, similar to reflections and illusions in that they deceptively appear to exist inherently although they do not. This wisdom enables bodhisattvas to bear suffering without physical or mental anguish and, thus, without anger.

Practicing fortitude and being compassionate do not mean our physical and verbal actions are always passive and pleasing. While calm behavior is appropriate in some situations, in others we may need to act forcefully or assertively to stop one person from harming another. Yet even in such a situation, we act without anger.

When someone harms us and then, realizing his error, sincerely apologizes, it is crucial that we forgive him and do not hold a grudge. Continuing to remind the person of his error or secretly wishing for harm to befall him runs counter to the bodhisattva spirit.

2) *The fortitude of voluntarily accepting suffering* is the ability to endure physical or mental suffering and hardship with calm. There are times in our lives when we willingly bear suffering. A woman in labor willingly bears the pain of childbirth. Similarly, we cultivate the capacity to bear suffering without becoming upset, because doing so will prevent future suffering and enable us to progress on the path to awakening.

When experiencing physical pain from illness or injury or mental pain from injustice or betrayal, we remember that this pain is the result of our own destructive actions. We can reflect, "It is better that this karmic seed ripens now as present suffering than in a horrible rebirth in the future." Or we can think, "May my suffering suffice for the misery of all sentient beings." We contemplate that enduring suffering with a calm mind dispels conceit, strengthens renunciation, fortifies our refuge in the Three Jewels, and increases our compassion.

3) *The fortitude of practicing the Dharma* enables us to happily continue to learn and practice for however long it takes to fathom the Dharma's deep and detailed meanings. Fear and resistance may arise along the path because the Dharma challenges our dearly held but afflictive preconceptions and prejudices. It takes fortitude not to retreat to the habitual emotions and behavior that are the very source of our misery and instead to arouse courage and continue practicing. Meditating on emptiness challenges the very root of innate self-grasping ignorance, so great fortitude and courage are required to dismantle it.

This fortitude includes accepting Dharma concepts that our wisdom has not yet completely penetrated by trusting the Buddha's word on the basis of the teachings we have already understood or experienced. This enables us to continue to investigate the teachings, knowing that time is needed to fully understand them. As we gain the fortitude born from reflecting on the Dharma, we become able to tolerate things that previously seemed intolerable.

Perfection of Joyous Effort

Joyous effort is an attitude that takes delight in virtue. Without it, actualizing our spiritual aspirations is impossible. But with joyous effort we happily practice the path for our own and others' welfare, without discouragement or exhaustion. With indefatigable effort, we will not give up when we undertake to fulfill the collections of merit and wisdom and liberate all sentient beings from saṃsāra. Thus joyous effort is said to be the source of all auspicious attainments.

The texts mention three types of joyous effort:

1. *Armor-like joyous effort* is enthusiasm for practice. It enables us to continue without falling prey to the laziness of procrastination, pursuing meaningless activities, or discouragement. With it, bodhisattvas vow, "I shall dedicate myself for eons to benefit even one sentient being."
2. *Joyous effort of acting constructively* is supported by a deep aspiration to benefit sentient beings, making our mind energetic and delighted to practice.
3. *Joyous effort of benefiting sentient beings* reaches out to help the same groups of sentient beings mentioned in the ethical conduct of benefiting others.

The *Abhisamayālaṃkāra* speaks of three types of joyous effort that counteract the three types of laziness:

1. *Joyous effort of not being attached to frivolous actions* counteracts the laziness of attachment to the eight worldly concerns. Remembering the disadvantages of cyclic existence jolts us out of our complacent distraction.
2. *Joyous effort of not becoming fatigued* opposes the laziness of sleep, lethargy, and procrastination. Contemplating death helps us appreciate the opportunity our present precious human life affords and dispels procrastination.
3. *Joyous effort of thoroughly upholding the path* opposes the laziness of discouragement that thinks, "I am incapable of practicing the Dharma," "The path is too difficult," or "The goal of awakening is too high."

Sometimes we want to develop a certain skill or to help others, but our work does not turn out as we wished and we feel discouraged. This happens to me too. But when I examine my motivation, my confidence returns. I began with a sincere desire to benefit. Regardless of what others may say, knowing that my motivation was genuine gives me courage and inner strength. Even though I may not be outwardly successful, I still feel satisfied. On the other hand, if my motivation is not sincere, then even if others praise me and I become famous, discomfort and self-doubt plague me.

It's important to counteract the laziness of discouragement. Do this by reflecting on the fact that you have the potential for liberation and full awakening. Reflect on the marvelous situation of freedom and fortune that you have with your precious human life. Recall that the Buddha was once a limited sentient being like you, but through his diligent practice, he attained full awakening.

Initially our ability to practice is quite weak. As we practice repeatedly, our capacity increases. When our capacity becomes strong, we will look back and see that what initially seemed almost impossible has now become possible and that we have accomplished what we did not think we could do. Our inner capabilities have grown because we made effort.

Four forces counteract the laziness inhibiting joyous effort: Thinking of the benefits of joyous effort and the faults of laziness, we generate *interest* in cultivating joyous effort and abandon laziness. With *stability* we continue whatever virtuous activities we begin, committing to do them only after examining whether we have the time and ability to complete these projects. With *joy*, we consistently and continuously act in beneficial ways. With *relinquishment*, we rest our body and mind when needed and later enthusiastically resume our virtuous activities.

Bodhisattvas cultivate three types of confidence enabling them to maintain their joyous effort: With *confidence in action*, they are prepared to act alone, without others' help. With *confidence in their capacity to work for others*, they engage in beneficial activities without self-doubt or hesitation. With *confidence to oppose afflictions*, they are determined to prevent and counteract afflictions.

Bodhisattas reflect, "Have I accumulated the collections today? What have I done to benefit sentient beings today?" In this way, they remember their heartfelt spiritual aspiration and encourage themselves to act upon it. Bodhisattas willingly take upon themselves the suffering of all beings and rejoice in their merit and virtues. They frequently recall the Buddha's great qualities and perform all actions motivated by bodhicitta. Whatever happiness they experience, they aspire for all beings to experience it as well. In this way, day by day, they accumulate the requisites for awakening.

Perfections of Meditative Stability and of Renunciation

While different in name, the Sanskrit perfection of meditative stability and the Pāli perfection of renunciation deal with the same practices: renunciation of sense pleasures and cultivation of concentration. The perfection of *meditative stability* involves developing concentration through the nine stages of sustained attention. The method to do this was described previously.

While bodhisattvas renounce the pursuit of sense pleasures to develop the eight meditative absorptions, these are not their main interest. Their ultimate aim is to use their concentration to develop the insight focused on emptiness and then use that to cut the root of saṃsāra and eliminate the two obscurations.

The pāramī of *renunciation* is grounded in realizing the unsatisfactory nature of saṃsāra. Based on a sense of spiritual urgency (*saṃvega*), bodhisattas abandon attachment to sense pleasures and to existence in all saṃsāric realms. Renunciation protects bodhisattas from extreme asceticism, involvement in the afflictions of others, and indulging in sense pleasures.

To reinforce renunciation, bodhisattas reflect on the dangers of sense pleasures, the distraction of the householder's life, and the benefits of monastic life. They see that career and family life lead to numerous entanglements that consume time and galvanize afflictions. Sense pleasures give limited pleasure and abundant harm, like honey smeared on the blade of a sword. They are fleeting like a flash of lightning, and they intensify our thirst like drinking salt water.

Seeing these disadvantages, bodhisattas contemplate the benefits of renunciation, simplicity, and solitude and become monastics. Living with ethical conduct, they cultivate contentment with robes, almsfood, and shelter, and through this they come to delight in meditation and attain the jhānas. Here Dhammapāla discusses the thirteen ascetic practices and the forty meditation objects for the cultivation of serenity.

Perfection of Wisdom

Cultivating the wisdom, intelligence, and knowledge to attain full awakening does not require a high IQ or educational degree. Rather we must be open-minded, have the ability to learn and analyze clearly, be sincere in our spiritual aspirations, and have created sufficient merit. Our intelligence and ability to understand can be increased in this life through learning, thinking, and meditating under the guidance of a wise and compassionate teacher.

In the Sanskrit tradition, the perfection of wisdom is of three types: wisdom understanding emptiness, wisdom of fields of knowledge and skills necessary to benefit sentient beings, and wisdom knowing how to benefit sentient beings. Here the wisdom realizing emptiness is emphasized, because without it we remain in saṃsāra and our ability to benefit others is restricted.

Meditation on emptiness is of two kinds: space-like meditation and illusion-like meditation. *Space-like meditation* is meditative equipoise on emptiness—the selflessness of persons and phenomena. It is called "space-like" because emptiness is unencumbered and limitless like space and the mind meditating on emptiness is spacious, uncluttered by the appearances of inherently existent objects and discursive conceptualizations.

After refuting inherent existence, what remains is mere nominal existence. It is obvious from our own experience that things exist and bring help or harm; our actions have effects. However, when we analyze *how* these things exist, we cannot find anything that exists "from its own side," in its own right. Everything exists by being merely designated.

After practitioners arise from meditative equipoise on emptiness, things once again appear inherently existent due to the latencies of ignorance. Bodhisattvas now do *illusion-like meditation*, reflecting that things are like illusions in that they appear one way (as inherently existent) but exist in another (as empty of inherent existence). This meditation enables practitioners to remain equanimous regarding the seemingly attractive and repulsive things they encounter. Mindfulness of the illusion-like nature of persons and phenomena reinforces their realization of emptiness in formal meditation sessions.

In the Pāli tradition, the perfection of wisdom understands the general and specific characteristics of phenomena. It arises based on concentration and knowledge of the four truths and clearly illuminates phenomena.

Wisdom purifies all the other perfections, enabling them to serve as the foundation for the omniscient mind of a buddha. Wisdom enables bodhisattas to *give* even their own bodies. It frees *ethical conduct* from afflictions such as craving. Recognizing the dangers of sense pleasures and the householder's life, wisdom knows the benefits of *renunciation*, jhāna, and nibbāna. It steers *joyous effort* in a proper direction, enabling it to accomplish all virtues. Wisdom gives bodhisattas *fortitude* when encountering others' wrongdoings and offensive behavior. Those with wisdom speak *truthfully*, have firm *determination*, *lovingly* care for the welfare of all beings, and maintain *equanimity* when serving and guiding them and while still abiding with the vicissitudes of saṃsāra.

To cultivate *wisdom arising from learning*, bodhisattas fully study the five aggregates, six sources, eighteen constituents, four ariya truths, twenty-two faculties, twelve links of dependent arising (Vism 14–17), four establishments of mindfulness, and classifications of phenomena. Bodhisattas also learn worthy fields of knowledge that could be useful to sentient beings. Bodhisattas cultivate the *wisdom arising from thinking* by reflecting on the specific characteristics of the phenomena that they have studied.

Then they engage in the *preliminary portion of the wisdom arising from meditation*, which is included under mundane kinds of full understanding (*pariññā*, *parijñāna*). Here bodhisattas discern the three general characteristics of the aggregates and understand all internal and external phenomena as follows, "This is mere name and form (*nāmarūpamatta*), which arise and cease according to conditions. There is no agent or actor. It is impermanent in the sense of not being after having been; unsatisfactory in the sense of oppression by changing; and not self in the sense of being unsusceptible to the exercise of mastery." Through this understanding bodhisattas abandon attachment and lead others to do so too. They mature sentient beings' minds in the paths of the three vehicles, helping them to attain the jhānas, meditative liberations, concentrations, attainments, and mundane superknowledges. They continue doing this until they reach the peak of wisdom and the qualities of the Buddha are in sight.

The *wisdom arising from meditation* may be spoken of in two ways: the five mundane superknowledges (Vism 12–13) and the five purifications. Purification of view, purification by overcoming doubt, purification by knowledge and vision of what is and is not the path, and purification by knowledge and vision of the way are mundane purifications. Purification by knowledge and vision is the supramundane knowledge of the four ariya paths (Vism 18–22).

Dhammapāla comments that the *Visuddhimagga* describes these topics for someone following the sāvaka path to arahantship. Bodhisattas should practice them with compassion, bodhicitta, and the skillful means of wisdom. In addition, bodhisattas develop wisdom up to and including purification by knowledge and vision of the way. They must wait to attain purification by knowledge and vision because this is the four ariya paths that realize nibbāna in stages. Before entering the ariya paths, bodhisattas must skillfully balance their development of compassion and wisdom, and only when the pāramīs are complete do they enter the ariya paths and attain full awakening. In this way their attaining nibbāna will coincide with their full awakening.

Perfections of Unshakable Resolve and of Determination

The Sanskrit perfection of unshakable resolve and the Pāli perfection of determination are similar. The *perfection of unshakable resolve* entails making strong aspirations and resolute determinations to do specific great deeds for the benefit of sentient beings. In the Sanskrit tradition, these include the twelve pledges of the Medicine Buddha, forty-eight pledges of Amitābha Buddha, and ten pledges of Samantabhadra. According to the *Gaṇḍavyūha Sūtra*, the latter are to pay homage to all buddhas, praise all buddhas, make abundant offerings, confess destructive actions, rejoice in others' virtues, request the buddhas to teach, request the buddhas to remain in the world, follow the teachings of the buddhas at all times, benefit and live harmoniously with all living beings, and dedicate all merit to sentient beings.

Bodhisattvas make unshakable resolves that may not be actualized, such as promising to lead each and every sentient being out of suffering. Making such pledges is not a pointless pursuit. It strengthens our determination to be of whatever benefit we can to whatever sentient being is in need, regardless of the difficulties it may entail for us personally. As ordinary beings with limited physical and mental abilities, we have to assess what we can actually do before acting. Nevertheless, making such wonderful resolutions, even if they seem unrealistic, expands the scope and strength of our minds so that gradually we will be able to increase our capacity to benefit others.

The *perfection of determination* is the unshakable resolve to fulfill our promise to liberate sentient beings and to perfect the ten pāramīs. It gives us the courage to remain steadfast in the practice, even when afflictive mental states threaten to dislodge us.

The above practices are shared by the Pāli and Sanskrit traditions. The following ones are found in the list of perfections from one tradition but not the other, although they are in fact practiced in both traditions.

Perfections of Skillful Means, Power, and Exalted Wisdom

Skillful means indicates the way in which buddhas and bodhisattvas, motivated by compassion, explain the teachings and adapt their behavior to best communicate with sentient beings, who have unique needs and capacities. Skillful means also includes bodhisattvas' ability to see all phenomena as empty without abandoning sentient beings, and to their ability to abide in deep states of concentration without being hindered by attachment to rebirth in the material and immaterial realms.

The *Bodhisattvabhūmi* describes two sets of skillful means. Regarding the first, *accomplishing all the qualities of a buddha within themselves*, bodhisattvas practice looking upon all sentient beings with compassion, taking rebirth in saṃsāra due to compassion and wisdom, knowing the ultimate nature of phenomena, not abandoning beings in saṃsāra, desiring the exalted wisdom of unsurpassed awakening, and spurring their enthusiasm with bodhicitta.

Regarding the second, *ripening all other living beings*, bodhisattvas cultivate the ability to teach sentient beings how to transform small actions into great virtue, cause them to accomplish great roots of virtue without hardship, eliminate anger in those who dislike the Buddha's doctrine, encourage those with a neutral attitude to enter into the Buddha's doctrine, ripen the mindstreams of those who have entered into the Dharma, and cause mature sentient beings to attain liberation.

Power is of many types: the power of no longer indulging in the afflictions because they have been abandoned, the power of superior thought to train in the exalted wisdom of ārya bodhisattvas, the power of remembering all Dharma teachings heard or read, the power to remain in deep concentration without being distracted, the power of knowing the behavior of each sentient being in the countless realms, the power to fulfill all our aims, the power of being skilled in distinguishing and examining the Buddha's qualities, the power to not give up engaging in the Buddhas' activities, the power to completely ripen the Buddha's qualities within self and others, the power of great love protecting all sentient beings without bias, the power of great compassion to eliminate the duḥkha of all sentient beings without bias, the power to experience the ultimate reality that is like an illusion, and the power of approaching the exalted wisdom of omniscience.

Contemplating these powers of ārya bodhisattvas gives us a glimpse of the qualities we will be able to gain by practicing the Bodhisattva Vehicle. Creating the causes for such powers and using them to benefit ourselves and others will bring us great satisfaction, confidence, and exuberance to practice.

The perfection of *exalted wisdom* knows the diversity of phenomena, conventionalities, and enables bodhisattvas to be of great benefit to all beings.

Pāramīs of Truthfulness, Love, and Equanimity

Truthfulness is speaking without deception. Through speaking truthfully and acting according to our promises, we remain true to our word to benefit sentient beings and do not abandon them. Through this, they will come to trust us, which opens the door to our benefiting them.

Bodhisattas speak the truth, whether others react by helping or harming them. They teach the Dhamma skillfully, according to the inclination of the audience, but do not alter the Buddha's word so that others will give them respect or offerings. Thus sentient beings can trust that bodhisattas' teachings are the actual Dhamma, not something adjusted or made up to indulge their afflictions.

With truthfulness bodhisattas accept the empty nature of beings. Not being deceived about the true nature of phenomena, they complete all collections for awakening and accomplish the bodhisatta path.

Love is the aspiration to give happiness to all sentient beings and create the conditions whereby they will be happy. Bodhisattas think, "It is good to wish others happiness, but that alone will not give them happiness. I must act with love and joyous effort to accomplish this." They also reflect that sentient beings are the incomparable field of merit with which they are able to cultivate virtue and fulfill the collections. In that way, bodhisattas consis-

Brian Harris (Tibetan Nuns Project)

BUTTER LAMP PUJA AT DOLMA LING NUNNERY IN DHARAMSALA, INDIA.

tently maintain a mind that cherishes sentient beings and never abandons them. With an unbounded heart they reach out to give happiness to others. To do that, they must eliminate sentient beings' misery and its cause, the afflictions. In this way they generate compassion wishing sentient beings to be free from suffering and its causes.

Equanimity is impartiality regarding the desirable and undesirable, the pleasing and displeasing. Remaining equanimous, bodhisattas continue to practice no matter what comes their way. With equanimity they benefit sentient beings without discriminating between those who help and those who harm.

Without equanimity the mind oscillates according to what we encounter from the people and things around us. This lack of balance impedes concentration, disturbs ethical conduct, and obstructs acting in ways that benefit sentient beings. Imbued with equanimity, we can face whatever comes in a balanced way, free from worry, discontent, and fear, thus increasing our determination to serve sentient beings and supporting the practice of all the pāramīs.

The Four Ways of Gathering Disciples

Found in both the Pāli and Sanskrit traditions, the four ways of gathering disciples are used by bodhisattvas to inspire people's interest in the Dharma and persuade them to learn and practice. These are also known as "four ways of promoting the good of others" and "four means of unification," in which we form a community unified by the common goal of Dharma practice.

1) *Being generous and giving material aid* involves helping others materially by supplying them with what they need. Others will be attracted by our generosity, and that opens the door for us to teach them the Dharma. Also, giving ensures that they have the material requisites to learn the Dharma, without which sincere disciples will be unable to practice. The Pāli and the Sanskrit traditions both attest that the gift of the Dharma is the highest gift, because it enables others to create the causes for temporal and ultimate happiness themselves.

2) *Friendly, pleasant speech* involves speaking to others in a variety of ways depending on the situation. We may talk with people about what interests them to make their acquaintance. When they are receptive to the Dharma, we speak pleasantly by instructing them in the Buddha's teachings and giving them wise advice when they face difficulties. Bodhisattvas speak politely, respect others, listen carefully to what they say, and do not force their ideas on others. They are not biased regarding who they teach—rich and poor, male and female, ordained and lay.

3) To *encourage others with beneficial conduct*, we praise their good qualities and support them so they can practice the Dharma and transform their physical, verbal, and mental actions into virtue. We may do this by organizing or leading Buddhist services, meditations, and retreats. By engaging in social welfare projects, Buddhists show the public that our compassion is not merely verbal, and they become attracted to the Dharma. Encouraging others who face karmic obstacles that make them resistant to the Dharma requires great patience and diligence but is worthwhile. In short, we try to arouse faith in the skeptic, virtue in the unethical, generosity in the stingy, and wisdom in the ignorant (AN 9:5).

4) *Acting congruently and living the teachings through personal example* inspires others to practice and increases their faith in the Three Jewels. Embodying the Dharma in our daily actions is essential to be worthy of others' trust and be able to continue to benefit them. Here we work and live with others, providing them with a good example of how to live a kind and ethical life. In skillful ways we lead others to adopt virtuous ways.

Teaching the Dharma is highly beneficial, but it is also a great responsibility that must be approached gradually and with the permission of our spiritual mentor. A compassionate motivation for teaching is of crucial importance, and we must continually reflect on and purify our motivation. The Buddha criticized monastics who taught in the hope that others would listen to them and express their appreciation by offering requisites and other gifts. Such a way of teaching is impure. The Buddha explained the pure way to teach (SN 16:3):

> But a bhikkhu who teaches the Dhamma to others with the thought: "The Dhamma is well expounded by the Blessed One, directly visible, immediate, inviting one to come and see, applicable, to be personally experienced by the wise. Oh, may they listen to the Dhamma from me! Having listened, may they understand the Dhamma! Having understood, may they practice accordingly!" Thus he teaches the Dhamma to others because of the intrinsic excellence of the Dhamma; he teaches the Dhamma to others from compassion and sympathy, out of tender concern. Such a bhikkhu's teaching of the Dhamma is pure.

To give the Dharma to others, we must know it well ourselves; otherwise we run the risk of giving incorrect teachings and damaging students. We should not teach topics we do not understand well. When we do not know the answer to a question, it is best to say, "I don't know," and then consult our teacher or research the topic in Dharma texts.

14 | The Possibility of Awakening and Buddha Nature

Is Liberation Possible?

If the possibility of ending duḥkha exists, then pursuing that aim is worthwhile. Two factors make liberation possible: the nature of the mind is clear light (*pabhassara, prabhāsvara*), and the defilements are adventitious.

According to the Sanskrit tradition, the clear-light nature of the mind refers to the basic, vivid nature of the mind—its clear and cognizant conventional nature that enables it to cognize objects. This capacity for the mind to be aware of or to know objects is already there; it does not have to be cultivated newly.

The mind's inability to know certain objects must then be due to obstructing factors. A material object, such as a wall, obstructs us from seeing what is beyond it. An object being too far away or too small makes it unperceivable to normal senses. Damage of the cognitive faculty—for example, being blind—inhibits our knowing a visual object. The type of cognitive faculties and brain of the realm we are born into can obstruct knowing objects. Human ears cannot hear sounds that many animals can, and animal brains inhibit elaborate conceptual knowledge and the use of language.

A further difficulty is that some things—for example objects known by the six superknowledges—are so subtle, profound, or vast that the ordinary mind is unable to cognize them. To know these, deep meditative concentration, sometimes coupled with correct wisdom, is needed.

The subtle latencies of ignorance on the mind and the mistaken appearances and perceptions they generate prevent us from knowing all phenomena. When the wisdom realizing the subtle selflessness of all phenomena has completely removed every last mental obscuration, the mind will naturally perceive all objects because there will be nothing to prevent this. Thus a buddha's mind is omniscient, capable of simultaneously realizing all phenomena, including their emptiness, in a single cognitive event.

The basic nature of the mind is clear like water. Any dirt in the water is not the nature of water and can be removed. No matter how murky the water is, its essential clarity is never lost. Similarly, afflictions are adventitious; they have not penetrated the basic nature of the mind. Not every instance of the mind's clarity and cognizance is associated with afflictions. If the afflictions were inherent to the mind, they would always be present, and it would be impossible to eliminate them.

The nature of the mind is also said to be clear light because the mind is empty of inherent existence. This is the mind's natural purity. If the mind existed inherently, the ignorance grasping inherent existence would be a correct knower and would thus be impossible to eliminate. However, the mind and all other phenomena exist dependently. Inherent existence does not exist, and ignorance that grasps it is a wrong consciousness.

Wisdom perceives the emptiness of inherent existence, how phenomena actually exist. Since it realizes the opposite of what ignorance grasps, wisdom has the ability to uproot ignorance. The more we become accustomed to wisdom, the more ignorance and other afflictions diminish, until they cease altogether. The afflictions that have beginninglessly obscured our mind are not abandoned by prayer, by requesting blessings from the Buddha or deities, or by gaining single-pointed concentration. They are eradicated only by wisdom that analyzes and then directly perceives ultimate reality. Because ignorance has an antidote, it can be removed, and liberation is possible. Destroying the afflictions does not destroy the mind itself; the pure nature of the mind remains. This is the meaning of ignorance and afflictions being adventitious.

Each Buddhist tenet system has a slightly different interpretation of liberation and nirvāṇa, but all agree that it is a quality of a mind that has forever separated from the defilements causing saṃsāra through the application of antidotes to those defilements.

When we examine that separation from defilements, we discover it is the ultimate nature of the mind that is free from defilements. This ultimate nature of mind has existed from beginningless time; it exists as long as there is mind. Within the continuum of a sentient being, the ultimate nature of the mind is called *buddha nature* or *buddha potential.* When it becomes endowed with the quality of having separated from defilements, it is called *nirvāṇa.* Therefore, the very basis for nirvāṇa, the emptiness of the mind, is always with us. It's not something newly created or gained from outside.

Furthermore, the mind's good qualities can be cultivated limitlessly, transforming our mind into a buddha's fully awakened mind. Three factors make this possible.

The clear and cognizant nature of the mind is a stable basis for the cultivation of all excellent qualities. The clear-light mind is firm and continual; it cannot be severed. Qualities cannot be cultivated limitlessly on an unstable basis such as the physical body. The more we train in excellent qualities based on this firm basis, the more those qualities will be enhanced limitlessly, until they are fully perfected in the state of buddhahood.

The mind can become habituated to good qualities that are built up cumulatively. Good mental qualities can be built up gradually, without having to begin all over again each time we focus on developing them. A high jumper cannot develop his ability limitlessly—each time the bar is raised, he must cover the same distance as before plus some. However, the energy from cultivating a mental quality today remains so that, if we cultivate that same quality tomorrow, we are able to build upon what we did yesterday. Because we do not need the same degree of energy to get to yesterday's level again, the same effort will serve to increase that good quality. Of course this requires consistent training on our part; otherwise like an athlete, our spiritual "muscles" will atrophy. But if we practice regularly, our energy can be directed to enhancing the good qualities continuously, until the point where they become so familiar that they are natural and spontaneous.

Good qualities are enhanced, not diminished, by reasoning and wisdom. Constructive attitudes and emotions have a valid support in reasoning and are thus never harmed by the wisdom realizing reality. Compassion, faith, integrity, and all other excellent qualities can be cultivated together with wisdom and are enhanced by wisdom. For this reason, too, they can be cultivated limitlessly.

All Buddhist traditions accept that vast good qualities can be cultivated and defilements can be entirely eliminated from the mind. Each tradition describes the basis upon which this occurs somewhat differently.

Pāli Tradition: Luminous Mind

In the Pāli scriptures the Buddha identified certain characteristics that reveal spiritual practitioners' aptitude for liberation. Having modest desire and a sense of contentment signify people are genuine spiritual practitioners aiming for liberation. Indicating their potential to gain attainments, these characteristics should be cultivated daily.

Some sūtras speak of the mind being luminous and this being the basis for mental development. The Buddha says (AN 1:51–52):

> This mind, bhikkhus, is luminous, but it is defiled by adventitious defilements. Uninstructed worldlings do not understand this as it really is; therefore for them there is no development of the mind.
>
> This mind, bhikkhus, is luminous, and it is freed from adventitious defilements. Instructed ariyas understand this as it really is; therefore for them there is development of the mind.

The Buddha also says (DN 11:85):

> Where consciousness is signless, boundless, all-luminous...

Yogācāra School: Buddha Nature

Buddha nature (*buddhagotra*)[33] is spoken of in Sanskrit texts such as the Prajñāpāramitā sūtras, Maitreya's *Abhisamayālaṃkāra* and *Uttaratantra*, and Asaṅga's *Bodhisattvabhūmi*. It is discussed from three perspectives: the Yogācāra, Madhyamaka, and Tantrayana.

According to Yogācāra, buddha nature is the seed or potency that has existed since beginningless time and has the potential to give rise to the three bodies of a buddha. A conditioned phenomenon, it is the seed of unpolluted exalted wisdom. Saying the buddha nature is a seed fits in well with the Yogācāra system that sees everything as arising due to seeds on the foundation consciousness. When this seed of unpolluted exalted wisdom has not yet been nourished by learning, reflecting, and meditating, it is called the *naturally abiding buddha nature*. When the same seed has been nourished by learning, reflecting, and meditating on the Dharma, it is called the *evolving buddha nature*. As the naturally abiding buddha nature, it is a simple seed that has three characteristics: (1) it has existed since beginningless time and has gone from one life to the next uninterruptedly, (2) it is not newly created but naturally abides in us, and (3) it is carried by the foundation consciousness according to Yogācāra Scriptural Proponents and by

CHINESE MONASTICS BOWING

the mental consciousness according to Yogācāra Reasoning Proponents. Both agree that because sensory consciousnesses are only intermittently present and therefore not a stable basis, they cannot be the buddha nature.

Later, when the naturally abiding buddha nature has been awakened and transformed by means of learning, reflecting, and meditating, it brings forth the realization of the ārya path and is called the *evolving buddha nature*. The Yogācāra Scriptural Proponents assert that these seeds or potencies are of three types, according to the three vehicles. Because these seeds are inherently existent, they cannot change into a seed for another vehicle; thus there are three final vehicles. Not every sentient being will become a buddha; some will become Śrāvaka or Pratyekabuddha arhats and abide forever in personal liberation.

Yogācāra Reasoning Proponents and Mādhyamikas both assert one final vehicle and say that all beings will eventually become fully awakened buddhas, including those who enter the śrāvaka and pratyekabuddha vehicles and attain arhatship first.

Madhyamaka School: Buddha Nature

The *Ratnagotravibhāga* defines buddha nature as phenomena having the possibility to transform into any of the buddha bodies. From the Madhyamaka perspective, *buddha nature* principally refers to the emptiness of the mind that is yet to abandon defilements. This empty nature of the mind is beyond time, beyond saṃsāra, and beyond constructive and destructive karma. Neither virtuous nor nonvirtuous, it can act as the basis for both saṃsāra and nirvāṇa. Because buddha nature is simply the mind's absence of inherent existence and a buddha's mind also lacks inherent existence, Nāgārjuna notes that the nature of a tathāgata is the nature of sentient beings (MMK 22:16). However, that does not mean sentient beings are already buddhas. For while sentient beings' minds have defilements, buddhas' minds do not.

The fact that the nature of the mind is empty does not mean we have already realized emptiness. Only when we realize the empty nature of the mind directly and use that realization to cleanse our minds of defilements will it serve as the basis for āryas' qualities.

An unconditioned phenomenon that does not depend on causes, the mind's emptiness of inherent existence is also called *natural nirvāṇa*. The emptiness of an ordinary being's mind exists as long as that ordinary being does. When that ordinary being becomes an ārya, the emptiness of that ordinary being's mind no longer exists, but the emptiness of an ārya's mind does. These two emptinesses are both the absence of inherent existence, and when perceived by a mind that realizes them directly, there is no difference between them.

As explained above, because the ultimate nature of the mind is empty of inherent existence, the mental defilements obscuring our vision of ultimate reality can be separated from it and removed. These defilements are not embedded in the ultimate nature of the mind.

Insight into the mind's emptiness, natural nirvāṇa, is the crucial element necessary to overcome all defilements. Cultivating this wisdom initiates the process of undoing the causal chain of the twelve links. By realizing natural nirvāṇa, we will attain the nirvāṇa that is the pacification of mental defilements. This nirvāṇa is the ultimate true cessation, the third truth of the āryas.

As explained in chapter 2, the nature of a buddha's mind has a twofold purity: its natural stainless purity free from inherent existence, and its purity from having eradicated all adventitious defilements. These two comprise a buddha's nature dharmakāya. While sentient beings' minds are empty of inherent existence and their defilements are adventitious, we cannot say their buddha nature is the nature dharmakāya of a buddha with this twofold purity. That is because sentient beings' minds are still obscured by defilements.

Like Yogācāras, Mādhyamikas also speak of naturally abiding buddha nature and evolving buddha nature, although they describe them differently. These two types of buddha nature exist in all sentient beings, whether or not they are on a path. *Naturally abiding buddha nature* is the emptiness of a mind that is not freed from defilement and is able to transform into a buddha's nature dharmakāya. *Evolving buddha nature* is the seed for the unpolluted mind. It consists of conditioned phenomena that will transform into a buddha's wisdom dharmakāya. Without this seed in our minds, there would be no way for the awakening activities of the Buddha to enter into us because there would be nothing in our minds that could germinate by coming into contact with the Buddha's teachings. The evolving buddha nature enables our minds to be affected and transformed by the teachings. The fact that the Buddha taught the Dharma indicates sentient beings have the potential to become buddhas. If we didn't, his turning the Dharma wheel would have been useless.

The evolving buddha nature includes neutral mental consciousnesses as well as love, compassion, wisdom, bodhicitta, faith, and other virtuous mental states that can be gradually developed as we progressively attain the ten bodhisattva grounds. At the time we become buddhas, our naturally abiding buddha nature will become the nature dharmakāya, and our evolving buddha nature will become the wisdom dharmakāya.

Afflictions cannot be transformed into any of the buddha bodies and do not have buddha nature. Although nonsentient phenomena such as rocks and grass are empty of inherent existence, they do not have buddha nature because they lack mind and cannot generate virtuous mental states.

No matter what realm a sentient being is born into, the naturally abiding buddha nature is always there. It does not decrease or increase. Gold may be buried in the ground for centuries, but uncovering it is always possible. It may be covered with dirt, but it doesn't become dirt. Although the dirt obscures it, it can be cleansed so that its natural radiance shines. Because the buddha nature exists, we can cleanse it and cultivate all good qualities limitlessly.

Tantrayāna: Buddha Nature

According to the unique description of highest yoga tantra, buddha nature is the subtlest mind-wind, whose nature is empty of inherent existence. The subtlest mind is an extremely refined state of mind, also called the *innate clear-light mind*. The subtlest wind-energy is its mount. The two are inseparable. All sentient beings have this subtlest mind-wind, and its continuity goes on until awakening. It is not a soul or independent essence; it changes moment by moment and is selfless and empty of independent existence. When we die, the coarser levels of mind dissolve into the innate clear-light mind, and when we are reborn, coarser consciousnesses again emerge from the basis of the innate clear-light mind. When these coarser levels of consciousness are present, constructive and destructive thoughts arise and create karma. The result of afflicted thoughts is saṃsāra, the result of virtuous mental states such as renunciation, bodhicitta, and wisdom is the attainment of nirvāṇa. In this way, the innate clear light is the basis for both saṃsāra and nirvāṇa. Sentient beings' subtlest mind serves as the substantial cause for a buddha's wisdom dharmakāya, and the subtlest wind-energy is the substantial cause for a buddha's form body.

In ordinary beings, the subtlest mind-wind manifests only at the time of the clear light of death, when it goes unnoticed. While it is neutral in the case of ordinary beings, special yogic practices can transform it into virtue, thus bringing it into the path to full awakening. Doing this is the heart of highest yoga tantra. Through special tantric practices this subtlest clear-light mind is activated, made blissful, and then used to realize emptiness. Because this mind-wind is so subtle, when it realizes emptiness directly, it becomes a very strong counterforce to eradicate both afflictive and cognitive obscurations. In this way buddhahood may be attained quickly.

Chan: Buddha Nature, Bodhicitta, and True Suchness

From the perspective of Chinese Chan, all sentient beings have the buddha nature that is by nature pure. Here "pure" means it transcends the duality of purity and impurity. When the buddha nature is fully manifested, that being is a buddha. But because of afflictions and defilements—especially ignorance—buddha nature is not presently manifest in sentient beings.

Pure mind and *buddha nature* refer to the same thing but approach it from different angles. *Pure mind* indicates that the nature of the mind is not and cannot be polluted by defilements. *Buddha nature* refers to the aspect of the mind that guarantees our potential and capability to become buddhas. When fully purified, it is called the *awakened mind* or *actual bodhicitta*, indicating that when ignorance was present we did not know our pure nature, and now with the removal of ignorance we see and understand it. From the perspective that unawakened beings do not yet recognize the pure nature of their mind, it is said they do not have the bodhi mind (bodhicitta), but from the perspective of the fundamental nature of the mind being pure of adventitious defilements, it is said they have the bodhi mind.

Here *bodhicitta* refers to the pure mind that can never be tarnished. It is like a pearl that has been covered with mud for thousands of years. Even though it is hidden in mud and its luster cannot be seen, none of its shining beauty has been lost; it is just temporarily obscured. It can be removed from the mud and cleaned so that its beauty is visible to all. Its luster did not decrease by being covered with mud, and its luster did not increase once it was removed from the mud. Similarly, our buddha nature is always pure. Its qualities do not decrease when it is covered with defilements, and they do not increase when the defilements are eradicated.

Bodhicitta is buddha nature. In the Chan tradition the terms *true suchness, buddha nature, original nature, ultimate reality, pure nature*, and so on have similar meanings. They refer to what cannot be fully known with words. To realize the buddha nature or bodhicitta is to realize that it is uncreated; it does not disappear, it is originally pure.

Peixiu, a Tang-dynasty layman praised by the Huayen and Chan patriarch Zongmi, explains that bodhicitta must be generated from our "true mind"—from the pure aspect of our mind that is part of our buddha nature. It does not arise from identifying with our saṃsāric body or the obscured mind obsessed by sense pleasure and worldly success. Our true body is "perfect and complete, empty and quiescent," and our true mind is vast in its scope and imbued with intelligence and awareness. The perfect and complete dharmakāya is replete with countless virtuous qualities; it is empty and quiescent in that it goes beyond all forms and characteristics and is forever free of disturbance. The true mind is vast in that it coincides with the dharmadhātu—the sphere of reality. It is imbued with intelligence and awareness because it is focused, penetrating, and clear, investigating illumination. Encompassing great virtuous qualities, it cuts through fallacious thinking, such as the wrong view that things arise from self, other, both, or causelessly. Like a full moon obscured by the clouds of afflictions, its original purity will manifest when the afflictions have been abandoned. As said in the

Avataṃsaka Sūtra, "The mind, the Buddha, and beings as well—in these three, there are no distinctions." This true mind is the same as the essence of the bodhicitta. When we do not see this, we become entwined with false conceptualizations and engage in actions that bind us in saṃsāra.

Understanding Tathāgatagarbha

In the Tathāgatagarbha sūtras popular in China and Tibet, the Buddha explains that each sentient being has a permanent, stable, and enduring *tathāgatagarbha*, or "buddha essence," that is a fully developed buddha body complete with the thirty-two signs. While some people take this literally and accept it as a definitive teaching, Mādhyamikas disagree, asking, "If a buddha existed within us in our present state, wouldn't we be ignorant buddhas? If we were actually buddhas now, what would be the purpose of practicing the path? If we had a permanent, stable, and enduring essence, wouldn't that contradict the teachings on selflessness and instead resemble the self asserted by non-Buddhists?" These same doubts were expressed by Mahāmati in the *Laṅkāvatāra Sūtra*:

> The tathāgatagarbha taught [by the Buddha] is said to be clear light in nature, completely pure from the beginning, and to exist, possessing the thirty-two signs, in the bodies of all sentient beings. If, like a precious gem wrapped in a dirty cloth, [the Buddha] expressed that [tathāgatagarbha] wrapped in and dirtied by the cloth of the aggregates, constituents, and sources, overwhelmed by the force of attachment, anger, and ignorance, dirtied with the defilements of thought, and permanent, stable, and enduring, how is this propounded as tathāgatagarbha different from the non-Buddhists propounding a self?

In examining the meaning of the tathāgatagarbha teachings, Mādhyamikas respond to three questions.

What was the Buddha's final intended meaning when making such a statement? When he spoke of a permanent, stable, and enduring essence in each sentient being, his intended meaning was the emptiness of the mind, the naturally abiding buddha nature, which is permanent, stable, and enduring. Because the mind is empty of inherent existence and the defilements are adventitious, buddhahood is possible.

What was the Buddha's purpose for teaching this? At present, some people are spiritually immature, and the idea of selflessness and emptiness frightens them. They mistakenly think it means that nothing whatsoever exists and fear that by realizing emptiness they will cease to exist. To calm their fear and gradually lead them to the full and correct realization of emptiness, the Buddha spoke in a way that corresponded with their current ideas, saying there was a permanent, stable, enduring essence, complete with the thirty-two signs.

What logical inconsistencies arise from taking this statement at face value? If this were a literal teaching, there would be no difference between this and the assertions of non-Buddhists who adhere to a permanent, inherently existent self. A permanent essence contradicts the definitive meaning—the emptiness of inherent existence—as expressed in the Prajñāpāramitā sūtras, and it is refuted by reasoning.

The emptiness of inherent existence—the ultimate reality and natural purity of the mind—exists in all sentient beings without distinction. In that sense, it is said a buddha is there. But an actual buddha does not exist in sentient beings. While buddhas and sentient beings are similar in that the ultimate nature of their minds is emptiness, that ultimate reality is not the same because one is the ultimate nature of a buddha's mind—the nature dharmakāya—and the other is the ultimate nature of a defiled mind. If the nature dharmakāya existed in sentient beings, the wisdom dharmakāya, which is one nature with it, would also exist in sentient beings. That would mean that sentient beings would be omniscient, which is not the case! Similarly, if the abandonment of all defilements existed in sentient beings, there would be nothing preventing them from directly perceiving emptiness, and they would have that realization. This, too, is not the case.

If the thirty-two signs were already present in us, it would be contradictory to say that we still need to practice the path to create the causes for them. If someone said that they were already in us in an unmanifest form and just needed to be made manifest, that would resemble the Sāṃkhya notion of arising from self, and Mādhyamikas refute that notion. The sūtra continues with the Buddha's response:

> Mahāmati, my teaching of the tathāgatagarbha is not similar to the propounding of a self by the non-Buddhists. Mahāmati, the tathāgata arhats, the completely perfect buddhas, having indicated the tathāgatagarbha with the meaning of the words

> *emptiness, the limit of complete purity, nirvāṇa, unproduced, signless, wishless*, and so forth so that the immature might completely relinquish a state of fear due to the selfless, teach the nonconceptual state, the sphere without appearance.

Here we see that the Buddha skillfully taught different things to different people, according to what was necessary at the moment to lead them on the path. We also learn that we must think deeply about the teachings, employ reasoning, and read widely in the sūtras and commentaries to discern their definitive meaning. By doing so, we will reach the correct understanding of the Tathāgatagarbha sūtras, which contain profound teachings hinting at the existence of the fundamental innate clear-light mind explained in tantra.

The purpose of learning about buddha nature and tathāgatagarbha is to understand that the mind is not intrinsically flawed and can be perfected, and that aspects of the mind already exist that allow it to be purified and perfected. Understanding this will give us great confidence and energy to practice the methods to purify and perfect this mind of ours so that it will become the mind of a fully awakened buddha.

15 | Tantra

ACCORDING TO the understanding of Buddhist Vajrayāna masters, Tantrayāna is an important part of the Buddhist heritage passed down through the Nālandā and Vikramaśīla masters in ancient India as well as by itinerant yogis. Buddhist tantra differs from non-Buddhist forms of tantra in that it is conjoined with refuge in the Three Jewels as a foundation and with renunciation, bodhicitta, and correct wisdom as the mainstays of the practice. Thus Vajrayāna evolves from ideas mentioned in the Pāli and general Sanskrit teachings.

In general, the uniqueness of Vajrayāna comes from its sophistication in concentration and meditation practices that make it possible to attain full awakening quickly compared to the three countless great eons required to accumulate merit and wisdom by following the Sūtrayāna. Ideally, Tantrayāna is practiced on the basis of both the Śrāvakayāna and general Bodhisattvayāna. When well trained in the three higher trainings and six perfections, bodhisattvas with exceptionally strong bodhicitta enter Tantrayāna. With great compassion that finds sentient beings' suffering in saṃsāra unbearable, these bodhisattvas request and receive tantric initiation (*abhiṣeka*), taking on the tantric ethical restraints and commitments. They then diligently engage in study and meditation on the tantric teachings in addition to the practices described in the sūtras.

Vajrayāna is widespread among followers of Tibetan Buddhism and the Japanese Shingon sect. Tantric practices are threads in the Buddhist fabric of China, Korea, and Vietnam as well. Interestingly, the Amitābha practice popular in these countries is found in Tibetan Buddhism as a tantric practice.

Unfortunately, misconceptions about Vajrayāna exist due to lack of correct information. While sexual yoga and intoxicants are permitted in some tantric practices, they are firmly restricted *only* to people on very high stages of the path. Only a very few people are qualified to do these practices, and they do them discreetly. Fancying themselves highly realized tantric practitioners, people who have entered Vajrayāna and yet engage in this behavior without having realized ultimate reality are transgressing the tantric precepts and creating destructive karma. Furthermore, some so-called tantric practitioners have reduced Tantrayāna to the performance of rituals done with a worldly motivation seeking wealth or prestige. Some people may give initiations to receive offerings. All this is wrong and outside the scope of the Buddhadharma. In this chapter, I explain how sincere and serious practitioners practice Vajrayāna.

Tantric Deities

Because the minds of ordinary beings are too obscured to receive teachings directly from the Buddha's omniscient mind, he appears in various form bodies according to the dispositions of sentient beings in order to teach them. Due to sentient beings' different mental inclinations and different physical constituents, various meditation deities appear. All tantric deities are one nature—the exalted wisdom of bliss and emptiness. They are not individual personalities with inherently existent selves.

Because a blissful mind is used to realize emptiness, many of the meditation deities in highest yoga tantra are depicted in union with consorts. The male deity symbolizes the method aspect of the path—compassion, generosity, and so forth—and the female deity symbolizes the wisdom aspect of the path. It is not the case that these awakened meditation deities have sexual desire.

A buddha's wisdom may manifest as either peaceful deities or fierce deities. The appearance of fierce deities illustrates the power and clarity of compassion and wisdom. Their ferocity is directed toward ignorance, afflictions, and self-centeredness, the real enemies that destroy our well-being. These awakened deities have compassionate minds and never angrily harm sentient beings.

Buddhists who do not understand tantric practice may incorrectly regard a deity as an external god to be worshiped. While tantric meditation manuals enjoin bowing, offerings, and prayers, the tantric path is not about worshiping an external being so that he or she will bless us and grant us nirvāṇa. The Buddha clearly said that we need to cultivate the path ourselves and transform our own minds. Bowing, offering, and so forth are methods to purify our destructive karma and create merit, which prepares the mind for meditation on serenity and insight.

Entering Vajrayāna

Receiving a tantric initiation marks formal entry into tantra. Before receiving an initiation from a spiritual master, it is important to examine the master's qualifications and qualities. A qualified vajra master has the qualities of a bodhisattva spiritual mentor, especially the correct understanding of emptiness complemented by bodhicitta. Such a master guards body, speech, and mind from destructive actions, practices the three higher trainings, is knowledgeable in both the sūtras and tantras, and is compassionate and free from pretense and deceit. He or she possesses the set of ten outer qualities and the set of ten inner qualities of a vajra master. This mentor must have received initiation into Vajrayāna, kept the precepts and commitments purely, studied the practices well, completed the appropriate retreats and concluding ceremonies, and experienced some deep insight through this path. Finding a qualified tantric guru may take many years, but careful selection is worthwhile.

Tantric texts instruct that initiations be given only to people who are properly prepared—those who have faith, renunciation, bodhicitta, and correct understanding of emptiness—not to people who lack understanding of the fundamentals of Buddhism. In spite of this, some Tibetan lamas allow newcomers to attend initiations. Their thought is to "plant good seeds" in the person's mindstream. In general this may be beneficial. However, detrimental results sometimes follow when initiation is given prematurely.

Ethical conduct is crucial in tantra. Tantric precepts are taken on the basis of the bodhisattva precepts, which, in turn, are based on refuge in the Three Jewels and preferably all five lay precepts.

Those with tantric initiation must study the various precepts and commitments and practice them diligently. Similarly, they must receive teachings and study the steps of meditation on emptiness, visualization of the deity, mantra recitation, and so forth in a tantric meditation, as well as practice these daily. Furthermore, Vajrayāna practitioners must continue to strengthen their renunciation, bodhicitta, and wisdom realizing emptiness, do purification practices to cleanse their mindstreams of destructive karma, and accumulate merit.

Vajrayāna teachings and practices should remain private or "secret" in that tantric practitioners should not boast about the initiations they have received or advertise to others that they do Vajrayāna practice. They should keep their Vajrayāna images private, taking them out only when they meditate. In this way, they avoid the danger of self-centeredness and arrogance, attitudes that hinder spiritual progress.

Excellent Features of Highest Yoga Tantra

According to one system of classification, Buddhist tantra can be divided into four classes—action, performance, yoga, and highest yoga. Highest yoga tantra reveals the ultimate meaning of buddha nature by explaining the subtlest level of mind—the fundamental innate clear-light mind. When this subtlest consciousness is transformed into the path, yogis are equipped with a very powerful instrument to quickly purify both obscurations and complete all a buddha's magnificent qualities.

Some of the factors that distinguish highest yoga tantra and make it profound are:

- One has a strong, urgent aspiration to become a buddha to benefit sentient beings, which brings forth special effort in practice.
- The object with which one cultivates serenity is very subtle, leading to deep concentration.
- Stabilizing meditation on subtle meditation objects and subtle levels of mind increases the clarity of the ascertainment of emptiness.
- Due to special meditative techniques, serenity and insight are attained simultaneously.
- Great bliss is generated to make manifest the subtlest clear-light mind, which is then used to realize emptiness directly and eliminate even the subtlest obscurations.
- Method and wisdom are cultivated simultaneously in a single mental event—enabling simultaneous accumulation of method and wisdom.
- One trains in perceiving the two truths simultaneously, preparing the way for buddhahood, where conventional and ultimate truths are perceived at the same time.
- The path of the union of bliss and emptiness that leads to an illusory body is a unique cause for attaining a buddha's form body.

- The illusory body and actual clear light actualized in Vajrayāna are substantial causes that are directly concordant with the resultant form and truth bodies.

The practice of transforming the bliss generated by desire into the path is governed by the tantric precepts that all practitioners of highest yoga tantra have taken. Transgression of these ethical restraints is extremely serious and leads to great nonvirtuous karma and adverse consequences. Yogis who take desire into the path must have stable renunciation, bodhicitta, and wisdom. Only a few, rare people have these prerequisites. Even if monastics are qualified, they do not engage in this practice since they are celibate.

Some people mistakenly believe, "Since everything is empty, there is no good or bad. When one realizes emptiness, one is beyond ethical precepts." This is flawed logic. Padmasambhava said that the higher one's realization of emptiness, the greater one's respect for karma and its effects and thus the stronger one's commitment to ethical conduct.

Contrary to misconceptions, tantric yogis do not practice magic, and tantra is not an excuse to behave in outlandish ways. The Buddha was always humble, and he is our guru. He worked very hard on the path—living simply and practicing diligently. We should follow the Buddha's example.

16 Conclusion

In the past, due to lack of knowledge, people had the impression that the Pāli and Sanskrit traditions were completely different and separate. That is a mistake. The Pāli tradition is the foundation of the Buddhadharma, and the practice of vinaya is essential for the existence of the Buddha's teaching. The Buddha himself shaved his head and became a monk, training in ethical conduct. He then did six years of meditation—training in concentration—followed by meditation under the bodhi tree—training in wisdom. Through that, he attained full awakening. So the Buddha's life illustrates the three higher trainings. As his followers, we must follow his example and practice these.

The Prajñāpāramitā sūtras found in the Sanskrit tradition elaborated on core Buddhist teachings practiced by all Buddhists. In these sutras, the Buddha extensively explained the possibility of completely eliminating ignorance from our mind and gave a comprehensive explanation of true cessation and true paths. He also elaborated on the bodhisattva path.

In the past there has been some distance between followers of the Pāli and Sanskrit traditions. This benefits nobody. We must come together and exchange. For example, we can learn from each other's prātimokṣa. We must have more regular meetings: not just ceremonial meetings, but serious ones with genuine exchange. Thoughtful discussion to learn about each other's tradition is essential.

I am Buddhist, but on a deeper level I am a human being, one of the seven billion on this planet. Human beings are social animals, so each individual's future depends on the rest of humanity. So, even for my own interest, I have to think seriously about all of humanity. Each one of us wants a happy life and does not want suffering, and each one has the right to attain that. There is no difference between people of different religious faiths or between religious and secular people in this regard. No matter our background—rich or poor, educated or uneducated, high social status or low—on this level we are all the same. Many of the problems humanity faces come from emphasizing these superficial differences among us.

The Buddha's teachings are now 2,600 years old and are still relevant to today's world. Even some top scientists are eager to learn Buddhist methods to tackle destructive emotions. But while the Buddha's teachings are wonderful, there are signs that the quality of our lamas, tulkus, and teachers is degenerating. If spiritual teachers and leaders do not lead a disciplined life, how can they teach other people? In order to show others the right path, we must follow it ourselves. We Buddhists—no matter what tradition we practice or how many titles we have—must be genuine followers of the Buddha. Changing our dress is not sufficient. Even a puppet can wear monastic robes! Real change must occur in our own hearts and minds. To become a genuine Buddhist follower or a true Buddhist monastic, we must seriously practice self-discipline.

The Buddha taught us the path to nirvāṇa, but whether we attain it is up to us. The Buddha cannot lead us to awakening by giving blessings. We are our own masters, and everything depends on our own actions. Whether an action is constructive or destructive depends on our motivation. By teaching us how to correct our motivation, the Buddhadharma makes a significant contribution to inner peace.

All major world religions have the potential to build inner peace and, through that, to create a better world. But one unique quality about Buddhism, Jainism, and part of the Sāṃkhya tradition is the emphasis on individual responsibility. We believe in the law of causality. If we engage in ethical actions, happy results will come. If we act harmfully, unpleasant events will occur. Because the law of causality is a natural law, no one else can save us from experiencing the results of our harmful actions, not even the Buddha.

Religious people sometimes act hypocritically, praying for all sentient beings but ignoring some beings' rights and exploiting others. We may have religious images and books in our homes, but our actions are corrupt. No great spiritual teacher tells us, "Exploit others as much as you can. Then I will bless you."

If you accept a higher being such as Buddha, Christ, Krishna, or Mohammed, you should be an honest and truthful person. In that way you will gain more self-confidence, thinking, "I have nothing to hide. I can say what I feel,

WESTERN NUNS FROM MANY BUDDHIST TRADITIONS AT THE NINETEENTH ANNUAL WESTERN BUDDHIST MONASTIC GATHERING, USA

and my actions are transparent." Others will trust you. So if you care about yourself, honesty and truthfulness are important sources of inner strength and self-confidence. Some people speak very nicely and smile a lot, but their motivation is something different. How can others trust or respect them?

We must be serious. As a Buddhist monk I always observe my mind. When I wake up every morning, I remember the Buddha and recite some of his teachings. Then I set my motivation, "As a student of the Buddhadharma, today I will live with honesty, truthfulness, compassion, peacefulness, and nonviolence." Whenever I have time, I study, think about, and meditate on the sūtras and commentaries. As a result of immersing my mind in these books, I have developed full conviction that the practice of the three higher trainings is indispensable.

We Buddhists have a responsibility to serve humanity. The very motivation for Gautama Buddha's awakening was to benefit sentient beings. His entire life and doctrine were meant for the welfare of all sentient beings. However, sometimes it seems that we think, "Let the Buddha work hard; we'll have a luxurious life." How can we think that? If we are Buddhists, we must follow the Buddha's own example: he lived simply and was content with what he received. My sincere hope for our Buddhist brothers and sisters is that when we talk about Buddhadharma and say, "Propagate the

Buddha's teachings," we ourselves first propagate the Dharma in our own hearts. That is essential.

Human intelligence has advanced scientific knowledge and technology, bringing both benefit and increased powers of destruction. Creating a happier world ultimately depends on individuals' motivations. Individuals living together with other individuals form communities and nations, and leaders arise from these. When individuals create inner peace in their own hearts, communities and eventually the world will become peaceful. This is the only way.

Notes

1. Please see the preface for the usage of these terms.
2. Permanent phenomena are phenomena such as unobstructed space, emptiness, and cessations that do not disintegrate moment by moment in dependence on causes and conditions.
3. These are the six faculties (five sensory and one mental); two regenerative faculties (the male and female organs); the life force; five faculties to experience results of constructive and destructive actions (mental happiness and unhappiness, physical pleasure and displeasure, neutral feelings); five faculties to depart from the mundane (faith, effort, mindfulness, concentration, and wisdom on the path of seeing); and three unpolluted powers (of seeing, meditation, and no-more learning). The first fourteen are causes of cyclic existence, the last eight causes of liberation and full awakening.
4. See chapter 5.
5. "Liberation of mind" refers to concentration because it is free from sensual attachment and malice; "liberation by wisdom" refers to wisdom because it is free from ignorance. In general, liberation of mind is the result of serenity, and liberation by wisdom of insight. When the two are unpolluted and conjoined, they are the result of the eradication of pollutants by an arahant's supramundane path.
6. Here "body" refers to a corpus or collection of qualities.
7. Anālayo, "The Buddha and Omniscience," *The Indian International Journal of Buddhist Studies* 7 (2006): 4n14.
8. Killing, stealing, sexual misconduct, lying, divisive speech, harsh speech, idle talk, covetousness, maliciousness, wrong views.
9. Vism 16:15 quotes the *Paṭisambhidāmagga* on the sixteen attributes. The following explanation is based on a teaching given by Ledi Sayadaw, http://mahajana.net/texts/kopia_lokalna/MANUAL05.html.
10. There are two kinds of concentration: serenity concentration (*samatha samādhi*) and insight concentration (*vipassanā samādhi*). In the former, the *nimitta* is the object, while in the latter, the five aggregates characterized by one or another of the three characteristics are the object.
11. Through a conflation of terminology, in Sanskrit texts these came to be called *samyak prahāna*, "supreme abandonings."
12. The Pāli explanation of the noble eightfold path was presented in chapter 3.
13. The first three metaphors are easy to understand. However, since the last metaphor seems true, we may think that perhaps the self is in the body. The meaning of this metaphor is that although a jewel is a distinct phenomenon from the box and can be removed from the box and examined separately from it, removing the self from the body and viewing it as a distinct entity from the body is not possible because the self is dependent upon the body.

14. Translated from Pāli. The words "dependent on" do not appear in the second verse, but the syntactical structure conveys this sense. The meaning of the second half of this verse is: the convention "a being" is used in dependence on the aggregates.
15. MN, p. 1346n1268. Translation was modified after personal communication with the translator, changing "truly" to "irreducibly" to avoid confusion with the Tibetan Buddhist presentation of true existence. "Reducibly" and "irreducibly" clarify that a distinction is being drawn between the mode of existence of the elements and of the person according to the Abhidhamma method of analysis.
16. Tsongkhapa, *Ocean of Reasoning*, translated by Geshe Ngawang Samten and Jay Garfield (New York: Oxford University Press, 2006), 97.
17. Translation by Nyanaponika Thera on www.accesstoinsight.org.
18. *Suttanipāta* 4:15, as translated by Andrew Olendzki on www.accesstoinsight.org.
19. *Suttanipāta* 3:12, as translated by Bhikkhu Bodhi.
20. Translation by Bhikkhu Bodhi in *The Great Discourse on Causation* (Kandy: Buddhist Publication Society, 1984).
21. Translation by Maurice Walshe on www.accesstoinsight.org.
22. Path consciousnesses correspond to uninterrupted paths and fruition consciousnesses to liberated paths in the Sanskrit tradition.
23. Bhikṣu Dharmamitra, *On Generating the Resolve to Become a Buddha* (Seattle: Kalavinka Press, 2009), 71.
24. This was elaborated in the section on Chinese Buddhism in chapter 9.
25. Walpola Rahula, "Theravada–Mahayana Buddhism," in *Gems of Buddhist Wisdom* (Kuala Lumpur: Buddhist Missionary Society, 1996).
26. *Dasabodhisattupattikathā* 1:1–2. Translated by Hammalawa Saddhatissa in *The Birth Stories of the Ten Bodhisattvas* (London: Pali Text Society, 1975).
27. Jeffrey Samuels, "The Bodhisattva Ideal in Theravaada," *Philosophy East and West* 47.3 (July 1997): 399–415.
28. Guy Armstrong, "The Paramis: A Historical Background," http://media.audiodharma.org/documents/paramis/HistoricalBackground.html. Chodron also heard this from monks during her stay at a Thai temple in 2007.
29. Rahula, "Theravada–Mahayana Buddhism."
30. *Cariyāpiṭaka* I 8:15–16. Translated by I. B. Horner in *The Minor Anthologies of the Pāli Canon* (Lancaster: Pali Text Society, 2007).
31. According to the Pāli tradition, one can become an ariya and arahant in a female body but not a buddha. According to the Tantrayāna, one can also become a buddha in a woman's body.
32. From the *Ugraparipṛcchā Sūtra*. Translated by Jan Nattier in *A Few Good Men* (Honolulu: University of Hawaii Press, 2005), 259.
33. Other terms found in the discussion of buddha nature include *buddha essence* (*tathāgatagarbha*) and *element of sentient beings* (*sattvadhātu*) or just *element*. Sometimes these terms are used interchangeably; sometimes they have slightly different meanings.

Index

NOTE

- *Page numbers followed by "ph" indicate photographs.*
- *Page numbers followed by "q" indicate quotations.*
- *Page numbers followed by "q+" indicate quotations plus discussions.*
- *Page numbers followed by "+q" indicate discussions plus quotations.*
- *Page numbers followed by "t" indicate tables.*
- *Page numbers followed by "+t" indicate discussions plus tables.*
- *Page numbers followed by "(2)" or "(3)" indicate multiple discussions.*

About the Authors

THE DALAI LAMA is the spiritual leader of the Tibetan people, a Nobel Peace Prize recipient, and an advocate for compassion and peace throughout the world. He promotes harmony among the world's religions and engages in dialogue with leading scientists. Ordained as a Buddhist monk when he was a child, Bhikṣu Tenzin Gyatso completed the traditional monastic studies and earned his geshe degree (equivalent to a PhD). Renowned for his erudite and open-minded scholarship, his meditative attainments, and his humility, the Dalai Lama says, "I am a simple Buddhist monk."

Peter Aronson

BHIKṢUṆĪ THUBTEN CHODRON has been a Buddhist nun since 1977. Growing up in Los Angeles, she graduated with honors in history from UCLA and did graduate work in education at USC. After years studying and teaching Buddhism in Asia, Europe, and the US, she became the founder and abbess of Sravasti Abbey in Washington State. A popular speaker for her practical explanations of how to apply Buddhist teachings in daily life, she is the author of several bestselling books, including *Buddhism for Beginners*. She is the editor of Khensur Jampa Tegchok's *Insight into Emptiness*. For more information, visit sravastiabbey.org and thubtenchodronbooks.org.

Also Available by the Dalai Lama and Thubten Chodron from Wisdom Publications

The Library of Wisdom and Compassion

A special multivolume series in which His Holiness the Dalai Lama shares the Buddha's teachings on the complete path to full awakening.

Volumes:

1. *Approaching the Buddhist Path*
2. *The Foundation of Buddhist Practice*
3. *Samsara, Nirvana, and Buddha Nature*
4. *Following in the Buddha's Footsteps*
5. *In Praise of Great Compassion*

More volumes to come!

Also Available by the Dalai Lama from Wisdom Publications

The Compassionate Life

Essence of the Heart Sutra
The Dalai Lama's Heart of Wisdom Teachings

The Good Heart
A Buddhist Perspective on the Teachings of Jesus

Imagine All the People
A Conversation with the Dalai Lama on Money, Politics, and Life as it Could Be

Kalachakra Tantra
Rite of Initiation

Meditation on the Nature of Mind

The Middle Way
Faith Grounded in Reason

Mind in Comfort and Ease
The Vision of Enlightenment in the Great Perfection

MindScience
An East-West Dialogue

Practicing Wisdom
The Perfection of Shantideva's Bodhisattva Way

Sleeping, Dreaming and Dying
An Exploration of Consciousness

The Wheel of Life
Buddhist Perspectives on Cause and Effect

The World of Tibetan Buddhism
An Overview of Its Philosophy and Practice

Also Available from Thubten Chodron

Insight into Emptiness
Khensur Jampa Tegchok
Edited and Introduced by Thubten Chodron

"One of the best introductions to the philosophy of emptiness I have ever read."—José Ignacio Cabezón

Practical Ethics and Profound Emptiness
A Commentary on Nagarjuna's Precious Garland
Khensur Jampa Tegchok
Edited by Thubten Chodron

"This work offers amazing spot-on advice for our times, especially for our leaders and policy-makers."—Jan Willis, author of *Dreaming Me: Black, Baptist, and Buddhist*

Buddhism for Beginners

Cultivating a Compassionate Heart
The Yoga Method of Chenrezig

Don't Believe Everything You Think
Living with Wisdom and Compassion

Guided Meditations on the Stages of the Path

How to Free Your Mind
Tara the Liberator

Living with an Open Heart
How to Cultivate Compassion in Daily Life

Open Heart, Clear Mind

Taming the Mind

Working with Anger

Additional Material

Wisdom Publications also offers an online course related to this book taught by Venerable Thubten Chodron. To check it out, visit:

Buddhism: One Teacher, Many Traditions
A Wisdom Academy Online Course
https://wisdomexperience.org/courses/buddhism-one-teacher/

Wisdom

About Wisdom Publications

Wisdom Publications is the leading publisher of classic and contemporary Buddhist books and practical works on mindfulness. To learn more about us or to explore our other books, please visit our website at wisdomexperience.org or contact us at the address below.

Wisdom Publications
199 Elm Street
Somerville, MA 02144 USA

We are a 501(c)(3) organization, and donations in support of our mission are tax deductible.

Wisdom Publications is affiliated with the Foundation for the Preservation of the Mahayana Tradition (FPMT).